The Cowboy Reader

The Cowboy Reader

Edited by

Lon Tinkle

and

Allen Maxwell

David McKay Company, Inc.
New York

Reissued 1976 by the David McKay Company, Inc.

Library of Congress Cataloging in Publication Data

Tinkle, Lon, ed.
  The cowboy reader.

  Reprint of the ed. published by Longmans, Green,
New York.
  1. Cowboys—The West—Addresses, essays, lectures.
2. Frontier and pioneer life—The West—Addresses,
essays, lectures. I. Maxwell, Allen, 1915-   joint
ed. II. Title.
F596.T55   1976   978   76-25042
ISBN 0-679-50677-2
ISBN 0-679-50678-0 pbk.

For
J. FRANK DOBIE
and
JOHN H. McGINNIS

two generous men whose vocation
—one as writer, one as editor—
has been to interpret
the West and Southwest
but who have never been
merely provincial

Contents

Part 6: The Daily Round

Part 7: Wine, Women, and Song

Part 8: No Life for a Lady

Part 9: Storytellers' Range

Part 10: The Summing-Up

Illustrations

The Cowboy Reader

Lots to Lasso

THE NATIVE VENTURESOMENESS of the American people finds its expression in many hero-types. But the one symbol or myth or pattern that most of the world has taken to heart as typical of life in the New World is the figure of the American cowboy.

Curiously, this image of excellence, or this image that spurs admiration and imitation, is rarely bodied forth in any actual person. He remains *the* cowboy rather than *a* cowboy. The latter could be such a specific human being as Andy Adams or Will Rogers or Charlie Siringo, who wrote about his stirring adventures on the deck, hurricane deck at that, of a Spanish pony, but we tend to think of the cowboy as a composite type.

The "bad man" is known as a specific individual: he is Billy the Kid or John Wesley Hardin or Sam Bass or one of a dozen others, each one a personality rather than a type. The "mountain man" has individual identity: he is Jim Bridger or Kit Carson or many another. The "law man" is known as a historically identifiable supershot, by the name of Wyatt Earp or Jeff Milton or Bat Masterson.

These western "types" exist separately and as private individuals for the public imagination. But the "cowboy" largely remains a composite figure, the sum not of just one human biography but of all the dangers and perils and all the gusto

1

and zest that surrounded the art and science of readying and trailing to market the world's best eating.

The cowboy's personal identity—in the sense that George Washington and Ben Franklin and Kit Carson and Mark Twain have identity—dissolves into the myth, into the generality. Above all it merges into his vocation. He was a man of action and therefore a man of acts. He was precisely defined, not by what he thought or believed but by what he did.

This is a book about what the cowboy did, a book about his peculiar, unique, still-envied vocation or occupation. His work was more than work, more than play, it was—in the fashionable term—a way of life. His life was, by sheer historical good luck, one of the few perfect weddings between man and his environment. Much more than the general public usually supposes, the cowboy's work, or life-style, required very special skills. But what made his work a way of life was not the skills required but the virtues exacted.

These virtues—and virtues are what distinguish a vocation from an occupation—were the virtues that naturally consort with the often-observed "native venturesomeness of the American people." They are the virtues of endurance and courage and daring and resourcefulness. Of the Western world's long adherence to the four theological virtues, the cowboy failed to measure up in regard to prudence, knowledge, and judgment, but he was mighty long on the fourth, fortitude.

Perhaps this is why the cowboy is always *the* cowboy: the common denominators the work required outweighed the differences that distinguished, say, forthright Teddy Blue from suave Jack Culley, or easygoing Charlie Siringo from animal-alert Andy Adams.

When innumerable old Homer twanged his lyre and celebrated the first great horsemen of the Western world, he made imperishable myths out of the virtues mankind most admires. Courage indomitable became Achilles, unbeatable resourcefulness became Odysseus or Ulysses, lionlike strength became Ajax, endurance became Hector. The myth of the cowboy, on millions of TV and movie screens and in thousands of western books, now has the currency with the populace that the Homeric sagas had with the Greeks.

The cowboy has never had his Homer, but he has his "literature."

Anybody tossing a lariat into the great plains of set-down-in-print cowboy lore and legend and history will swiftly rope a mighty herd. This collection of cowboy stuff, as any other of necessity must, faced the inevitable embarrassment of riches. You have to edit such an anthology, no doubt, to be amazed at the quantity of writing, some of it superlatively interesting, about American life's most picturesque occupation. Another collection of equal size and equal interest could easily be made from what has had to be omitted to keep this volume in manageable proportions.

Frank Dobie, emphasizing that the cowboys themselves were given to idealizing their life, writes:

Heaven in their dreams was a range better watered than the one they knew, with grass never stricken by drought, plenty of fat cattle, the best horses and comrades of their experience, more of women than they talked about in public, and nothing at all of golden streets, golden harps, angel wings, and thrones; it was a mere extension, somewhat improved, of the present. . . . For every hired man on horseback there have been hundreds of plowmen in America, and tens of millions of acres of rangelands have been plowed under, but who can cite a single autobiography of a laborer in the fields of cotton, of corn, of wheat? Or do coal miners, steelmongers, workers in oil refineries, factory hands of any kind of factory, the employees of chain stores and department stores ever write autobiographies? Many scores of autobiographies have been written by range men, perhaps half of them by cowboys who never became owners at all. . . . They realized that they had been a part of an epic life. . . . Sympathy for the life biases my judgment; that judgment, nevertheless, is that some of the strongest and raciest autobiographic writing produced by America has been by range men.

Of the more than thirty selections that make up this Reader, a large majority come from the actual reminiscences or writings of cowboys themselves, going back to the first great work in the field, when Illinois-bred Joseph G. McCoy recorded his life on the range and his converting Abilene, Kansas, into a cow town in his *Historic Sketches of the Cattle Trade of the West and Southwest* (1874). What Dodge City was like in those early days when the million cattle the Civil War had dammed up in Texas needed a shipping point by rail to the East is reported at first hand by the greatest cowboy writer of them all, Andy Adams. These accounts are authentic, as are the others in this book. Our first standard of choice was the reliability of the report, second its readability. Luckily the two coincide to an astonishing extent. The reader who finds that rollicky, roisterous Charlie Siringo is very casual and flip in tone has only to compare the hum of truth in his account with the events and the same hum of truth between the lines that one finds all the way from old-timers like Andy Adams and W. S. James on down through the more recent recollections of such tough-minded and realistic cowboys as "Teddy Blue" Abbott and Fred Gipson's "Fat" Alford.

Only a few of these selections are by "scholars," and in each of these cases we have been able to offer interpretations of the American cowboy by men as much at home on the range as they are at home in the techniques and disciplines of trained scholarship. J. Frank Dobie is a prime example. Dobie, generally known as "Mr. Texas," was born on the famed Dobie spread, adjoining the King Ranch, in the brush country of Rio Grande Texas; his family, in considerable numbers, came out to Texas before its liberation from Mexico, before the Texas Republic of 1836–1846. Dobie grew up working cows and uncertain whether he wanted to be a ranch man or a poet. He has switched back and forth in his career, but has taught long enough to have made many a conspicuous Southwesterner aware of his heritage by virtue of Dobie's famed course at the University of Texas on "Life and Literature of the Southwest."

Dobie probably knows more than any other man alive about this field, but he has never lost his critical standards and never fails to apply them. This book, of course, is overwhelmingly indebted to his invaluable *Guide to Life and Literature of the Southwest.*

Other contributors here who share Dobie's personal experience of ranching as well as his training in historical investigation are Walter Prescott Webb, president in 1959 of the American Historical Association, Douglas Branch, Wayne Gard, and Paul Horgan, whose *Great River: The Rio Grande in North American History* won the 1954 Pulitzer Prize.

Except for four pieces of fiction by men who had personally experienced ranch life—O. Henry, Owen Wister, Stewart Edward White, Alfred Henry Lewis—the remaining selections are historical accounts by men whose lives have been identified with the cattle tradition, whether such painters and writers from past and present as Charlie Russell and Frederic Remington and Tom Lea or such cowpunchers, part time or full time, as Teddy Roosevelt and Jack Potter and Ross Santee.

Reliability, yes, but also variety and uniqueness have governed our choices. Women, unique of course anywhere, were especially so in early ranch life. We are happy, therefore, to signal the attention of readers to an excerpt not to be missed, the one from Agnes Morley Cleaveland's delightful *No Life for a Lady.*

Editors owe an obligation to state the principles that govern their choices and an obligation to explain, if not justify, omissions. Plus the reasons above, our principle has been to offer in as handy and agreeable a way as possible a "treasury of the best that has been written about the American cowboy." Not the rarest or least accessible material (Ramon Adams has already done that to perfection) but a meshed cluster of the most representative, most reliable, and most readable pictures of life on the open and shut range.

That is why we should like to explain certain omissions. For example, the matter of Eugene Manlove Rhodes will leap at once to many minds. We have omitted him here because we think his best work lies in his long fiction, especially in the wonderful *Pasó por Aquí.* To have represented so sterling a man as Rhodes by his lesser work would be to diminish him unfairly; to include a long work would have required omitting, to make place, too many other items. In the same way, certain books have a quality that is lost in a sampling or an excerpt; this we felt to be true of such a first-class memoir as John Culley's *Cattle, Horses, and Men* (typical of the many intelligent Britishers who came out to try ranching in the West). Other works that lost none of their quality in excerpts nonetheless duplicated similar accounts of trailing or of the roundup. You could make a "Trail Reader" or a "Roundup Reader" alone, though monotony might set in early. Or, again, we were loyal to the key word "cowboy"; gun fights, Indian scrapes, no matter how interesting, we tended to regard as incidental, not central, to the cowboy's working day.

Finally, there are some very good interpretations and summaries of cowboy life we should have liked to represent in these pages, but here too there was duplication. For our purposes, the "summing up" could not be done more superlatively in short space than in Paul Horgan's much admired set-piece, reprinted here, from his *Great River: The Rio Grande in North American History*. Readers wanting book-length treatment of this theme will delight in, among others, the standard *The Cowboy* of Philip Ashton Rollins and *The American Cowboy: The Myth and the Reality* of Joe B. Frantz and Julian Ernest Choate, Jr.

The idea for *The Cowboy Reader* originated with our editor, John L. B. Williams. We are grateful to him for selecting us to execute the project and for his constant editorial help. To the writers and their publishers whose work comprises this volume, our debt is as visible as our gratitude is real.

And now like the chuck-wagon cook we say: "Come and get it!"

Dallas, Texas
June 20, 1959

LON TINKLE
ALLEN MAXWELL

PAUL HORGAN

The Cow Boy Revisited*

⟨ PAUL HORGAN of Roswell, New Mexico, has been a consistent prize winner with his books ever since his first novel, *The Fault of Angels*, won the Harper $10,000 Novel Prize in 1933. Among many other awards since then, his *Great River: The Rio Grande in North American History* won the 1954 Pulitzer Prize in history. Horgan was born in Buffalo, but his family moved to New Mexico when he was a boy. He has been identified with the Southwest ever since, but he is a world traveler and his most recent book is titled *Rome Eternal*. This excerpt is a celebrated chapter from *Great River*.

EVER SINCE the eighteenth century the raising and tending of large herds of beef cattle had been practiced on the Rio Grande's wide flat borderlands. All descended from animals brought to Mexico in the sixteenth century by Spaniards, there were several types of cattle on the river plains, of which the most distinctive had tremendously long horns doubled up and backward for half their length; heavy thin heads; tall legs, and narrow, powerful flanks. They were haired in various colors, with white patches. By the hundred thousand, wild

* From *Great River: The Rio Grande in North American History* by Paul Horgan. Copyright, 1954, by Paul Horgan. Reprinted by permission of Rinehart & Company, Inc., New York, Publishers.

7

cattle roved at large over the uninhabited land on both sides of the border, and constituted its prevailing form of wealth. As such they were always prizes for Indians, Mexicans, and Americans who in an unbroken tradition of border violence raided the herds—preferably those already gathered into ownership by other men—and drove away thousands of animals to sell on the hoof, or to kill for their hides which were baled and sold to traders, while the carcasses were left to carrion, and the bones to workers who gathered them up and hauled them for sale as fertilizer to Texas farming towns.

Even in the face of such hazard a few cattle traders drove herds east to New Orleans, north to Missouri, and west even as far as California, before the Civil War. But the trade was unorganized, and the principal markets, New Orleans and Mobile, were supplied by cattle steamers that sailed out of the Texas Gulf ports. The longhorn cattle they carried were called "coasters" or "sea lions." The coast-wise cattle trade was limited by a monopoly held on Gulf shipping by the Morgan Line. "To anyone outside of the ship company," wrote an early cattle trader, "an enormous rate of freight was exacted, practically debarring the ordinary shipper." And when the Civil War took levies of man power from the cattle business, the trade was further constricted. In consequence of such conditions, "for a quarter of a century or more," the trader remarked, "the herds of Texas continued to increase much faster than the mature surplus was marketed. In fact, no market accessible existed sufficiently to consume this surplus, and of course the stock [became] less valuable in proportion as it became plentiful." But shortly after the Civil War the cattle trade was revived, and by the seventies, the herds of Texas owners were the largest in the United States. Of these, some of the largest belonged to great companies operating where the nation's range cattle industry had its origin—along the Rio Grande between the Pecos and Mexico Bay.

It was the *brasada*, the brush country, stretching from the Nueces to the Rio Grande. It was profuse in growths—but almost all were thorned. It was either swept with gray dust

Composite Cowboy, the Texan Archetype

Drawing by José Cisneros, from *The Typical Texan: Biography of an American Myth,* by Joseph A. Leach (Southern Methodist University Press, 1952)

borne on blistering winds or beaten by deluges that hissed as
they first struck the hot ground or raked by blizzards that came
whistling out of the north. In its interlocking thickets that
enclosed small clearings where grew curly mesquite grass,
cattle could graze by thousands and hardly be seen by horsemen who sought them. There cicadas sang of the heat, and
sharp-haired peccaries rooted among the thorns, and blue
quail ran amidst the wiry shadows, and rattlesnakes sought
the cool and sometimes were drummed to death by wild turkey
gobblers at whose destroying wings they struck and struck
with no effect on nerveless quill and feather. It was a land
of hard secrets, the best kept of which was the location of
water. Its few rivers ran in abruptly cut trenches walled with
pink or yellow or slate blue limestone, and could not be seen
except from their very brinks. In every direction the wilderness
looked the same. There were no distant mountains to be seen.
The land swelled away toward the white sky in slow rolls and
shimmered in the heat that blended the ashen color of the
ground with the olive greens of the brush until across the
distance there seemed to hang a veil of dusty lilac.

It was astonishing how much human activity there was in
a land so hostile to man's needs. It was the scene of habitual
Indian travels, and of the military campaigns of the Mexicans
and Texans in their wars, and of the United States Army in its
Rio Grande movements, and of traveling traders, missioners,
and criminals. In its thickets there was even an occasional
small ranch, locked in isolation by sun, distance, and the poverty of its occupants, who possessed even few wishes. And it
became the scene of organized work in the cattle business.
Animals born and grown there were taken in herds to the
milder prairies above the Nueces, and across the rest of Texas
and Oklahoma to beef markets in the north. ". . . The cow
boys, as the common laborers are termed," said a cattleman
who saw the industry develop, "go in squads of four or five
scouting over the entire range, camping wherever night over-
takes them, catching with the lasso upon the prairies every
young animal found whose mother bears their employer's

brand." It was "legal and a universal practice to capture any unmarked and unbranded animal upon the range and mark and brand the same in their employer's brand, no matter to whom the animal may really belong, so be it is over one year old and unbranded. . . ."

The cow boy was the last of the clearly original types of Western American to draw his general tradition and character from the kind of land he worked in, and the kind of work he did. His forerunners were the trapper of the mountains and the trader of the plains. Of the three, he left the fullest legacy of romance; and to see him as he first was, it would be necessary in a later century to clear a way back to him through a dense folk literature of the printed page, the moving picture film, and the radio that in using all his symbols would almost never touch the reality that supported them.

His work was monotonous in hardship and loneliness, and occasionally it was shot through with excitement that rose from danger. The country where he worked was in its dimensions and character his enemy; and yet it was also in an intimate way almost a completion of his nature, that reveled in vast vacant privacies, and fixed its vision on the distance as though to avoid any social responsibility. He had for his most constant companion not a man or a woman, but an animal—his horse, on whom his work and his convenience and even at times his life depended. His duties took him endlessly riding over range country, where he sought for cattle to capture, calves or yearlings to brand, herds to drive to water, individual cows or bulls of a proper age or condition to cut out of a herd for segregation into another group. Such a group would then be driven to another location—a different pasture or a market.

In dealing with cows through the consent of his horse, the cow boy needed to know much of the nature of both animals. Through experience he learned to anticipate the behavior of cattle, and to judge the effect upon them of every stimulus. He saw that the laws that governed them were the laws of the crowd; and he developed extraordinary skill in handling great crowds of cattle at a time. His horse, broken to riding, and subject to his will, he had to know as an individual creature, and dominate relentlessly its nature by turns sensitive, stubborn, and gentle. Living with these two animal natures, the cow boy seemed to acquire as his own certain of their traits, almost as though to be effective at living and working with them, he must open his own animal nature to theirs and through sympathy resemble them. If he could be as simple as a cow, he could also be as stubborn; as fearless as a wild mustang, and as suspicious of the unfamiliar; as incurious as an individual bull, and as wild to run with a crowd when attracted. Even in his physical type, the cow boy might tend to resemble his animal companions—a certain flare of nostril and whiteness of eyelash could recall the thoughtless face of a calf; a leanness of leg and arm was a reminder of a horse's fine-boned supports and further suggested the physique best adapted to, and developed for, the horseman's job—the hard, sinewy body, light of weight but powerful, tall for high vision over the animal herd, long-legged for gripping the mount around its breathing barrel. His state of body and nerve had to be ready to fight, for his job sometimes included battle, when Indians or organized cattle and horse thieves came down upon his herd. Then like any soldier he had to shoot to kill, under the sanction of his duty. For his labors, he was paid in the 1870's from fifteen to twenty dollars a month in gold or silver. He saw himself at his task, and his self-image survived in his anonymous folk literature:

> All day long on the prairie I ride,
> Not even a dog to trot by my side:
> My fire I kindle with chips gathered round,
> My coffee I boil without being ground.

In any group of nineteenth-century cow boys, more were bearded than clean-shaven. Their costumes were much alike, though with individual variations. But all their garments were "coarse and substantial, few in number and often of the gaudy pattern." The cow boy wore a wide-brimmed hat with its crown dented into a pyramid or flattened. If the brim in front

was sometimes turned up off his face, it could be turned down
to protect him from the pressing light of the sky under which
he spent all day. Around his neck he wore a bandana of tough
silk. It served many purposes. Tied over his face it filtered
dust before his breath. It served to blindfold a calf or tie its
legs. It was a towel, a napkin, a bandage, a handkerchief, or
simply an ornament. His shirt was of stout cotton flannel, in a
bright color or loud design of checks or stripes or plaids. Over
it he sometimes wore a cloth or leather vest but rarely a jacket.
His trousers were either of heavy denim, dyed dark blue, sewn
with coarse yellow thread, and reinforced at points of great
wear with copper rivets; or were of odd colors and materials,
mostly dark, that could stand tough use. They fitted tightly.
The trouser legs were stuffed into boots that reached almost to
the knee. At work, the cow boy often wore leggings—two long
tubes, with wide flaps at each side cut into fringes or studded
with silver disks, that reached from ankle to groin, and were
tied to a belt as though to the string of a breechclout. Their
purpose was to shield him against thorns in the brush he rode
through, and the violent rub of haired animal hides, and the
burn of rope when he pulled it against his leg as he turned his
horse to control a lassoed creature. On his boots he wore large
spurs, of silver or iron. He wore gloves to work in, and around
his tight hips he wore a cartridge belt from which depended
his pistol—most often a Colt's single-action, 45 caliber revolver
called the Peacemaker. He had no change of clothing. He went
unwashed and unbathed unless he camped by a stream or a
pond. He said in his multiple anonymity,

> I wash in a pool and wipe on a sack;
> I carry my wardrobe all on my back. . . .

Like the object of his work and its chief instrument—the cow
and the horse—his Texas saddle, in its essential form, came
from Spain. Its high pommel and cantle, heavy stirrups, and
great weight suggested the squarish, chairlike saddle of the
jousting knight, though its design was modified by Mexican
saddlers until all contours were rounded and smoothed, and

the pommel, of silver or other metal, was developed to serve as a cleat about which to secure the lariat whose other end was noosed about a captive cow or horse. When not in use the lariat was coiled and tied to the saddle. There was little other baggage on the saddle, except now and then a leather scabbard containing a short rifle. If two cow boys traveled together they carried their camp equipment and bedrolls on a pack animal. Otherwise, when a large group worked daily out of a central camp, their equipment was carried in the camp wagon to which they returned during the day for meals and at night for fire, food, and companionship.

The wagon, pulled by four horses and driven by the camp cook, was a roving headquarters for the grazing party. Its form was invented in the 1850's by Charles Goodnight, who adapted an army vehicle to the needs of the cow camp. Rolling in movement, it had a compact look, with its sheets over bows that concealed the contents, which consisted of bedrolls for the workers, and at its free end a high, square chest standing upright. Parked, free of its horses, and with its sheets extended and supported by poles to make a generous pavilion of shade to one side, the wagon seemed to expand into several times its own size. It was amazing how much it carried, and how much immediate ground its unpacked equipment could cover. The chest at the rear was faced with a wooden lid which when opened downward became a worktable supported by a central leg. Then were revealed in the chest many fitted drawers and hatches in which the cook kept every necessity for cooking and every oddment, including medicines. Behind it in the wagon bed, along with the bedrolls, he carried his heavy pots and skillets and tin dishes. Beneath the wagon frame hung buckets and to its sides were lashed water barrels.

The cooking fire, which at night served also to give its only light to the camp gathering, was made a few feet from the wagon and its profuse scatter of equipment. There the cook prepared his meals, always the same. If brush or wood were scarce, he made his fire of dried animal droppings, like the Spanish soldiers who centuries before had found these the only useful product of fabled Quivira. If he had no matches he could start his fire by pouring gunpowder into his pistol, wadding it loosely, and firing it with its muzzle close to a scrap of cloth or other dry kindling. He prepared a great pot of coffee boiled from whole beans. A cow boy drank a quart or more every day. Of such coffee it was said that "you would hesitate, if judging from appearance, whether to call it coffee or ink." It was drunk without cream or sugar. There was a kettle full of stew in which using his pocket-knife—his only table service —the cow boy probed for a lump of meat. With thick biscuit or cornbread he soaked up the gravy and like an Indian ate from his fingers. There were no green vegetables to be had. A pot of kidney beans finished the meal. The cow boys squatted near one another, or stood idling by the wagon, and ate in silence and with speed. A meal was not an occasion of social interest. It was an act of need, disposed of without grace or amenity. Inseparable from it were the taste and smell of dust and cow-hair and horse sweat and leather—sensory attributes of everything in the cow boy's working life.

> For want of an oven I cook bread in a pot,
> And sleep on the ground for want of a cot.

But before the bedrolls were opened up from their heavy canvas covers, and the work party went to sleep, there was a little while for talk and other diversion. Such a miniature society created its own theater. There was always someone who would be moved to perform, while the rest gazed at the intimate, never-failing marvel of how one whom they knew—a man just like them—became before their very eyes somebody else. The campfire put rosy light over the near faces of the gathered men and their cluttered possessions, and threw their shadows like spokes out on the flat ground until the immense darkness absorbed all. At the very center of light a fellow rose. He had a joke to tell. He acted it out. It may have been well known to all, but they listened in fixity. It was likely to be an obscene jape. The cow boy, observed a cattleman of the seventies, "relishes . . . a corrupt tale, wherein abounds much vulgarity and animal propensity." His delight was a practical joke on one of his fellows. The joke was good if it made a fool of someone. It was better if it mocked the victim's peculiarity, and it was even better if it played upon "animal propensity"— for the sake of symbolic relief of the enforced continence under which the work party lived on the range.

There were other stories to hear—many dealt with experiences in the Civil War, to which the early cow boys were still close in time. There were wrestling and other trials of strength to perform. There were songs to sing, some of whose texts were lewd parodies of sentimental ballads. All knew the songs of the cattle trail, and could sing them together. If in one of his cubbyholes the cook carried a violin for its owner, there would be fiddle music of an astonishing legerity that yet managed to seem tuneless, while a cow boy danced a clog in firelighted dust, and the rest clapped hands. Often a mournful piety stirred in someone, and when he began to sing a hymn, others joined him, and like a sigh of innocence, their united voices rose over their lonely fire where they camped, a little knot of men with every potentiality, to one or another degree, for every human attribute. The bedrolls came out of the wagon and were spread. Nobody had a book to read, and in any case, the firelight was dying and would soon be down to coals.

> My ceiling's the sky, my floor is the grass;
> My music's the lowing of herds as they pass;
> My books are the brooks, my sermons the stones,
> My parson a wolf on his pulpit of bones. . . .

As his artless song implied, the cow boy belonged to the type of man who was not, actually, domesticated. He chose freedom in the wilds over responsibilities of hearth and home. He thought more about work than he did of a family. He made love on almost a seasonal schedule, as though in rut. He visited a prostitute, or took a sweetheart, only to leave her, with sighs about how he must go roaming, as though all would understand his natural state. He departed for work or went off to fight wherever he would find other men like himself. He pre-

ferred the society of men to that of women: for only with men
could he live a daily life that was made up of danger, and hard
exposure, and primitive manners. These did not seem like
disadvantages to him, for he liked them for themselves; and,
further, they brought into his life excitement, freedom, and
wilderness, all of which he sought.

If he saw himself as a simple creature, and if tradition so
accepted him, both were wrong. His temperament and character were full of tempestuous contradictions and stresses. The
life he chose resembled the Indian's more than any other, but
it lacked the sustaining spiritual power of the Indian's nature-
mythology, and so it could not really hold for him the unques-
tioned dignity of a system that tried to explain—in whatever
error—the whole of human life. He was close to the frontiers-
man, many of whose ways he repeated, but he was neither in-
novator, builder, nor explorer. His love of hardness and
primitive conditions could be turned either to serve his comrades in unbreakable loyalty, or to lead him, as it did in individual cases, to a career as gunman or cattle thief. His longing for love was so great that he felt an exaggerated chivalry
for womankind, but in his worship he made women unreal;
and yet through his song literature he lamented, ". . . between
me and love lies a gulf very wide." He sanctioned his state by
romanticizing it in ballad and story; but he refuted it sym-
bolically by his periodic violent outbreaks of gunplay, drunken-
ness, and venery. And with all his hardness, he gave in to a
soft core of sentiment whose objects were the animals he
worked with, and the comrades who worked with him.

"I and they were but creatures of circumstance," said a cow
boy of his fellows in his domesticated old age, "—the circumstances of an unfenced world." From their unfencedness came
their main characteristics. Solitude was put upon them by their
chosen environment, which thus modified their character. "Ad-
hesiveness," in the jargon of the nineteenth-century parlor science, was a human trait. The nearest living being to whom the
cow boy could turn with affection was his horse. It was his
daylong companion and helper. It obeyed his orders and made

him master of distance and took him in and out of danger. Responding to his signals, it seemed to him to possess more than animal intelligence. His horse, a masterpiece of anthropomorphism, joined him in a partnership, and was paid every honor due to such a position. Continued the retired cow boy,

My horse was something alive, something intelligent and friendly and true. He was sensitive, and for him I had a profound feeling. I sometimes think back on . . . remarkable horses I owned in much the same way that I think back on certain friends that have left me. . . . I went hungry sometimes, but if there was any possible way of getting food for my horse or if there was a place to stake him, even though I had to walk back a mile after putting him to graze [and cow boys hated to walk] I never let him go hungry. Many a time I have divided the water in a canteen with a horse.

If it was expedient to take care of his horse in order to assure his own mobility and safety, and if it was ordinary human kindness to care for a dumb creature, there was yet more than such promptings in the cow boy's devotion to his mount, as many a song and story attested. The professional cow boy rarely had a cultivated mind; and in his incurious thought he was lowered and his horse was elevated until they drew together in common identity. It was a process typical of a juvenile stage of character, and it may have suggested why the cow boy and his legend should appeal forever after as a figure of play to little boys. In much the same sort of emotion the cow boy felt a mournful fondness for the animals he herded—the little "dogies" to whom he sang on the trail to keep them quiet, and to whom he attributed something of himself as they were objects of his vigilance and labor, day and night. In its innocence and pathos his system of projected sentimentality for his animals suggested that only by making of them more than they were could he have survived his lonely and arduous duty with them. One of his songs said of the cow boy that "his education is but to endure. . . ."

Another song celebrated the life of cow boys together in their wandering yet coherent community. "The boys were like

brothers," they sang of themselves, "their friendship was
great. . . ." Alike in their extreme individualism, their self-re-
liance, their choice of a life wild, free, and rude, the companions of the cow camp gave to one another an extreme
loyalty. It seemed like a tribute to the hard skills they had to
master to do their jobs. A man who proved himself able at it
deserved membership in a freemasonry unlike any other. Its
physical tasks caused a high value to come upon the life of
action, in which there was no place for the values of mind and
spirit. These were relegated to the world of women; and in the
towns and cities that later completed the settling of the last
frontier West, for the better part of a century it would be
the women's organizations that would try to rescue the fine
arts, education, religion, and social amenity from being held
as simply irrelevant to civilized life—an attitude even more
withering to mankind's highest expressions than one of mere
contempt. For its purpose in its time, the brotherhood of the
cow camp was all that was needed to make an effective society. Diverse like all individuals, and sprung from various backgrounds and kinds of experience, the cow boys taken together
seemed to merge into a type more readily than most workers
in a common job. Their environment directly created the terms
of their work, and their work in its uncomplicated terms created
their attitudes and points of view. And if they were like one
another in their principal traits, it was because so many of
them chose their calling for the same general reason.

This—it was attested to again and again in the cow boy's
anonymous ballad literature—this was flight from one kind
of life to another. Many cow boys left home, said a ballad,

> Each with a hidden secret well smothered in his breast,
> Which brought us out to Mexico, way out here in the West.

In this lay a suggestion of doom, a rude Byronism that was
echoed in other songs by allusions to unhappiness, guilt, escape.
Some were driven to the new society of the cow range by a
faithless girl at home, or a dissolute life, or a criminal past;
others by inability to become reconciled to their home societies

following the Civil War, or by bitterness in family life, or even by a cruel stepmother. Romantic conventions of behavior in the nineteenth century could move the cow boy, who punished those who had betrayed him. "I'll go," he threatened,

> . . . to the Rio Grande,
> And get me a job with a cow boy band.

He did not mean a band of musicians, for not until the next century would the cow boy's public identity be chiefly that of an entertainer who in a commercial adaptation of the cow boy costume would spend more time with a microphone than with either horse or cow. No, with companions on the cattle range, the cow boy, deaf to dissuasion by loved ones who had proved faithless, promised to go

> . . . where the bullets fly,
> And follow the cow trail till I die.

Unable for whatever reason to accept the bindings of conventional society, within the one he sought and helped to make on the last frontier he was capable of sure dependability in any cause for the common good of his comrades, whom he did not judge, even if sometimes a propensity to go wrong should overtake them in the very land where they had thought to escape their doom. Who knew when a man might encounter the moral frailty of one of his friends of the brushlands?

> As I walked out in the streets of Laredo,
> As I walked out in Laredo one day,
> I spied a dear cow boy wrapped up in white linen,
> Wrapped up in white linen as cold as the clay.

It was a dirge for a young man who in his dying words revealed a longing for a gentler land than the dusty empire of his work, and confessed his errors. "Oh, beat the drums slowly," he said,

> . . . and play the fife lowly,
> Play the Dead March as you carry me along;
> Take me to the green valley, there lay the sod o'er me,
> For I'm a young cow boy and I know I've done wrong.

Unashamed of their grief that sprang from their close living, his bearers saw themselves in him, and if he had sinned, they could not condemn him.

> We beat the drum slowly and played the fife lowly,
> And bitterly wept as we bore him along;
> For we all loved our comrade, so brave, young and
>   handsome,
> We all loved our comrade although he'd done wrong.

For here was a clan feeling, a solidarity, with a realistic view of character and its capacity for error. Idealizing one another in the all-male society of their work and play, the cow boys remained loyal above, or even because of, the weaknesses they shared and assuaged with violence. In conclusion, the dirge moved from the individual to the group.

> Then beat your drum lowly and play your fife slowly,
> Beat the Dead March as you carry me along;
> We all love our cow boys so young and so handsome,
> We all love our cow boys although they've done wrong.

In another valedictory the cow boy spirit, after reciting the perils of "some bad company" which could only lead to being "doomed for hell," ended in the presence of the hangman with an admonition to morality.

> It's now I'm on the scaffold,
> My moments are not long;
> You may forget the singer
> But don't forget the song.

In the cow boy's lonely character there were extremes of feeling and behavior. If in his work there seemed to be a discipline of dedicated steadfastness, a purity of vocation, then when he went to town, he threw himself into indulgence. Perhaps the town was a reminder of the coherent social life he had fled at home, and perhaps it was now a guilty joy to outrage it by his behavior. Certainly the town was the very opposite of the desolate open range from which even the cow boy needed periodic change.

His best chance for it came when men of the range party were told off to drive a herd of cattle to the marketing and shipping towns. The main trails along which he drove went north from the Texan Rio Grande to Kansas, and another—the Goodnight-Loving Trail—led westward to New Mexico and California. It passed the Pecos River at Horsehead Crossing about a hundred miles above the Rio Grande, and presently divided into two forks. One pointed north to Colorado. The other crossed the Rio Grande at Las Cruces and followed the old road to San Diego.

The cattle made trails that showed many narrow grooves side by side—marks of the strict formation in which the animals in their thousands were driven for upwards of a thousand miles. A cow boy said that trail life was "wonderfully pleasant" —this in spite of continuing hazards. There still might be trouble with Indians. All the cattle were wild, and were easily stampeded by attacks, or by thunderstorms, or by hail. If the weather was wet, rivers rose, and to take thousands of cattle across swollen waters was at best a tedious job, and often a perilous one. Against the drovers on the move there pressed at one period a whole organized enterprise of thievery. Outlaws captured drovers, tortured them, sometimes killed them, and stole their herds. When one drover was captured, he tried to talk his way out of his trouble, but the bandits were immovable and a reporter of the incident said bitterly that "it was like preaching morality to an alligator."

But in swelling volume the animal trains passed through to their destinations, and the cow boys were happy on the trail. They played tricks on one another, and shot game on the prairies, and after supper sang, told stories, danced to a fiddle, lay back to look at the stars and speculate about them, and listened for the sounds of the herd settling down for the night. "I do not know anything more wholesome and satisfying," mused a cow boy long after his trail days, "than seeing cattle come in on their bed ground at night so full and contented that they grunt when they lie down." It was like a communion of creature comforts in which man and animal could meet.

Three shifts of night guards were posted over the herds. A sleepy cow boy rubbed tobacco juice in his eyes to keep awake. Morning must come, and another day to be spent at the pace of cattle walking with odd delicacy in their narrow grooved trails, and after enough such days, the shipping town would take form like a few scattered gray boxes on the severe horizon, and the cow boy would feel his various hungers begin to stir.

It was in town that he got into most of his trouble. Every facility was here to help him do it. As a cattle shipper observed, in frontier towns "there are always to be found a number of bad characters, both male and female; of the very worst class in the universe, such as have fallen below the level of the lowest type of brute creation." These pandered to the cow boy's howling appetite for dissipation.

Sometimes he rode into town and without cleaning himself or changing his clothes but just as he had dismounted in hat, damp shirt, earth-caked trousers, and boots and spurs, he strode into a dance house, seized a "calico queen" or a "painted cat," as he called the dancing women, and with Indian yells and a wild eye went pounding about the dance floor under a grinding necessity to prove in public, most of all to himself, that he was at last having a good time. The music to which he danced was "wretched . . . ground out of dilapidated instruments, by beings fully as degraded as the most vile. Few more wild, reckless scenes of abandoned debauchery can be seen on the civilized earth," remarked the cattle shipper, "than a dance house in full blast in one of the many frontier towns. To say they dance wildly or in an abandoned manner is putting it mild. . . ."

And sometimes the cow boy, at large in town with his accumulated pay, went first to improve his looks. In a barbershop he had a bath, and then had his three to six months' growth of hair trimmed, and his full beard cut down, shaped, and dyed black. In a clothing store he bought completely new clothes, from hat to boots; and then, strapping on his pistol, he was ready to impose himself like shock upon the town. Gambling rooms, saloons, a theater, a row of prostitutes' quarters like cattle stalls, dance houses—from one to the next the cow boy could make his explosive way, to be catered to by "men who live a soulless, aimless life," and women who had "fallen low, alas! how low . . . miserable beings." Among the conventions of the cow boy's town manners was free use of his firearm, whether he might harm anyone or not. The pathos of folly long done and half forgotten would make his murderous antics seem unreal to later view. But they were real enough to the frontier towns of the 1870's. Sighed the cattle shipper in that decade,

It is idle to deny the fact that the wild, reckless conduct of the cow boys while drunk . . . have brought the *personnel* of the Texan cattle trade into great disrepute, and filled many graves with victims, bad men and good men. . . . But by far the larger portion of those killed are of that class that can be spared without detriment to the good morals and respectability of humanity. . . .

And "after a few days of frolic and debauchery, the cow boy is ready, in company with his comrades, to start back to Texas, often not having one dollar left of his summer's wages." All he had was a memory that found its way into one of his songs, about "The way we drank and gambled and threw the girls around. . . ."

The cow boy triumphed at a lonely work in a beautiful and dangerous land. Those of his qualities that did the job were the good ones—courage, strength, devotion to duty. His worse traits, exercised for relief, were not judged in relation to his task. All aspects of his complex nature entered into his romance. He saw himself for his own achievement, and like the earliest individuals of the frontier, he consciously created his character and his tradition, and whether his emotion was honest or not, it was so energetic that by it he made his nation see him in his own terms. In him, the last American to live a life of wild freedom, his domesticated compatriots saw the end of their historical beginnings, and paid him nostalgic tribute in all their popular arts. Soon, like them, he would lose his nomadic, free, and rough form of life before the westward sweep of machine techniques by which Americans made their lives physically more easy—and socially less independent and self-reliant. In the very exercise of their genius for convenience in living, the Americans sacrificed to the social and commercial patterns of mass techniques some part of the personal liberty in whose name the nation had been founded. The cow boy in his choice of solitude held on to his whole liberty as long as he could. But domestication of his West by machine techniques began in the 1860's and, once started, went fast.

For in response to such techniques, the cattle industry grew with suddenness, and then became stabilized. The first of these was the westward advance of the railroads with which the northbound cattle drives could make a junction. It was not easy to arrange for the earliest rail transport of western cattle. A young Illinois cattle shipper who was the first to establish a livestock market in Kansas was astonished to have his new idea rejected by two railroad presidents and the leading businessmen of several Kansas towns to whom he went in turn. Finally the Hannibal & St. Joe Railroad gave the young shipper a contract "at very satisfactory rates of freight from the Missouri River to Quincy, thence to Chicago." He selected Abilene, Kansas, as the site for his stockyards, and in 1867 the first cattle were driven there from Texas. During the next four years 1,460,000 head of cattle were brought to Abilene. Other trails and shipping centers were soon established, and it was estimated that during a period of twenty-eight years nearly ten million cattle worth almost a hundred million dollars were moved from the Texas ranges to market. In the process of developing so great a business, the whole practice of cattle raising became formalized through changes that sought greater efficiency.

One of these used a technical machine product that soon conquered the open range where wild cattle once drifted according to weather. It was barbed wire, first used in 1875 to fence pastures in which with fewer and less skillful cow boys the herds could be restricted and more easily managed. When

land was enclosed, ranch dwellings were needed. Permanent
headquarters buildings followed. Cattle no longer were driven
to rivers but found their water in earth tanks supplied by dug
wells, with still another machine product to keep it flowing—
the metal windmill. The main trunk lines of the railroads ran
east to west across the continent; but soon feeder lines were
built—sometimes following the flat terrain of the old trails—
and machine transportation reached nearer and nearer to the
great ranches of the border where the whole cattle industry
had had its beginnings. The Missouri, Kansas and Texas Railroad was the great Texas cattle line. It tapped the Rio Grande
brush country ranges. The Atchison, Topeka and Santa Fe
main line crossed New Mexico and a branch line ran from
Belen on the Rio Grande all the way down the valley to El
Paso. The Texas and Pacific reached eastward from San Diego
to El Paso in 1877, and bridges now came back to the Rio
Grande to stay. The whole river empire was soon tied to the
rest of the nation by rails. When packing houses were established at Kansas City, Fort Worth, and other southwestern
cities, the final pattern of the organized beef cattle industry
was realized. In it there was little room for the figure, the temperament, of the original cow boy, with his individual lordship
over great unimpeded distances and his need of freedom as he
defined it. His cow camp literature recorded yet another stage
—the last—of his history. "The cow boy has left the country,"
he could sing, "and the campfire has gone out. . . ."

On barbed-wire fences, like symbols of the new order of
affairs over the controlled range lands, dead, skinned coyotes
were impaled in a frieze—twenty or thirty of them at a time.
They were stretched in mid-air with a lean, racing look of un-
earthly nimbleness, running nowhere; and their skulled teeth
had the smile of their own ghosts, wits of the plains. In the
dried varnish of their own amber serum they glistened under
the sun. The day of unrestrained predators was over.

J. FRANK DOBIE

In the Brush Country*

⟦ J. FRANK DOBIE, one of the great authorities on the American West, is Texas' chief contribution to American letters, author of a score of books with such southwestern titles as *The Longhorns, The Mustangs, The Voice of the Coyote, Coronado's Children.* But he is also author of *A Texan in England.* Dobie, professor of English literature as well as of American history, served as guest professor at Cambridge University during World War II. Born on a famed ranch, he typifies the kind of civilized mind that is magnetized by indigenous material but is able to view it from a nonregional outlook.

ONE DAY along in the early 'eighties a long, lanky, thirsty cowboy from up on the Esperanzas rode a Mexican bronco into the only town of McMullen County. He fetched up at the main store of the place with a yell that made the old mesquite tree outside shake its leaves, dragged his spurs inside, took three deep swigs of undiluted "white mule," and then announced that he was going to wake up everybody and every dog in town. He did. After he had yelled a while, interspersing his "yahooing" with more drinks of straight whiskey, he got

* From *A Vaquero of the Brush Country* by J. Frank Dobie. Copyright 1929 by J. Frank Dobie. Reprinted by permission of Little, Brown & Co.

on his bronc, let out what he proposed to be a climactic whoop, and dug in his spurs. The bronco began pitching and with each jump the cowboy gave a merry squall.

The dogs, which had been awakened, soon gathered around the horse and rider, all yelping. There were more than fifty of them. The natives seemed to be enjoying the show as much as the dogs, for they gathered also, joining in the noise to encourage both dogs and cowboy. Some of the dogs began to bite at the horse's heels and others at the rider's toes. The horse pitched a little higher and the cowboy yelled a little louder. He was having a bigger celebration than in his dreamiest hours out beyond in the ascetic prickly pear and black chaparral he had ever dreamed of having. Then he quieted down and his horse quieted down and the dogs fell silent, but they kept a ring around the mounted man just the same. "What next?" their ears and noses seemed to be saying.

The answer was a pretty hoarse squawk that the cowboy meant for a farewell, and he headed his bronc down the road. Perhaps the bronc did not understand. He went to pitching again and the dogs again began snapping at his heels and at the toes of the rider. The whole performance was repeated; when the cowboy had again quieted his horse, the dogs quieted too, but still kept their watchful circle. After a while the rider, who was sobering up a little, told the dogs very plainly to go home. If they understood they made no sign of understanding. Then the cowboy talked to the dogs in a language that even some of the men could not understand; apparently the dogs did not understand this language either.

Finally, however, a good Samaritan broke the circle of canine beleaguerers with a stick. The cowboy started off, and had he ridden on away slowly and quietly all would have been well; but he could not resist the temptation to express the buoyancy of his unconquerable soul. At the first whoop all the dogs took in after him. They outran him, and out near the Boot Hill Graveyard—nobody had heard of a "memorial park" in those days, and "cemetery" was still a literary word—they rounded him up again and kept him there for an hour. At last, however, he got ahead of the pack, and the music those dogs made behind him would have set any old fox-hunter wild with delight. How far they chased him nobody ever knew; some of them did not get back home until the next day.

Home was Tilden, on the Frio River. Before the presidential election of 1876 the name of Tilden was Dog Town, and Dog Town, despite the Post Office Department, it was for many years still called. The old name was more fitting than the new, but so far as one of the early postmasters of the town was concerned there was no difference between the two—at least not in print. When the stage brought the mail in, he would dump it on the floor of the post office and then shout: "There's your mail, boys! Pick out what belongs to you."

The half-dozen or so ranchmen of McMullen County who built their log houses in a bend of the Frio River, coming together for mutual protection against the Indians and Mexican bandits, had no intention of establishing a town. Eventually, however, some man put in a few groceries and a barrel of whiskey; then a stage route that was established between San Antonio and Laredo passed through the place. It had to have a name, and as every cowman had a pack of dogs with which to catch wild cattle out of the brush, it was logically and naturally christened Dog Town. Forty miles southwest of it was Fort Ewell on the Nueces in La Salle County, and Fort Ewell and Dog Town were the principal stage stands between San Antonio and the Rio Grande. From the big bend of the Nueces River in McMullen County to the thin line of Mexican *ranchitas* on the Rio Grande sixty or seventy-five miles southward the country was eighty years ago practically uninhabited.

The stagecoaches, which were light, were drawn by six little Spanish mules that usually went in a long lope and often in a run. These mules had to be circled by the driver and checked by the helper at each stage stand before they would come to a halt. If anybody wanted to get on or off at a point between the stands, all the driver could do was to circle the mules, thus reducing the speed somewhat, while the passenger jumped off or on as best he could. Stage robbers could make a hold-up

only by killing the mules. The few passengers who rode the
stage always got a thrill for their money.

McMullen County is on the border. Because of its limited
rainfall its lands were late in being sought by westward-push-
ing home-seekers, and, indeed, the dry farmer has not yet to
any considerable extent succeeded in growing crops on its soil.
Its brush makes excellent covert for anything, man or beast,
that is hunted. Hence it was in the early 'eighties a refuge for
outlaws not only from the counties to the north and east, where
law was becoming established, but from Mexico, where the
rurales President Diaz had inspired were running bandits into
their holes. Some of these outlaws purported to be mustangers;
all of them stole horses and cheated at cards.

Dog Town was the capital of the brush country—not the
splintering cedar brakes of the Colorado and the Llano, nor
the blackjacks of the country east of the San Antonio; not the
huisache of the lower Nueces, nor the clawing *tornillo* of the
upper Rio Grande. All of this is bad, but none of it is quite so
bad as the highly varied aggregation of thorns and limbs that
makes up the thickets of McMullen, Webb, Live Oak, Duval,
and other Texas counties lying between the Nueces River and
the Rio Grande. Mexicans used to refer to the big area of brush
in Webb and McMullen counties as the Brasada. *Brasada* is a
good word.

Perhaps no other widely dispersed tree growth responds more
apparently to climate, altitude, and latitude than the mesquite.
In the southern part of Live Oak County, where it seems generally to thrive best, it grows into great trees; on the Llano
and out on the Edwards Plateau it is gnarled and black-barked,
the tops conspicuously thin; on the plains it is just "switch
mesquite." The thorns on it vary in size and number as much
as the tree itself varies. In the Brasada the mesquite is as
nearly covered with thorns as it is possible for bushes to be
covered, and their length is at the maximum. But the mesquite
is just one among many thorned growths that characterize the
Brasada. Here are great *mogotes* (thickets) of the evergreen,
stubborn *coma* with dirk-like thorns two inches long. Here

are *granjeno,* cat's-claw, *agarita* (wild currant), *junco* ("all-thorn"), prickly pear—in some places higher than a man on horseback—devil's head, Spanish dagger, *huajilla* (another kind of cat's-claw), *brasil,* white brush, and black chaparral—all thorned and all showing their thorough adaptation to the country by diverging into many varieties.

To work effectively in this brush a *vaquero* had to have *tapaderos* (toe-fenders) on his stirrups, boots on his heels, heavy leather leggins (never called *chaps* in Southwest Texas) on his legs and up to his waist, ducking jacket for the protection of his arms and the trunk of his body, gauntleted gloves for his hands and wrists, and stout hat for the protection of his head. The hat frequently had a *barboquejo* (chin-strap), but even when strapped on it was likely to be torn off a *vaquero's* head in fierce struggles against the tenacious brush. Such was the skill of many brush hands, however, that they could dispense with much of this armor and still "tear a hole" through the worst thickets. A good gun alone does not make a good shot; a good saddle does not make a good rider; nor does a pair of high-heeled shop-made boots give a man the true cowboy walk.

Perhaps in dealing with the art of the brush hand the present tense rather than the past should be used. The Brasada is still a *brasada,* the openings in it fewer and smaller. It is still a cow country, and brush hands, mostly Mexicans now, still "kill up" their horses running wild cattle. However, the wild cattle are few indeed compared with their former numbers; the country is all cut up into pastures and the waterings are controlled by fences. Perfection in any art requires constant practice, and present conditions do not demand so much hard running in the brush as formerly. Nevertheless, although this account is of times and conditions that have passed away forever, the thorned land and the class of men who rode through the thorns have not, like so many other things, utterly vanished. As nearly as the present-day cowboy on the wide broken ranges of Arizona approaches the old-time cowboy, the present-day brush hand of Southwest Texas approaches the brush hand of the time when the Brasada was as wild as the cattle that hid in it.

In running in the brush a man rides not so much on the back of his horse as under and alongside. He just hangs on, dodging limbs as if he were dodging bullets, back, forward, over, under, half of the time trusting his horse to course right on this or that side of a bush or tree. If he shuts his eyes to dodge, he is lost. Whether he shuts them or not, he will, if he runs true to form, get his head rammed or raked. Patches of the brush hand's bandana hanging on thorns and stobs sometimes mark his trail. The bandana of red is his emblem.

If the brush is low and thick, the brush hand, while he may not have to dodge it with his head and body, still has to ride with every muscle active in order to stay on his leaping, crashing, swerving horse. Now the horse, in a bound that curves in mid-air so that he may secure footing on the other side, shows skylight under his belly. Here is a race with thorns for handicaps and every step a hurdle. It is a race that the Derby or Newport would hardly recognize.

Unseen and unapplauded, the brush hand almost daily exerts as much skill and grit as any rodeo star ever displayed in conquering the most savage outlaw horse. The bronco-buster is constantly on exhibition. Millions of people have seen him and thrilled at his daring. Great painters and able writers have glorified him. He has become the darling of the cowboy tradition. But nobody ever sees the brush-popper in action. When he does his most daring and dangerous work he is out of sight down in a thicket. An "observer" might hear him breaking limbs, but that is all. He has never been pictured on canvas or in print. If in the romance of range tradition he ever comes into his own, he will come through faith in somebody else's description and not by sight of rodeo fans.

A brush hand can work on the prairie as well as any prairie-trained cowboy. After he has struggled in the brush, any kind of horseback work on the prairie seems as "soft" to a brush hand as a cushioned rocking-chair seems to a leg-weary ditch-digger. No ditch-digger ever exerted himself more or sweated more profusely than a brush hand exerts himself and sweats in a thicket on a hot day. A prairie-trained cowboy is as helpless in bad brush as any tenderfoot.

Like the brush hand, the brush horse is a distinct type. A horse raised and trained on the open prairie is no more to be depended upon in the brush than in steep gorges and rocky mountains, though a brush horse is all right on the prairie provided it is clear of prairie-dog holes. These require a special skill. The chances are that the untrained hand who gets on a good brush horse and starts after a wild cow through a thicket will never get through. A good brush horse is not going to stop when he gets after something in the thorns any more than a game hound will stop when he gets hot on the trail of a panther. A little horse is better for dodging under low limbs; a big horse is better for clearing the way for his rider. A few horses, powerful and fearless, have a way of hitting the brush sidewise. Plenty of brush hands are afraid to ride these powerful horses: in the heat of the chase they are apt to become "cold-jawed" (hard-mouthed) and uncontrollable. But a rider who trusts to one will get there—if he doesn't get killed.

Let us draw a picture. Down in a *ramadero* of spined bushes and trees that seem to cover all space except that occupied by prickly pear, a man with scratched face, frazzled ducking jacket, and snagged leggins is sitting on a horse, one leg thrown over the horn of his saddle. He is humped forward and seems almost asleep. The horse has grey hairs in his flanks; his knees are lumped from licks and thorns of past years. He is an old-timer and knows the game. He is resting one hip and he seems to be asleep. The man is waiting, for some other *vaqueros* have entered the *ramadero* above him to start up the wild cattle. Presently he thinks that he catches the high note of a yell far up the brush; he feels a quiver in the muscles of his horse. The horse thinks that he hears too; he no longer appears to be asleep; his ears are cocked. A minute later the sound of the yell is unmistakable. The brush hand takes down his leg; the horse plants down the leg he has been resting and holds his head high, ears working. Again the yell, closer.

Pretty soon the popping of brush made by the running cattle

will be heard. There will not be many cattle in the bunch, however—just three or four or a half-dozen. Outlaws like company but they are not gregarious. The *vaquero's* feet are planted deep in the stirrups now. *Pop—scratch*—silence. In what direction was that sound? The old horse's heart is beating like a drum against the legs of his rider. *Pop—scr-r-ratch*—rattle and rake of hoofs. Man and horse hit the brush as one. They understand each other. They may get snagged, knocked by limbs that will not break, cut, speared, pierced with black thorns, the poison from which sends cold chills down the back of the man and makes him sick at the stomach. No matter. The horse and rider go like a pair of mated dogs charging a boar. The brush tears and pops as if a pair of Missouri mules were running through it with a mowing machine. Hell pops. The brush hand is in his element.

Walter Billingsley used to say that "if Sam Dickens was running a cow across a prairie a section wide and there was a chaparral bush in the middle of it, Sam would head his horse right through the bush." Sam was a brush-popper. Like many another brush rider, Sam was wont to emerge from a thicket with enough wood hanging in the fork of his saddle to cook a side of yearling ribs.

Winter has always been the best time in which to run wild cattle. Then some of the brush sheds its leaves, allowing greater visibility, although much of the brush, like the *coma* and black chaparral, is evergreen. Wild cattle that have been run hard and become "over-het," often die. In hot weather they will literally run themselves to death; running in cold weather is much less disastrous. In winter time, too, a horse can run farther and work harder without becoming *solado,* or *solyowed* (*solaoed*) as the border people have Anglicised the Spanish word meaning "wind-broken." Half of the cow ponies of the brush country used to be *solado.* The heat and exertion suffered by a horse that is ridden recklessly and relentlessly through the brush of South Texas in summer time are overpowering.

A brush-popper does not ask for room in which to swing his rope. He is lucky if he strikes a little opening big enough to allow him to toss a clear loop over the horns or head of the animal he is running. If he misses his throw at this little opening, he will probably not get such an opportunity again. Often he is right at the animal's heels without space in which to cast any kind of loop. If he can keep up with the animal long enough, however, he is almost sure to come to a place where he can rope it by one or both hind legs. Sometimes he leans over and pitches the loop up instead of down, as is done on the prairie, thus avoiding low-hanging limbs. This kind of side-and-up throw generally catches a cow *media cabeza*—by the half-head. To rope in the brush a *vaquero* wants a much shorter rope—one about twenty-five feet long is right—than is used on the plains, where ropes forty feet long, and even forty-five, can be managed. Carrying a rope in the brush without getting it entangled is an art in itself. In the old days the rawhide *reata* was used a great deal, for it could, on account of its weight, be thrown through the small brush much more effectively than lighter ropes of fiber.

The number of horses required to mount a man who was running regularly in the Brasada was very large—probably three times the number required in an open country, for they were always getting crippled. As long as a horse keeps warm he can run, no matter how many thorns are in him; he becomes crippled only after he has cooled off. The morning after a *corrida* of men had run all day in the brush, a third of their horses would sometimes be unable to walk to the corral with the *remuda*.

Prickly-pear poultices and kerosene oil were the principal remedies against thorns in the flesh of either man or horse, though "Volcanic Oil" and "Sloan's Liniment" were widely used. When a horse got a thorn from the *biznaga* (devil's head) in his foot, no poultice or caustic could draw it out. The devil made the *biznaga* thorn so that it will work in, in, and it is plated with a hard substance that will hardly decay at all. A big mesquite or *coma* thorn in the joint of a horse's leg is as bad as a *biznaga* thorn in his foot.

Thorns were just one item that brush ranchers had to contend with in trying to keep enough horses to work on. Horse-thieves were another item. Mustangs, constant enticers of gentle horses, were still another. Then, sometimes saddle stock would wander from their accustomed range looking for better grass. A few months later they might return fat; again, they might never return. Sometimes a rancher even in the midst of cow work might find himself afoot and compelled to buy a new *remuda*.

After the "Big Steal" of the 'seventies—a story in itself—most of the cattle left in the Brasada country were literally wilder than the deer. When Pat Garrett, in his *Authentic Life of Billy the Kid*, wished to give an idea of how fast some outlaws ran on a certain occasion, he said, "They ran like a bunch of wild Nueces steers." To *run like a Nueces steer* used to be a com-mon—and expressive—saying to keep company with *kicking like a bay steer*. These native wild cattle of the Nueces did not know that the brush grew thorns. Among them were old maverick cows and bulls that belonged to anybody who could catch them. Some of the cows and steers that bore brands were not worth catching. If roped they would only "sull" and fight; they weighed nothing and "looked as if they had but one gut in them." The best thing to do with them was to shoot them in order to prevent their spoiling other cattle. Out in the Brasada ten and fifteen miles from permanent water were old Mexican longhorns that could subsist for months on prickly pear and dagger blooms without coming to water at all. Such cattle were exceedingly wary. Only dogs could rouse them.

It used to be a common saying that Texas was all right for men and dogs but was hell on women and horses. In the Brasada country the dogs had as hard a time as the women and horses. Every cowman had his pack for trailing and rallying the wild cattle; when an outfit was working regularly it had to change dogs just as it changed horses, for thorns, rocks, and the prevailing warm weather would wear down the hardiest of dogs. Three dogs were regarded as the right number for two or three *vaqueros* working together to run with. In the brush there could be no round-ups; the cow hands just "worked," "hunted," and "ran" cattle. Running them with dogs did not make them any gentler.

On moonlight nights the *vaqueros* often took stands near the river and roped *ladinos*—outlaw cattle. Low-hanging elms and other growth line the banks of the Frio and Nueces in this part of the country; then there used to be—and to an extent yet are—openings between the river brush and back-lying thickets. Outlaw cattle that stayed in the thickets all day crossed these openings at night in order to get to water, and they liked also to come out and graze in the openings. It was best to let them fill up on water, so that they would not be so active, before tying into them. Often the men lying in wait had to run through scattering brush in order to get to the cattle; night roping then became dangerous business. Old Dan Mc-Closkey was right: he used to say that it took just two things to make a good brush roper, especially at night—"a damned fool and a race horse."

When an outlaw animal was roped out in the brush it was tied to a tree and then later necked to a lead ox and thus brought in. The lead oxen were, of course, gentle. They were kept around ranch headquarters, and one of them with a rope around his horns would lead, following a *vaquero*, as well as a horse. After an outlaw "critter" had been necked to a well trained ox, the ox would be turned loose and left alone to make his way back to the ranch, frequently through many miles of brush. In the course of a day or two he would come in, his mate considerably subdued. However, many of the lead oxen with their yoke-mates had to be driven.

At the ranch the outlaw cattle, some with forked sticks on their necks, some with heads tied down to a front foot, some necked together, might be held in a small pasture until enough cattle were gathered to make a bunch; or they might be held under herd with gentler cattle during the day and then penned at night. Getting them out of the country even after they were caught was a job. They were generally put into a herd of cattle that were manageable.

Excessively wild cattle in a brush country have never been

money-makers. In order to gentle their cattle the Brasada ranch people kept their cows and calves up in a pen, turning the cows out to pasture by day and the calves out by night. Several months of this sort of handling would gentle the cows, and the calves would start life in a civilized manner. Sometimes a ranchman would have two or three hundred head of cows and calves up at one time. A few of the cows were so wild that they would not come to the pens even for their calves. In that event the calves might be released to their mothers, or they might be suckled to other cows and thus raised as *sanchos* (dogies).

The Brasada—the brush country—marked the meeting of the East and the West. Desperados from eastern states as well as from Texas counties to the east sought the border brush and its security. Raiding Mexicans from below the Rio Grande slipped over the unguarded river, rendezvoused with the American bad men, stole, murdered if necessary, and rode back into Mexico before they could be discovered, though plenty of them were trailed far beyond the borders of Texas and there ceased making tracks forever. In short, the Brasada was a strategic point for stealing and smuggling.

The white men who operated with the Mexicans were even worse thieves and more hardened criminals than the *bandidos;* in some ways they were worse than the Comanches had been. They could steal a bunch of horses as far east as the San Antonio River, ride hard all night and a part of one day, and then, having crossed the Nueces River, lie up in some wild thicket of the Brasada. There Mexican confederates with a bunch of "wet" horses—horses stolen in Mexico and smuggled across the river—would meet them; the two outfits would exchange stolen stock; then each would turn back with horses to trade. Such operators could afford to offer horses at attractive prices. Many a Texas cowman bought Mexican horses for which his own *remuda* stolen a week or ten days before had been swapped.

JACK POTTER

·─·→·──◆►●◄◘──·◆··

Coming off the Trail in 1882*

❨ JACK POTTER survived the high jinks he relates here
to become a prosperous stockman at Kenton, Oklahoma, a
ranch manager known throughout the cattle industry. His
memoir of 1882 experiences appeared in *The Trail Drivers
of Texas* compiled and edited by the late J. Marvin Hunter
and is, as Frank Dobie says, "about the livest thing in that
monumental collection." Son of a famed West Texas
preacher, Jack Potter the "Fighting Parson," the younger
Potter was characterized by George W. Saunders, president
of the Old Time Trail Drivers' Association, as a "rip-roar-
ing, hell-raising cowpuncher" who "was considered to be
the most cheerful liar on the face of the earth."

I N THE SPRING of 1882, the New England Livestock Co.
bought three thousand short horns in Southwest Texas, and
cut them into four herds and started them on the trail to
Colorado. . . . There was no excitement whatever on this
drive. It was to me very much like a summer's outing in the
Rocky Mountains. . . . After leaving Cheyenne we pulled out
for Powder River and then up to Sheridan. The weather was
getting cold and I began to get homesick. . . . When we
arrived at the Crow Agency the boss received a letter from
the manager instructing him to send me back to Texas, as the

* From *The Trail Drivers of Texas* (2nd ed., rev.; Nashville, Tenn.: Cokes-
bury Press, 1925).

company were contracting for cattle for spring delivery, and I would be needed in the trail drives. The next morning I roped my favorite horse and said to the boys: "Good-bye, fellows, I am drifting south where the climate suits my clothes." That day I overtook an outfit on the way to Ogallala, and traveled with them several days, and then cut out from them and hiked across the prairie one hundred and fifty miles to the Crow ranch, where I sold my two horses and hired a party to take me and my saddle to Greeley, where I expected to set out for home.

Now, reader, here I was, a boy not yet seventeen years old, two thousand miles from home. I had never been on a railroad train, had never slept in a hotel, never taken a bath in a bath house, and from babyhood I had heard terrible stories about ticket thieves, money-changers, pickpockets, three-card monte, and other robbing schemes, and I had horrors about this, my first railroad trip. The first thing I did was to make my money safe by tying it up in my shirt tail. I had a draft for $150 and some currency. I purchased a second-hand trunk and about two hundred feet of rope with which to tie it. The contents of the trunk were one apple-horn saddle, a pair of chaps, a Colt's 45, one sugan, a hen-skin blanket, and a change of dirty clothes. You will see later that this trunk and its contents caused me no end of trouble.

My cowboy friends kindly assisted me in getting ready for the journey. The company had agreed to provide me with transportation, and they purchased a local ticket to Denver for me and gave me a letter to deliver to the general ticket agent at this point, instructing him to sell me a reduced ticket to Dodge City, Kansas, and enable me to secure a cowboy ticket from there to San Antonio for twenty-five dollars. Dodge City was the largest delivering point in the Northwest, and by the combined efforts of several prominent stockmen a cheap rate to San Antonio had been perfected for the convenience of the hundreds of cowboys returning home after the drives.

About four P.M. the Union Pacific train came pulling into Greeley. Then it was a hasty handshake with the boys. One of them handed me my trunk check, saying, "Your baggage is loaded. Good-bye, write me when you get home," and the train pulled out. It took several minutes for me to collect myself, and then the conductor came through and called for the tickets. When I handed him my ticket he punched a hole in it, and then pulled out a red slip, punched it, too, and slipped it into my hatband. I jumped to my feet and said, "You can't come that on me. Give me back my ticket," but he passed out of hearing, and as I had not yet learned how to walk on a moving train, I could not follow him. When I had become fairly settled in my seat again the train crossed a bridge, and as it went by I thought the thing was going to hit me on the head. I dodged those bridges all the way up to Denver. When I reached there I got off at the Union Station and walked down to the baggage car, and saw them unloading my trunk. I stepped up and said: "I will take my trunk." A man said, "No; we are handling this baggage." "But," said I, "that is my trunk, and has my saddle and gun in it." They paid no attention to me and wheeled the trunk off to the baggage room, but I followed right along, determined that they were not going to put anything over me. Seeing that I was so insistent one of the men asked me for the check. It was wrapped up in my shirt tail, and I went after it, and produced the draft I had been given as wages. He looked at it and said, "This is not your trunk check. Where is your metal check with numbers on it?" Then it began to dawn on me what the darn thing was, and when I produced it and handed it to him, he asked me where I was going. I told him to San Antonio, Texas, if I could get there. I then showed him my letter to the general ticket agent, and he said: "Now, boy, you leave this trunk right here and we will recheck it and you need not bother about it." That sounded bully to me.

I followed the crowd down Sixteenth and Curtiss Streets and rambled around looking for a quiet place to stop. I found the St. Charles Hotel and made arrangements to stay all night. Then I went off to a barber shop to get my hair cut and clean up a bit. When the barber finished with me he asked if I wanted a bath, and when I said yes, a Negro porter took me down the hallway and into a side room. He turned on the water, tossed me a couple of towels and disappeared. I commenced undressing hurriedly, fearing the tub would fill up before I could get ready. The water was within a few inches of the top of the tub when I plunged in. Then I gave a yell like a Comanche Indian, for the water was boiling hot! I came out of the tub on all fours, but when I landed on the marble floor it was so slick that I slipped and fell backwards with my head down. I scrambled around promiscuously, and finally got my footing with a chair for a brace. I thought: "Jack Potter, you are scalded after the fashion of a hog." I caught a lock of my hair to see if it would "slip," at the same time fanning myself with my big Stetson hat. I next examined my toe nails, for they had received a little more dipping than my hair, but I found them in fairly good shape, turning a bit dark, but still hanging on.

That night I went to the Tabor Opera House and saw a fine play. There I found a cowboy chum, and we took in the sights until midnight, when I returned to the St. Charles. The porter showed me up to my room and turned on the gas. When he had gone I undressed to go to bed, and stepped up to blow out the light. I blew and blew until I was out of breath, and then tried to fan the flame out with my hat, but I had to go to bed and leave the gas burning. It was fortunate that I did not succeed, for at that time the papers were full of accounts of people gassed just that way.

The next morning I started out to find the Santa Fé ticket office, where I presented my letter to the head man there. He was a nice appearing gentleman, and when he had looked over the letter he said, "So you are a genuine cowboy? Where is your gun and how many notches have you on its handle? I suppose you carry plenty of salt with you on the trail for emergency? I was just reading in a magazine a few days ago about a large herd which stampeded and one of the punchers mounted a swift horse and ran up in front of the leaders and began throwing out salt, and stopped the herd just in time to

keep them from running off a high precipice." I laughed
heartily when he told me this and said, "My friend, you can't
learn the cow business out of books. That yarn was hatched
in the brain of some fiction writer who probably never saw a
cow in his life. But I am pleased to find a railroad man who will
talk, for I always heard that a railroad man only used two
words, Yes and No." Then we had quite a pleasant conversation. He asked me if I was ever in Albert's Buckhorn saloon in
San Antonio and saw the collection of fine horns there. Then
he gave me an emigrant cowboy ticket to Dodge City and a
letter to the agent at that place stating that I was eligible for
a cowboy ticket to San Antonio.

As it was near train time I hunted up the baggage crew and
told them I was ready to make another start. I showed them
my ticket and asked them about my trunk. They examined it,
put on a new check, and gave me one with several numbers on
it. I wanted to take the trunk out and put it on the train,
but they told me to rest easy and they would put it on. I stood
right there until I saw them put it on the train, then I climbed
aboard.

This being my second day out, I thought my troubles should
be over, but not so, for I couldn't face those bridges. They
kept me dodging and fighting my head. An old gentleman who
sat near me said, "Young man, I see by your dress that you
are a typical cowboy, and no doubt you can master the worst
bronco or rope and tie a steer in less than a minute, but in
riding on a railway train you seem to be a novice. Sit down
on this seat with your back to the front and those bridges will
not bother you." And sure enough it was just as he said.

We arrived at Coolidge, Kansas, one of the old landmarks
of the Santa Fé trail days, about dark. That night at twelve
o'clock we reached Dodge City, where I had to lay over for
twenty-four hours. I thought everything would be quiet in the
town at that hour of the night, but I soon found out that they
never slept in Dodge. They had a big dance hall there which
was to Dodge City what Jack Harris' Theater was to San
Antonio. I arrived at the hall in time to see a gambler and a

cowboy mix up in a six-shooter duel. Lots of smoke, a stampede, but no one killed. I secured a room and retired. When morning came I arose and fared forth to see Dodge City by daylight. It seemed to me that the town was full of cowboys and cattle owners. The first acquaintance I met here was George W. Saunders, now the president and chief remudero of the Old Trail Drivers. I also found Jesse Pressnall and Slim Johnson there, as well as several others whom I knew down in Texas. Pressnall said to me: "Jack, you will have lots of company on your way home. Old 'Dog Face' Smith is up here from Cotulla and he and his whole bunch are going back tonight. Old 'Dog Face' is one of the best trail men that ever drove a cow, but he is all worked up about having to go back on a train. I wish you would help them along down the line in changing cars." That afternoon I saw a couple of chuck wagons coming in loaded with punchers, who had on the same clothing they wore on the trail, their pants stuck in their boots and their spurs on. They were bound for San Antonio. Old "Dog Face" Smith was a typical Texan, about thirty years of age, with long hair and three months' growth of whiskers. He wore a blue shirt and a red cotton handkerchief around his neck. He had a bright, intelligent face that bore the appearance of a good trail hound, which no doubt was the cause of people calling him "Dog Face."

It seemed a long time that night to wait for the train and we put in time visiting every saloon in the town. There was a big stud poker game going on in one place, and I saw one Texas fellow, whose name I will not mention, lose a herd of cattle at the game. But he might have won the herd back before daylight.

I will never forget seeing that train come into Dodge City that night. Old "Dog Face" and his bunch were pretty badly frightened and we had considerable difficulty in getting them aboard. It was about 12:30 when the train pulled out. The conductor came around and I gave him my cowboy ticket. It was almost as long as your arm, and as he tore off a chunk of it I said: "What authority have you to tear up a man's ticket?"

He laughed and said, "You are on my division. I simply tore off one coupon and each conductor between here and San Antonio will tear off one for each division." That sounded all right, but I wondered if that ticket would hold out all the way down.

Everyone seemed to be tired and worn out and the bunch began bedding down. Old "Dog Face" was out of humor, and was the last one to bed down. At about three o'clock our train was sidetracked to let the westbound train pass. This little stop caused the boys to sleep the sounder. Just then the westbound train sped by traveling at the rate of about forty miles an hour, and just as it passed our coach the engineer blew the whistle. Talk about your stampedes! That bunch of sleeping cowboys arose as one man, and started on the run with old "Dog Face" Smith in the lead. I was a little slow in getting off, but fell in with the drags. I had not yet woke up, but thinking I was in a genuine cattle stampede, yelled out, "Circle your leaders and keep up the drags." Just then the leaders circled and ran into the drags, knocking some of us down. They circled again and the news butcher crawled out from under foot and jumped through the window like a frog. Before they could circle back the next time, the train crew pushed in the door and caught old "Dog Face" and soon the bunch quieted down. The conductor was pretty angry and threatened to have us transferred to the freight department and loaded into a stock car.

We had breakfast at Hutchinson, and after eating and were again on our way, speeding through the beautiful farms and thriving towns of Kansas, we organized a kangaroo court and tried the engineer of that westbound train for disturbing the peace of passengers on the eastbound train. We heard testimony all morning, and called in some of the train crew to testify. One of the brakemen said it was an old trick for that engineer to blow the whistle at that particular siding and that he was undoubtedly the cause of a great many stampedes. The jury brought in a verdict of guilty and assessed the death penalty. It was ordered that he be captured, taken to some place on the Western trail, there to be hog-tied like a steer, and then have the road brand applied with a good hot iron and a herd of not less than five thousand long-horn Texas steers made to stampede and trample him to death.

We had several hours' lay-over at Emporia, Kansas, where we took the M., K. & T. for Parsons, getting on the main line through Indian Territory to Denison, Texas. There was a large crowd of punchers on the through train who were returning from Ogallala by way of Kansas City and Omaha.

As we were traveling through the Territory old "Dog Face" said to me: "Potter, I expect it was me that started that stampede up there in Kansas, but I just couldn't help it. You see, I took on a scare once and since that time I have been on the hair trigger when suddenly awakened. In the year 1875 me and Wild Horse Jerry were camped at a water hole out west of the Nueces River, where we were snaring mustangs. One evening a couple of peloncias pitched camp nearby, and the next morning our remuda was missing, all except our night horses. I told Wild Horse Jerry to hold down the camp and watch the snares, and I hit the trail of those peloncias which headed for the Rio Grande. I followed it for about forty miles and then lost all signs. It was nightfall, so I made camp, prepared supper and rolled up in my blanket and went to sleep. I don't know how long I slept, but I was awakened by a low voice saying: "Dejarle desconsar bien por que en un rato el va a comenzar su viaje por el otro mundro." (Let him rest well, as he will soon start on his journey to the other world.) It was the two Mexican horse thieves huddled around my campfire smoking their cigarettes and taking it easy, as they thought they had the drop on me. As I came out of my bed two bullets whizzed near my head, but about that time my old Colt's forty-five began talking, and the janitor down in Hades had two more peloncias on his hands. Ever since that night, if I am awakened suddenly I generally come out on my all fours roaring like a buffalo bull. I never sleep on a bedstead, for it would not be safe for me, as I might break my darn neck, so I always spread down on the floor."

It was a long ride through the Territory, and we spent the

balance of the day singing songs and making merry. I kept thinking about my trunk, and felt grateful that the railroad people had sent along a messenger to look out for it. At Denison we met up with some emigrant families going to Uvalde, and soon became acquainted with some fine girls in the party. They entertained us all the way down to Taylor, where we changed cars. As we told them good-bye one asked me to write a line in her autograph album. Now I was sure enough "up a tree." I had been in some pretty tight places, and had had to solve some pretty hard problems, but this was a new one for me. You see, the American people go crazy over some new fad about once a year, and in 1882 it was the autograph fad. I begged the young lady to excuse me, but she insisted, so I took the album and began writing down all the road brands that I was familiar with. But she told me to write a verse of some kind. I happened to think of a recitation I had learned at school when I was a little boy, so I wrote as follows: "It's tiresome work says lazy Ned, to climb the hill in my new sled, and beat the other boys. Signed, Your Bulliest Friend, JACK POTTER."

We then boarded the I. & G. N. for San Antonio, and at Austin a lively bunch joined us, including Hal Gosling, United States Marshal, Captain Joe Sheeley and Sheriff Quigley of Castroville. Pretty soon the porter called out "San Antonio, Santonnie-o," and that was music to my ears. My first move on getting off the train was to look for my trunk and found it had arrived. I said to myself, "Jack Potter, you're a lucky dog. Ticket held out all right, toe nails all healed up, and trunk came through in good shape." After registering at the Central Hotel, I wrote to that general ticket agent at Denver as follows:

San Antonio, Texas, Oct. 5th, 1882.
Gen. Ticket Agt. A. T. & S. F.,
1415 Lamar St., Denver, Colo.:

DEAR SIR—I landed in San Antonio this afternoon all O. K. My trunk also came through without a scratch. I want to thank you very much for the man you sent along to look after my trunk. He was very accommodating, and would not allow me to assist him in loading it on at Denver. No doubt he will want to see some of the sights of San Antonio, for it is a great place, and noted for its chili con carne. When he takes a fill of this food, as every visitor does, you can expect him back in Denver on very short notice, as he will be seeking a cooler climate. Did you ever eat any chili con carne? I will send you a dozen cans soon, but tell your wife to keep it in the refrigerator as it might set the house on fire. Thank you again for past favors.

Your Bulliest Friend,

JACK POTTER.

WAYNE GARD

Grub for the Trail*

《 WAYNE GARD, editorial writer for the Dallas *Morning News*, has published five books on the frontier West, his subjects ranging from the badman tradition (*Sam Bass, Frontier Justice*) to the great days of quarter-horse racing (*Fabulous Quarter Horse: Steel Dust*). "Grub for the Trail" is from his comprehensive history of one of the main cattle-driving routes, *The Chisholm Trail*. Gard's latest work is *The Great Buffalo Hunt*.

IN THE ERA of trail driving, the cook was a key man in any cattle outfit. Usually he was older than the punchers and drew higher pay. In authority he ranked next to the trail boss. Often he was a veteran cow hand who, from some accident, had been disabled for work in the saddle and had learned the art of pots and kettles. A successful drover chose his cook carefully to have one who could keep the men satisfied with good grub.

On the trail, according to James H. Cook,

a camp cook could do more toward making life pleasant for those about him than any other man in the outfit. A good-natured, hustling cook meant a lot to a trail boss. A cheery voice ringing out at daybreak, shouting, "Roll out there, fellers, and hear the little birdies

---

* From *The Chisholm Trail* (Norman, Okla.: University of Oklahoma Press, 1954).

sing their praises to God!" or "Arise and shine and give God the glory!" would make the most crusty waddy grin as he crawled out to partake of his morning meal—even when he was extremely short of sleep.

As a rule, though, the camp cook had a reputation for being grouchy and cantankerous. "Crossin' a cook is as risky as braidin' a mule's tail," said some. Many a cook gloried in this reputation for crankiness and tried to keep the trail drivers in awe of him. In addition to cooking, he drove the chuck wagon, kept it and the harness in repair, and served as doctor for men and horses. He was custodian of the personal belongings of the trail hands and often stakes-holder for bets. Sometimes he would condescend to pull a tooth, trim hair, or sew on a button.

The wagon at which the cook presided was the outcome of an evolutionary process and was a highly functional vehicle. In the earliest cattle drives from Texas, as in the cow hunts of that period, each of the few men involved had carried his own food. It might be taken in a saddle bag or in a sack tied behind the cantle of the saddle. As the drives became larger, an outfit might take along a Negro slave or a Mexican to do the cooking. In this event, the food would be carried by a pack horse or mule. In later years, one that persisted in this method was called a "greasy sack" outfit, and the mule a "long-eared chuck wagon."

As trails became longer and herds larger, the pack mule gave way to the oxcart. But the cart was too clumsy, and the oxen were too slow. More speed was needed to enable the cook to arrive at the camp site early and to have a hot supper ready for the tired men. At the close of the Civil War, cowmen began adapting wagons for trail use. Some of the first ones they called commissaries. In the spring of 1866, Charles Goodnight bought the gear of a government wagon, with axles of iron instead of the usual wood. He had a Parker County woodworker rebuild the wagon of tough, seasoned bois d'arc and put a chuck box on the back end. The wagon carried a can of tallow for greasing the axles.

Although Goodnight had this early chuck wagon pulled by

six oxen, it soon became the custom to use horses or mules—
usually four. Almost any good wagon could be converted for
trail use. The drover preferred one with wide tires that gave
better traction in rough country. The narrow-tired wagon of
the farmer he disdained as a "butcher-knife" wagon. In use,
the trail wagon or chuck wagon usually was referred to merely
as "the wagon." It had a standard bed, often with extra side-
boards, for carrying the men's bedrolls and other equipment.
As a rule, it had bows over which a canvas wagon sheet could
be tied as a shield against sun and rain.

"Come and Get It!"

Drawing by Harold D. Bugbee, from *Son-of-a-Gun Stew: A Sampling of the Southwest*, edited by Elizabeth Matchett Stover
(Southern Methodist University Press, 1945)

The chuck box, which Goodnight had had built into his
trail wagon in 1866, was several years in coming into common
use. "At first we just had kegs for our supplies," said Mark
Withers.

Our first mess boxes were goods boxes. We put bacon, coffee, and
flour in a box in the middle of the wagon. We had hides stretched
under the wagon and put utensils there. We also had a water barrel
with the spout out in front of the wagon. Later we turned it so the
spout was out on one side. I liked the barrel spout out in front better
because it didn't get broken as often.

"The outfit of a Texas drover is a scientific fit," noted one who saw the wagons being loaded in front of the grocery stores at Matagorda early in 1874.

There seldom is a cover to the wagon—it's too much trouble. The whole is exposed to public gaze. There are kegs of molasses, jugs of vinegar, boxes of bacon, sugar, and a variety of other provisions. Some things are strapped to the sides in a helter-skelter but perfectly secure manner. Sometimes bundles of kindling are tied to the hind axle.

The chuck box, the most distinctive feature of the later wagon, was built into the back end. This was a closed cupboard with partitions, shelves, and drawers for food and utensils. Its rear end sloped outward from top to bottom, like the front of an antique writing desk. The piece across the sloping end was hinged at the bottom so that it could be lowered to a horizontal position. This allowed it to serve as a kitchen table in front of the cabinet. The cabinet door was held in this position by ropes or chains or, more often, by a prop resting on the ground.

The chuck box held cutlery or "eatin' irons," a five-gallon keg or jar of sourdough, a sack of flour, cans of coffee, a supply of salt, and a variety of other foods and condiments. These might include beans, salt pork, dried fruits, canned tomatoes, a few onions and potatoes, sugar, molasses, pepper, and lard. One drawer might contain a few simple remedies, such as liniment, quinine, and some kind of laxative. There might be a bottle of whiskey for snake bite. If so, it would be the only intoxicant allowed with the outfit.

Some wagons had beneath the chuck box a smaller box for the heavier utensils, such as skillets, pots, and Dutch ovens. A water barrel, usually with a wooden spigot, was fastened on one side of the wagon. Balancing it on the other side was a tool box containing branding irons, horseshoeing equipment, an ax, and a shovel. Usually the wagon carried grain for its harness horses or mules. The cow ponies had to get along on grass.

Stretched under the bottom of most wagons was a rawhide hammock into which the wrangler put spare wood for fuel.

Where there was no wood at hand, it carried buffalo chips or cow chips, which the punchers called prairie coal. This hammock was called the cooney, from the Spanish *cuna,* or cradle. Some called it the 'possum belly. Occasionally, when not needed for storing fuel, it was put to other use. "It was a splendid place," said G. E. Lemmon, "for a small person to crawl into on a stormy night when all hands were not required with the herd—which was seldom. I have many times crawled into the cooney and come out dry and warm the next morning."

The cook, whose art Ramon Adams describes in detail in his book, *Come an' Get It,* was wakened by his alarm clock ahead of the others. He tried to have meals ready on time. If, in a big outfit, he needed help, he called on the wrangler. Besides bringing in fuel, the wrangler could grind coffee, keep the water barrel filled, and help with the dishes.

When breakfast was ready, the cook yelled, "Roll out! Come an' get it! Come a-runnin'!" Or a more imaginative one might call out:

> Bacon in the pan,
> Coffee in the pot!
> Get up and get it—
> Get it while it's hot!

The trail afforded less variety in fare than did the ranch. Pancakes usually were out of the question in a big trail outfit, while eggs and fresh vegetables were served only on those rare occasions when the men could swap a calf or a shoulder of beef to some nester.

Always there was hot coffee—hot and strong. "I have yet to see a cowboy who isn't a coffee drinker," observed Bill Poage, who went up the trail in 1874. The cook put plenty of Arbuckle's in the pot and boiled it for half an hour. Some called it six-shooter coffee. It was so strong, they said, that it would float a pistol. Almost always it was taken without sugar and without any of the condensed milk that the cook might have in a can.

The breakfast that the coffee washed down might include

bacon or salt pork, sourdough biscuits, and some sort of dried fruit such as prunes, raisins, or apples. The sourdough biscuits came with almost every meal. They were the main test of a cook's ability. Heavy or doughy "sinkers" might get the cook a reputation as a "belly cheater." Light, fluffy ones would draw appreciative murmurs and calls for more.

The sourdoughs were made without yeast. At the start of the drive the cook mixed batter in a keg or jar and let it ferment a day or two. Then, each day, he took out some of the batter, added soda and lard, and worked it into dough. When he did this, he put into the jar more flour, salt, and water. Thus the fermenting continued all through the drive. The biscuits were baked in a Dutch oven set over coals and with other coals piled on its lid. Some trail hands boasted that their cook made sourdoughs so light that, unless he mixed in blueberries or raisins, the mosquitoes and gnats would carry them off.

The noon meal, although called dinner, was usually light. Its preparation and content depended largely on the time the cook had after reaching the nooning site. Supper was the big meal for the meat-eating cowboys. There always was plenty of beef. Whenever the supply in the wagon ran low, it was easy for the men to kill another steer or heifer. Often they would rope a stray from some other herd and thus avoid killing one of their own. If not, they picked a young one with poor markings or one that had been giving trouble on the trail. The killing was done at some distance from the herd, since the smell of blood excited the longhorns. The meat was hung overnight to cool, then wrapped in slickers and placed in the wagon.

For a day or two after each killing, the trail hands would feast on son-of-a-gun stew. It had everything in it, some said, except the horns, hide, and hoofs. It was a mixture of tongue, liver, heart, and other small parts that needed to be cooked promptly where there was no refrigeration. Although some cooks made the stew in water, others used only the juices of the meat. It was made from beef alone, except for salt and pepper and, in some cases, an onion or a pinch of chili powder.

With the stew out of the way, the men settled down to roasts and steaks, especially the latter. The cook cut the steaks in generous slabs, covered them with flour, and cooked them in sizzling suet in his Dutch oven. Just before they were done, he added salt. Often he served potatoes and onions with the roasts. Dried beans, after being soaked overnight, frequently were cooked over a slow fire, with pieces of dry salt pork for seasoning. Most cowmen liked the beans, which some called Pecos strawberries. Occasionally a wagon had a keg of mixed pickles. Canned tomatoes, often used between meals to quench thirst, sometimes appeared as a dessert. A more common dessert was molasses, called lick, which the trail men sopped up with their sourdough biscuits. On rare occasions the cook baked pies, usually with raisins or dried apples.

Dennis Collins told of the time when he and a fellow puncher, out with a mixed herd, had a hankering for custard pie. The cook, who had some turkey eggs that had been found the day before, told the cowboys they would have to get the milk.

Bill and I chose a cow that seemed to have more milk than her calf required. Bill roped her, threw her, and hog-tied her. I held her down while he was endeavoring to separate her from her milk. With much labor and some protests against her restlessness, he extracted about a pint. I proudly gave it to the cook, but he informed me that it was not enough for a pie. It took wrangling with two more of those restless creatures to persuade them to favor us with some of their milk, but we succeeded.

When the herd was delayed in the Indian country, some of the men might bring the cook fish, venison, or wild turkey to vary the diet. At other times the trail hands, although usually "hungry enough to eat a saddle blanket" and not choosey about food, might find the fare monotonous and complain in song:

> Oh, it's bacon and beans 'most every day—
> I'd as soon be eatin' prairie hay.

At meals on the trail, the men, often leaving their hats on, helped themselves to food and coffee. Then, with legs crossed, they sat on the prairie and ate their fill. When through, they dropped their tin plates, cups, and cutlery in the dishpan or tub, the "wreck pan." If they didn't like the food, they seldom dared complain within hearing of the cook. But, after a hard day in the saddle, almost any grub was likely to taste good. Most of the trail men preferred the rough cow-camp fare to that of town restaurants, whose "wasp-nest" bread they rated a poor substitute for fluffy sourdough biscuits.

TOM LEA

Cattle Raids on the King Ranch*

⟦ TOM LEA of El Paso began as a painter (he trained at the Art Institute of Chicago and later in Rome) and while serving as war correspondent-illustrator for *Life* magazine with the Marines in the Pacific in World War II he turned also to words and writing. His first novel following the war, *The Brave Bulls*, was a smash hit as well as a critical success. His most recent work is the famed two-volume *The King Ranch*, a national best seller despite the $17.50 price. Readers got their money's worth, as can be seen from this selection, which was rewritten and condensed from *The King Ranch* (Little, Brown, 1957) for publication in *The Atlantic Monthly*.

1

CATTLE THIEVES started to plague the ranges of Southwest Texas immediately after the end of the Civil War. The stealing began as a consequence of the severe winter of 1863–1864, when huge numbers of strayed cattle from north of the Nueces drifted before the punishing winds into the south tip of Texas. Owners could do little toward recovery of this stock; most of it was left unclaimed, untended, bearing its increase.

* © *The Atlantic Monthly* (May, 1957); condensed by the author from Chapter 10 of *The King Ranch*.

Uncounted thousands of cattle so far from home ranges and so close to an international boundary were an open invitation to theft; a traffic in stolen livestock sprang up. Any foot-loose horseman could drive cattle wearing any Texas brand across the river into Mexico and get two to four dollars cash for a cow that cost nothing but the effort to deliver it. Scattered thievery soon became wholesale depredation. A spawn of border ruffians, operating mostly from lairs south of the Rio Grande, began to raid and terrorize the ranches of the border country as far north as the Nueces.

The risk was very small. Texas suffered a sorry lack of means to enforce law and to put down the disorder that followed in the wake of a ruinous war. The Texas Rangers were disbanded, abolished by order of the Reconstruction regime. Local law administrators were powerless to provide peace officers who would even attempt to cope with the brigands adrift along both banks of the convenient river. The only real presence or semblance of force against unbridled border lawlessness were garrisons of United States troops. And, as Rip Ford, ex-Texas Ranger and ex-Confederate colonel, wrote later, "It might have been the powers of government remembered the course of Texas during the Civil War, and left her to take care of herself in the emergency brought about by Mexican raiders."

To this sorry lack of means for the enforcement of law in Texas there was joined a cynical lack of interest on the part of Mexican authorities in stopping thieves from bringing stolen Texas cattle to Mexico. The old hatreds and mistrusts between the two races were still alive and needed only a little fanning to burst again into flame.

Plunder of the ranches along the Texas side of the river soon assumed the guise of race war. The operations of the brown-faced marauders were so surprisingly successful they were soon bragging, "The gringos are raising cows for me." They justified themselves, if they had any qualms, by saying that the cattle and everything else between the Nueces and the Rio Grande originally belonged to Mexicans, that they had every right to take back their own. They called the cattle they stole "Nanita's" cattle, meaning "grandma's." Grandma's cattle brought quick cash money.

The raiding of Texas ranches and the theft of almost incredible numbers of Texas livestock were continuous from 1865 until 1878. In the years when raiding was at its height, Texas stockmen estimated that as many as 200,000 head of their cattle were stolen annually. By 1875, there remained in the region between the Rio Grande and the Nueces only one fourth to one third the number of cattle there had been in 1866.

The raiding was often accompanied by brutal murder. Isolated ranchmen had no recourse, no protection, but that which they could furnish themselves. "Old and young were subjected to every form of outrage and torture, dragged at the hooves of horses, burned and flayed alive, shot to death or cut to pieces with knives, their homes and ranches looted and destroyed." Defenseless travelers were ambushed; the roads over the lonely prairies became too dangerous to travel without armed escorts.

Not all the thieves drove away the stock they stole. Gangs of hide-peelers killed cattle on the range, skinned them, and hauled the hides to market—a thievery practiced with greater dispatch, if less profit, than delivering herds of cattle on the hoof. Hide-peelers displayed unspeakable cruelty in their operations. Many of them used the *media luna,* a scythe-like knife in the shape of a half-moon mounted on a long shaft, handled from horseback to hamstring cattle. The knocked-down animals were sometimes skinned while still alive. Ranchers pursuing hide-peelers would come upon suckling calves bawling by their mothers' raw carcasses still warm and jerking with signs of life.

In the midst of this trouble, rancher Richard King was no novice at defending himself. He fought the gangs of spoilers by every means he could muster, from firearms to political pressures, but the thieving was so stealthy and endless, the raiding so malign, it threatened the survival of his ranch.

From a post-war roundup of stock on the Santa Gertrudis in 1866, R. King & Co. had estimated it owned 84,000 head of cattle. Yet at the division of the property in 1869, King and Kenedy managed to gather just 48,664 cattle which, added to an estimated 10,000 head ungathered, made a total of 58,664. This startling decrease, after three years in which few cattle were sold and in which an undisturbed breed herd would ordinarily double in size, was some indication of the plunder in progress even before the raiding reached its full fury. During the next three years, from 1869 to 1872, Richard King claimed loss by theft of 33,827 head of cattle.

Losses like these came in spite of constant vigilance. Since its first establishment in 1854, the ranch on the Santa Gertrudis had been forced to maintain its own defense. A band of *Kineños* commanded by their foreman, Captain James Richardson, had stood guard against thieves for years. There was nothing new in keeping the brass cannon at headquarters loaded or in manning the lookout atop the commissary, high on the rise in the prairie. As the livestock thefts increased regardless of his vaquero patrols, King bought "some thirty stands of Henry rifles and a supply of ammunition." He hired extra riders, probably as many a dozen, who were handy with the Henrys. And while foreman Richardson and his riders patrolled, King built fence. A visitor to the ranch in 1872 said that Captain King calculated "it would cost $50,000 to fence his ranch, and that he would be repaid in one year by the prevention of these thefts and proceeded to fence his ranch . . . and has now built 31 or 32 miles and has 8 or 9 miles now under way. This is directly a preventative against theft. Guard stations to be placed on each of the four sides of this enclosure."

Direct action, in trying to keep thieves off his ranch and in fighting them with guns when they came anyway, was not enough. King paid agents along the Rio Grande and even in Mexico to spot stolen cattle bearing his brand. He hired men to ride after this stock to try to bring it back. He found that once the cattle had crossed the river, attempts at recovery were futile.

Facing conditions like these, ranchmen on the north bank of the river banded together in 1870 as the Stock Raisers Association of Western Texas, to help each other gun for thieves, to find and return each other's stolen stock, to prosecute in court every criminal that could be caught, and to bring pressure on the state and national governments for protection. Mifflin Kenedy presided over the first meeting; he and King not only supported but led the activities of the organization. Among these was the advertisement of the stockmen's registered brands in the local newspapers, so that the legal owners of cattle wearing such brands might be unmistakable. The list of brands used by Richard King, followed by a long array of brands he held by purchase, appeared regularly.

In 1869, official hide and cattle inspectors appointed by the Army post commanders on the Rio Grande were authorized to examine all cattle and hides in the commerce crossing the river. The inspectors gathered facts and figures, but were armed with no power whatever to check the traffic they daily observed. A too earnest pursuit of their duties proved unhealthy for reasons clearly discernible in a typical Matamoros hide yard dealer's instructions to his help: "Shoot the first damned gringo son of a bitch who comes here and attempts to look at a hide."

When the thievery increased rather than diminished, and especially when it became clear that there was some connection between the official Mexican Commander of the Line of the Bravo and the depredation north of the Bravo, United States Army details were at times ordered into the field to pursue reported raiders. As usual, regulation soldiers on limited scouts were incapable of countering the nonregulation elusiveness of brush-riding bandits. What the border needed, and missed sorely, was a troop of Texas Rangers.

2

Both the Mexican government and the U.S. government set up investigating commissions in 1872. In 1875, a Permanent Committee of Brownsville citizens prepared and printed an exhaustive account of the depredations suffered at the hands of Mexican thieves and bandits; a Congressional Committee of the 44th Congress in 1876 drew up an even longer list of specific murders, burnings, losses, thefts to which the south tip of Texas had been subjected. Yet all this documentation produced little more than prime source material for the writing of history in a later day. At the time, the reports brought no comfort and very little direct aid to the ravaged citizens above the Line of the Bravo.

In January of 1874, Governor Richard Coke, elected by the people of Texas and not by the ballot-stuffing of Carpetbaggers, had taken the reins of office from E. J. Davis. A Democratic legislature had already abolished the Texas State Police; late in 1874, the Texas Rangers had been re-established, to the relief of every decent citizen in every frontier county of the state. In the spring of 1875, an extraordinary officer named L. H. McNelly, former Rebel, one of the few men with a fine record in the Texas State Police, was commissioned as a captain of Texas Rangers to enlist a company for special duty on the lower Rio Grande.

On April 18, 1875, authorities at Austin received a telegram from Sheriff John McClane of Nueces County:

IS CAPT MCNELLY COMING. WE ARE IN TROUBLE. FIVE RANCHES BURNED BY DISGUISED MEN NEAR LA PARRA LAST WEEK. ANSWER.

Captain McNelly came, made short work of the villainous excesses of "disguised men," then late in May led his rangers south to Brownsville.

His arrival there coincided with a burst of activity on the part of cattle thieves in the area. Their chieftain, General Juan Cortina, happened to be gathering livestock in Texas to fill a contract for the delivery of 3500 beeves to Spanish army garrisons in Cuba. A ship was waiting at Bagdad; Cortina was watching it load.

McNelly hit like a bolt of lightning from a clear sky. Early in the morning of June 12, on the Palo Alto prairie fourteen miles north of Brownsville, the ranger captain with twenty-two of his men struck a band of about a dozen bandits driving three hundred stolen cattle toward the river. In the blazing fight one ranger was killed; not one of the thieves got away alive. Next day the bandits' dead bodies were hauled in and dumped on the market square in Brownsville. As a public notice, it was a statement bandits could understand, published in their own language. The bodies were quickly identified as some of Cortina's more notorious bravos; the display aroused a great wrath across the river. And after ten long years of banditry unpunished, the dead bodies left for relatives to claim on the market square of Brownsville that day in June aroused an entirely unaccustomed caution on the part of men who made their living stealing cattle.

The 31-year-old Leander H. McNelly was a leader exactly formed for the work he found on the border. With less than fifty men, in less than a year, he broke the back of a long war with hundreds of organized brigands. He burned himself out at it, dying young from the tuberculosis his life of exposure and hardship brought him. But while he lasted—there were never any like him.

He had a soft voice, an even temper, and a cold-steel disdain for personal danger. Beneath this unassailable cool steadiness burned a flame that made him a brilliant leader, a fire that warmed the hearts of the men he led, that kindled them with respect for him in camp, with emulation for him in a fight. The men he enlisted to follow him were all young and they did not stay unless they were daring. There were only a handful of Texans; their captain preferred to recruit from backgrounds remote from any locale of ranger duty. The basic requirements for service were unflinching bravery and disregard of hardship; skill with firearms and horses came next. McNelly was a demanding master who made his demands by example. The western frontier seems not to have had at any time a more fearless band of disciplined fighters than McNelly's border company of Texas Rangers.

The only way McNelly could catch bandits—he never had more than forty rangers to patrol the whole area—was to be in the right place at the right time. To be there, it was necessary to have advance information, and the only way to get that information was from spies or captives. McNelly used both.

The bandits had their informers among the rancheros in Texas. Fighting fire with fire, McNelly set about acquiring spies among the bandits in Mexico. He said, "I made inquiry about the character of the men who composed the various bands on the opposite bank and I found they were organized into bands of fifteen or twenty or thirty. . . . I made inquiries into the personal character and reputation of the individuals of the bands and I selected those whom I knew to be tricky." To these tricky ones McNelly offered more money than they could make by raiding, a regular salary of sixty dollars a month plus additional rewards depending on the number of thieves identified with any foray for which the spy furnished advance information. McNelly said he found the informers "reliable and trustworthy. I did not propose to interfere with their own individual stealing. I gave them liberty, when I was not in their neighborhood, to cross over with their friends, and get cattle and return again." The money required to pay these spies was clearly outside any ranger service budget; some of the members of the Stock Raisers Association were furnishing McNelly with a war chest. At the time, Richard King was supplying the rangers with beef. He doubtless supplied more, including his own network of informers and contacts with border characters whom McNelly could trust.

McNelly also got information from the thieves he captured. Fighting ruthless enemies, McNelly used ruthless methods. Among the recruits he took into his company was a strange figure named Jesús Sandobal, who from his knowledge of the language and of the country was given charge of forcing information from prisoners. Sandobal often hanged them afterwards. His cruelty stemmed from vengeance: the ranch he owned in Texas had been destroyed and his wife and daughter violated by raiders. McNelly used "Casuse" Sandobal as a harsh instrument in a harsh operation. The border war with cow bandits was at no time, on either side, a tournament of chivalry.

3

For five months following the fight on the Palo Alto prairie the rangers had no major encounter with any big band of raiders. During that time McNelly's men caught scattered thieves and recovered herds of stolen livestock north of the river, while McNelly entertained the growing conviction that the only way to end the border's trouble was to hit the heart of the matter: to strike with full force *south* of the river.

Through his spies McNelly learned that the principal lair of the organized brigands was a fortified ranch called Las Cuevas belonging to a General Juan Flores, located in the brush three miles south of the river, twelve miles below Rio Grande City and Ringgold Barracks. The proximity of Las Cuevas to a post of newly arrived troopers belonging to the Eighth Cavalry at Ringgold suggested an augury for the operation McNelly began to plan. He lost no opportunity to meet Army officers and to work at an Army promise for coöperation with a ranger thrust across the Rio Grande—where it would do the most good. Though the Army was hampered by its usual instructions not to violate neutrality by pursuing bandits into Mexico, field officers stationed on the border lent the ranger captain a sympathetic ear.

Early in November, McNelly learned that Las Cuevas was to be the gathering point of eighteen thousand head of Texas cattle which Mexican traffickers in stolen livestock had contracted to deliver to purchasers in Monterrey within ninety days. He made this information known to the Army; on November 12, McNelly had seen the commander at Ringgold, Major A. J. Alexander, and had gotten a promise from him that he would "instruct his men to follow raiders wherever I will go." Alexander's promise was backed by a similar commitment from his superior in command at Brownsville, Colonel Potter. Sharpened with this prospect and alerted for the expected raiders bringing stolen herds south toward Las Cuevas, McNelly took the field planning to pursue the raiders into Mexico, when necessary, and to wipe them out with United States Army help.

Events did not conform to McNelly's plans.

While he and his men were in the brush near Edinburg fifty-five miles downriver late in the afternoon of November 17, a scouting company of the Eighth Cavalry found a gang of bandits chasing a herd of cattle into Mexico at the Las Cuevas crossing. In the firing, two thieves were killed and another wounded, but the troopers did not cross the river in pursuit. Instead, they made camp on the Texas riverbank, to await further orders.

No dispatch rider was needed. That evening the old wilderness warfare on the remote Rio Grande partook of a new time: a telegraph line now ran along the river close by the cavalry camp. A field telegrapher was soon in communication with Ringgold Barracks and Fort Brown. And the wires went on to Washington.

During the night, Colonel Potter at Brownsville ordered Major Alexander at Ringgold to reinforce and to assume command of the encamped troops at the Las Cuevas crossing; at dawn another cavalry unit came from downriver and joined the force.

There were at least a hundred troopers perched on the riverbank doing nothing when Captain McNelly, riding alone, came into the camp at noon on November 18. He quietly announced he intended to go into Mexico after the stolen cattle as soon as his rangers arrived, and he dispatched a messenger for them. They rode the fifty-five miles to the Las Cuevas crossing in five hours.

The telegraph wires had already tangled the troops with Army red tape and with second thoughts on the part of the command. When McNelly asked the senior officer present on the riverbank, Major Clendenin, for troops to go with the rangers into Mexico, the request was refused, though Clendenin said, "If you are determined to cross, we will cover your return." Knowing the odds his rangers faced on the other side of the river, McNelly replied that not one of them could get back alive without the aid of the troops.

McNelly shoved off that night. Five men swam their horses to the other bank; the others, including McNelly, crossed three at a time in a leaky Mexican scow. At four o'clock in the morning on November 19, the ranger company stood gathered in the dark on the Mexican side of the Rio Grande: thirty men, five mounted, each man carrying only pistol and rifle, with forty rounds of ammunition for each weapon, and a little broiled goat meat prepared before the crossing. With this force McNelly expected to attack a fortified ranch he knew was defended by at least ten times his own number. He expected no quarter from them and he expected to give none. He took the risk believing that his action would bring the United States Army into Mexico and into decisive war against the brigands.

Standing in the dark before daybreak he said, "Boys, the pilot tells me that Las Cuevas Ranch is picketed in with high posts set in the ground with bars for a gate. We will march single file as the cowtrail is not wide enough for you to go in twos. The mounted men will go first, and when we get to the ranch the bars will be let down and I want the five men on horses to dash through the ranch yelling and shooting to attract attention and the rest of us will close in behind and do the best we can. Kill all you see except old men, women and children. These are my orders and I want them obeyed to the letter."

At first dawn they arrived before the heavy picket posts they thought enclosed Las Cuevas. McNelly inspected his little invasion force in the dim light. "Boys," he said, "I like your looks all right—you are the palest set of men I ever looked at. That is a sign you are going to do good fighting. In the Confederate army I noticed that just before battle all men get pale."

Gate bars were let down. The rangers charged in yelling and shooting, killing four men surprised while chopping wood for breakfast fires. In the growing light, the guide suddenly told McNelly that he had made a mistake, that he was in the wrong rancho, that this was a place called the Cachattus, that the Las Cuevas headquarters was a half mile up the trail.

By the time the rangers had made their way on to Las

Cuevas itself, more than two hundred mounted Mexican soldiers were dashing into the stronghold, stirred up by the
shooting they had heard at the outlying rancho. McNelly
formed a line and opened fire but soon decided to withdraw.
"Our surprise is gone," he explained. "It would be suicide to
charge them with only thirty men. We will go back to the
river."

At the river's edge, McNelly had no thought of recrossing
to the Texas side. Posting two pickets in the brush, he hid the
rest of his men under the cover of the riverbank, hoping the
Mexicans would come in pursuit—and still hoping to bring
United States cavalrymen into Mexico for a fight.

The bandits were not long in coming. About twenty-five
horsemen dashed from the brush expecting to catch their
enemies swimming the river. The rangers charged up from the
riverbank and opened fire, advancing. After a hot exchange
the horsemen wheeled back into the thickets. They left a dead
man on the open field. When the rangers moved up firing to
where he lay, they found they had killed the bandit chief himself, the *dueño* of Las Cuevas, General Juan Flores. McNelly
tucked Flores' gold- and silver-plated pistol into his own belt
and ordered the rangers back to the cover of the riverbank.

Meanwhile, Captain Randlett of D Company, Eighth Cavalry, had crossed the river with forty troopers. At the beginning
of the action McNelly had shouted across the river—in carefully
exaggerated distress—while his men were charging up the
riverbank and out of sight, "Randlett, for God's sake come over
and help us!" Randlett had decided that the rangers were "in
danger of annihilation" and had come over to keep the Army's
promise.

When the rangers got back to the river and found Randlett
with his troopers ready on the Mexican side, McNelly tried
to persuade Randlett to go with him to assault the ranch. The
Army captain replied he was not unwilling to stay on the
Mexican riverbank until his commander, Major Alexander,
arrived on the other side and could give orders, but he refused
to consider McNelly's proposal for a move inland.

They did not find it necessary to leave the river to find a fight. The enemy returned in force to avenge the death of Flores. At intervals from eleven that morning until nearly five that afternoon, the Mexicans came charging. Each time the rangers and the troopers beat them back.

At five o'clock, Mexicans suddenly appeared with a white flag of truce. They presented a note which was interpreted at great variance by Randlett and McNelly in separate reports later.

Randlett said the truce proposal promised that the stolen cattle would be returned to Ringgold next day, that every effort would be made to arrest the thieves, that a withdrawal of American troops was requested. McNelly said the note as written demanded that the troops vacate Mexico—and only promised to consider any Texan complaint afterwards. He said that Randlett was ready to agree to such terms but that he, McNelly, refused to leave Mexico until the stolen cattle and the thieves were brought to him. The Mexicans then asked a cessation of hostilities for the night. When this was arranged, McNelly and Randlett moved back to the riverbank. It was dusk; Alexander had arrived at the campfires across the river. He ordered Randlett and his troopers out of Mexico immediately.

As night came on, the handful of Texas Rangers stood alone in Mexico, and stayed alone. An overwhelming force of brigands and soldiers enveloped them. Yet with the bearing of a man who led a fire-eating regiment, not a company of thirty, McNelly in the truce arrangements had agreed to give the enemy "an hour's notice before I commenced active operations." In the dark of the long night he had his men dig a trench by the riverbank.

4

The next morning, November 20, the wires on the poles along the other side of the river made a high hum. The affair at Las Cuevas had reached Washington. Through channels,

Colonel Potter at Fort Brown received orders which he relayed to Major Alexander, "Commdg. in the Front":

ADVISE CAPT MCNELLY TO RETURN AT ONCE TO THIS SIDE OF THE RIVER. INFORM HIM THAT YOU ARE DIRECTED NOT TO SUPPORT HIM IN ANY WAY WHILE HE REMAINS ON THE MEXICAN TERRITORY. IF MCNELLY IS ATTACKED BY MEXICAN FORCES ON MEXICAN SOIL DO NOT RENDER HIM ANY ASSISTANCE. KEEP YOUR FORCES IN THE POSITION YOU NOW HOLD AND AWAIT FURTHER ORDERS. LET ME KNOW WHETHER MCNELLY ACTS UPON YOUR ADVICE AND RETURNS.

The clatter of the telegraphers reached past the Army, into the State Department. The United States Consul at Matamoros was wiring the United States Commercial Agent of Camargo, standing in readiness at Ringgold:

I UNDERSTAND MCNELLY IS SURROUNDED AND TREATING FOR TERMS OF SURRENDER. IF SO GO TO HIM IMMEDIATELY AND ADVISE HIM TO SURRENDER TO THE MEXICAN FEDERAL AUTHORITIES AND THEN YOU GO WITH HIM TO THIS CITY TO SEE THAT NOTHING HAPPENS ON THE WAY. INSTRUCTIONS HAVE BEEN SENT FROM HERE TO AUTHORITIES IN CAMARGO TO ALLOW YOU TO ACT IN THE MATTER. ANSWER.

Copies of both these communications, accompanied by every official pressure, were hurried across the river to save the "doomed" rangers.

At four o'clock that afternoon, McNelly notified the Mexicans, according to his truce agreement to give one hour's advance warning, that he was *advancing to attack* unless his demands were met. He demanded the delivery of the stolen cattle and the thieves who stole them, with no legal dodges nor any excuses for delay. The ruffians facing this man with the lethal eyes, this *hombre de verdad,* gave in. They agreed to deliver to Rio Grande City at ten o'clock the next morning all the stolen stock that could be rounded up and all the thieves that could be caught. With that promise, McNelly withdrew— "reserving the right, if I saw proper, to go to Camargo and take the cattle."

The next morning McNelly took ten rangers to Rio Grande

City to get the cattle; he was fairly certain he would get no thieves. Instead of cattle, he got a note. The *jefe* in Camargo wrote: "Because of excessive work on hand, I do not send you the cattle today, but early tomorrow morning . . ." McNelly wrote a note in return, which ended: "As the Commanding Officer of the United States forces is here awaiting your action in this matter, I would be glad if you would inform me of the earliest hour at which you can deliver these cattle and any of the thieves you may have apprehended."

The Commanding Officer was not "awaiting" and would have done nothing about it if he had been. But McNelly's acute mention of the United States Army was not lost upon the *jefe* in Camargo, who forthwith changed the schedule of his excessive work on hand. He wrote a note informing McNelly that the cattle would be delivered at three o'clock that afternoon.

Seventy-five stolen cattle close-herded by twenty-five Mexicans armed with Winchesters and pistols came to the river's edge at three. McNelly with his ten men, armed, had come over on the ferry to meet them. McNelly asked the drovers to put the cattle on the Texas side, as agreed. The *caporal* refused, saying it was impossible until the cattle "were inspected." McNelly told his interpreter to tell the *caporal* that the cattle were stolen from Texas without being inspected and they were going back that way. The *caporal* said no. McNelly rapped out an order. The startled drovers were instantly looking down the barrels of the rangers' cocked guns. One of the men holding one of the cocked guns said later that McNelly told the interpreter "to tell the son of a bitch that if he didn't deliver the cattle across the river in less than five minutes he would kill all of them, and he would have done it too, for he had his red feather raised. If you ever saw cattle put across the river in a hurry those Mexicans did it."

In the herd that came back at last, after the long years in which herds moved only one way, there were thirty-five head of cattle wearing the brand of Richard King.

The McNelly rangers brought an abrupt change of demeanor to the outlawry on the border. The stealing of cattle from

Texas, formerly such an attractive pursuit, lost its appeal. It began to be dangerous. Though the raiding continued for another five years, it became desultory and increasingly furtive. The wholesale depredation ceased, the outrageous open traffic in stolen livestock came to an end with the affair at Las Cuevas. The raffish practitioners of border banditry and the purveyors of border race hate lacked the guts to hunt a fight with men like L. H. McNelly and his rangers. When the rangers hunted them, they quit.

W. S. JAMES

How Cow-Boys Guy a Greener*

⟨ W. S. JAMES was a cowboy who wrote his memoirs with the subtitle of *27 Years a Mavrick* after he had turned frontier preacher. This evolution in vocation is not so rare as it might seem; several other cowboy-parsons felt the call to set down their memories. Plus the later saving of souls, James saved in his book some precious details about range life.

IT IS CALLED exaggerating, a stretch of the imagination, misrepresentation, prevarication, and numerous other very palliating aliases, but the unvarnished, unpolished cow-boy calls it "lying." Many good credulous fellows have read those exaggerated stories of life in the far west on a Texas cow ranch and have had education quite bitter in the school of experience for their ignorance and want of judgment.

They come to Texas perhaps with good capital, the result of years of patient work and economy on the part of a good and indulgent father, who has "divided unto them his living." They wish to engage in business that promises fabulous returns. The first thing they do, in the majority of cases, is to show how much they know, and in the presence of an outfit of

* From *Cow-Boy Life in Texas: 27 Years a Mavrick* (Chicago: M. A. Donohue & Co., 1893).

regulars, they make complete donkeys of themselves. They often play out in three rounds, some of them make good use of their experience, and some of them let some sharper invest for them and they go halves in the proceeds; the result is the old story of "capital and experience," the two soon swap places (however, the rule is not without exceptions).

One circumstance that I recall was a young man who came to Texas in '82; he had in cash $30,000 to invest in a ranch. He landed in a western town, met some of the boys, and made known his intentions; he also made free to state that he was "onto" cow-boys, but wished to thoroughly learn the ropes, etc.; so they took him in hand, learned first his ideas concerning the business, blowed him in for $100, for an old stove-up pony, a sixty-five dollar saddle, a pair of flashy red blankets, spurs, quirt, rope and leggings, cow-boy hat, two six-shooters and a long keen knife; after tanking him up on red liquor they started him out to paint the town red, taking care all the while to keep their own necks out of the halter, which a cow-boy knows just how to do.

This young man allowed himself rushed into making a ridiculous picture of himself by appearing on the streets whooping like an Indian on the war-path, firing off his pistols and running that old stove-up pack pony up and down the streets until the sheriff got hold of him and run him in; he then allowed himself further imposed upon, by cursing the judge, according to instructions; the fine and costs amounted to $150, before he got through. He made bond for his appearance and then went with the outfit to the ranch. Next morning when he awoke, he was all alone, horse, saddle, blankets and everything he had started with, gone. They had made him drunk and robbed him of everything while he was asleep, and were in hiding to see the effect on him. He looked all around, and then hit the road and began to cut dirt for town, a sadder but wiser man. Some of the boys followed him at a safe distance with his outfit, and when they saw him get in a farmer's wagon, they surrounded him, beat him to town and hitched his horse where he could find him when he came in. The man of whom he bought the horse went to him and gave him back his money, took the old horse off his hands and gave him five hundred dollars worth of good advice in a few words. That young man, unlike many who started just as he did, took the advice, went to work, learned the cattle business and afterward became a reasonably good cattleman, but like a great many of the more visionary among the boys went under in the great rise and fall of cattle from 1880 to 1885.

At one time there came an old gentleman from the Eastern States to western Texas and bought two thousand choice steers; he was one of those genial characters sometimes to be met with in most any station in life, who are as happy at one time as another, no difference what their surroundings may be, and let me tell you right here that this is the most fortunate disposition for one to possess who goes among cow-men.

He will have less trouble and get less skin knocked off his shins. But of all the unfortunate characters who ever came into the clutches of a cow-boy, the braggadocio, self-important smart Aleck is the worst. But I am deviating. This old gentleman came to receive the cattle, and drove out to the camp in a two-horse spring wagon, or hack as it is called in the West. He wore a silk hat. The camp was located near a spring of water, under a large live oak tree, whose evergreen foliage covered "way up yonder" close to a quarter of an acre of ground. It was a lovely summer day, a trifle too warm in the sun, but a gentle breeze made it delightful in the shade.

Our Mr. N—— had located his claim on the southern boundary of the massive roots of the tree, and was enjoying a snooze. He laid his hat by his side; the cook was busy about the dinner, so the old fellow was left to enjoy himself according to his own sweet will. Chuck time drew near and the boys, fifteen or twenty of them, came riding into camp for the purpose of eating something up. As they approached the place where Mr. N—— was, the tramp of their horses' feet disturbed his slumbers and when once fairly awake he heard the boys, who had stopped within twenty or thirty feet of where he lay, commenting on something. One said: "What must we do," another said, "What is it?" one said "It's a bear," another, "It's the venomous kypoote," another said, "It's one of those things that flee up and down the creek and hollowed 'walo wahoo,' in the night time." One called out, "Boys, it's a shame to stand peaceably by and see a good man devoured by that varmint," and calling loudly to the now thoroughly excited old man to "Look out there, mister, that thing will bite you," at the same time drawing his pistol. Mr. N. sprang to his feet like a ten-year-old boy (as some of the boys put it, got a ten-cent move on him), and didn't stop to get his hat. He had perhaps gotten ten or fifteen feet from his pre-emption when almost every man in the outfit, fired (some of them two or three bullets,) into that silk hat, simply shooting the crown off.

The bewildered old fellow was so thoroughly scared that it was some time before he noticed what it was that had come so near devouring him; in fact not until one of the boys dismounted, took a stick and turned it over and said, "Boys, it's shore dead." Our good-natured old friend, after recovering from his scare, took a hearty laugh over the little jamboree and called the boys all 'round to his wagon and drew out a jug of sixteen-shooting liquor—thus they celebrated the death of the terrible varmint. . . .

This is one of the methods used by the cow-boy to guy a greener, but not the only one. The name is legion. I remember once when a number of gentlemen came into camp out on the Leon river, two of them in a buggy and three others on horseback. Before leaving the East they had provided themselves umbrellas and the little leather saddles used in New York and all of the Eastern and some of the Southern States, which are very good in town, or when a man has but little riding to do, but in working cattle a man wouldn't last until he was all gone. When the gentlemen above referred to came in sight of camp with their umbrellas stretched, every cow-boy in the outfit made a rush for his horse and ran, like a troop of wild Indians had made their appearance, and those who had no horses took it a-foot, some of them calling at the top of their voice: "Mister, please don't turn that thing loose";

others calling out: "Don't shoot, I'll give up." Some of the older fellows, whose days of such fun had passed, laughingly told the gentlemen that they needn't be frightened, as the boys were only scared at their umbrellas, but advised them to put their saddles in a good, safe place. Some of them took the joke nicely, and others got mad. They didn't say anything, however, but showed it by their looks. Finally, being assured of protection, the boys came into camp very cautiously; then they opened the conversation among themselves, each telling what he thought it was, some declaring they were so bad scared they didn't have time to think. . . . By and by one of the boys made it in the way to run over one of the saddles and fell full length on the ground, turning the saddle over into full view of the boys; it had been covered with a blanket or partly so. This was the occasion for another general stampede, but they rallied and gathered around the saddle and held another consultation. The final decision was that it was the chief of the hairy tribe, or something good to eat, and that as a band of civilized cow-boys they would desist from doing it bodily harm as the thing seemed to be quiet and willing to do the square thing. Then they dispersed and each went about his business, joking each other about the adventures of the morning, one of them declaring that he intended to go to meeting next Sunday, he was so glad he was alive. . . .

The cow-boy is the roughest character on a stale joke you will find in a week's travel. In fact, it matters very little how new or spicy a story may be if the outfit wish to hack a fellow they will guy him in a hundred different ways. When the subject they wish to hack tells anything, some one will start it by saying: "That sounds to me," then every man in the outfit usually takes it up and carries it 'round "that sounds to me" and when it has gone the rounds some one will turn to another and say: "What do you think of that?" First one answer and then another will be given, one heard it in '47, another wants a little evidence on it, says that it would look real nice with a little evidence, another don't believe a word of it, still another believes part of it but can't swallow it whole.

In this way they test a man's metal, if he takes his medicine and does not get angry, it is much easier; when they see that he is disposed to stand the test they are not nearly so hard on him. But if he gets mad and sulks he is a very unfortunate man. After they have tested a man, if anyone tries a second time to hack that one, they turn the tables on him. . . . When a greenhorn comes into a range he will have all sorts of impositions practiced on him until he cuts his eye-teeth. Never anything very serious, but sometimes very annoying, and mortifying always, unless one is very genial and accepts it as part of his training which is by far the better way.

CHARLES M. RUSSELL

···✦···━━▶►●◄◆━━···✦···

The Story of the Cowpuncher*

❡ CHARLES M. RUSSELL was a legend while he was
still living in Montana; his sketches and paintings of the
Old West were recognized by many as the truest ever rendered. Frank Dobie does not hesitate to call him "the greatest painter that ever painted a range man, a range cow, a
range horse or a Plains Indian." Like Frederic Remington,
Russell was an artist with words too; his yarns and anecdotes were rounded up in *Trails Plowed Under*, a collection
"saturated with humor and humanity," as Dobie says. "The
Story of the Cowpuncher" leads off the book.

S PEAKIN' of cowpunchers," says Rawhide Rawlins, "I'm glad
to see in the last few years that them that know the business have been writin' about 'em. It begin to look like they'd
be wiped out without a history. Up to a few years ago there's
mighty little known about cows and cow people. It was sure
amusin' to read some of them old stories about cowpunchin'.
You'd think a puncher growed horns an' was haired over.

"It put me in mind of the eastern girl that asks her mother:
'Ma,' says she, 'do cowboys eat grass?' 'No, dear,' says the old
lady, 'they're part human,' an' I don't know but the old gal
had 'em sized up right. If they are human, they're a separate
species. I'm talkin' about the old-time ones, before the country's
strung with wire an' nesters had grabbed all the water, an' a

* From *Trails Plowed Under* by Charles M. Russell. Copyright 1927 by
Doubleday & Co., Inc. Reprinted by permission of the publisher.

cowpuncher's home was big. It wasn't where he took his hat off, but where he spread his blankets. He ranged from Mexico to the Big Bow River of the north, an' from where the trees get scarce in the east to the old Pacific. He don't need no iron hoss, but covers his country on one that eats grass an' wears hair. All the tools he needed was saddle, bridle, quirt, hackamore, an' rawhide riata or seagrass rope; that covered his hoss.

"The puncher himself was rigged, startin' at the top, with a good hat—not one of the floppy kind you see in pictures, with the rim turned up in front. The top-cover he wears holds its shape an' was made to protect his face from the weather; maybe to hold it on, he wore a buckskin string under the chin or back of the head. Round his neck a big silk handkerchief, tied loose, an' in the drag of a trail herd it was drawn over the face to the eyes, hold-up fashion, to protect the nose an' throat from dust. In old times, a leather blab or mask was used the same. Coat, vest, an' shirt suits his own taste. Maybe he'd wear California pants, light buckskin in color, with large brown plaid, sometimes foxed, or what you'd call reinforced with buck or antelope skin. Over these came his chaparejos or leggin's. His feet were covered with good high-heeled boots, finished off with steel spurs of Spanish pattern. His weapon's usually a forty-five Colt's six-gun, which is packed in a belt, swingin' a little below his right hip. Sometimes a Winchester in a scabbard, slung to his saddle under his stirrup-leather, either right or left side, but generally left, stock forward, lock down, as his rope hangs at his saddle-fork on the right.

"By all I can find out from old, gray-headed punchers, the cow business started in California, an' the Spaniards were the first to burn marks on their cattle an' hosses, an' use the rope. Then men from the States drifted west to Texas, pickin' up the brandin' iron an' lass-rope, an' the business spread north, east, an' west, till the spotted long-horns walked in every trail marked out by their brown cousins, the buffalo.

"Texas an' California, bein' the startin' places, made two species of cowpunchers; those west of the Rockies rangin' north, usin' center-fire or single-cinch saddles, with high fork an' cantle; packed a sixty or sixty-five foot rawhide rope, an' swung a big loop. These cow people were generally strong on pretty, usin' plenty of hoss jewelry, silver-mounted spurs, bits, an' conchas; instead of a quirt, used a romal, or quirt braided to the end of the reins. Their saddles were full stamped, with from twenty-four- to twenty-eight-inch eagle-bill tapaderos. Their chaparejos were made of fur or hair, either bear, angora goat, or hair sealskin. These fellows were sure fancy, an' called themselves buccaroos, coming from the Spanish word, *vaquero.*

"The cowpuncher east of the Rockies originated in Texas and ranged north to the Big Bow. He wasn't so much for pretty; his saddle was low horn, rimfire, or double-cinch; sometimes 'macheer.' Their rope was seldom over forty feet, for being a good deal in a brush country, they were forced to swing a small loop. These men generally tied, instead of taking their dallie-welts, or wrapping their rope around the saddle horn. Their chaparejos were made of heavy bullhide, to protect the leg from brush an' thorns, with hog-snout tapaderos.

"Cowpunchers were mighty particular about their rig, an' in all the camps you'd find a fashion leader. From a cowpuncher's idea, these fellers was sure good to look at, an' I tell you right now, there ain't no prettier sight for my eyes than one of those good-lookin', long-backed cowpunchers, sittin' up on a high-forked, full-stamped California saddle with a live hoss between his legs.

"Of course a good many of these fancy men were more ornamental than useful, but one of the best cow-hands I ever knew belonged to this class. Down on the Gray Bull, he went under the name of Mason, but most punchers called him Pretty Shadow. This sounds like an Injun name, but it ain't. It comes from a habit some punchers has of ridin' along, lookin' at their shadows. Lookin' glasses are scarce in cow outfits, so the only chance for these pretty boys to admire themselves is on bright, sunshiny days. Mason's one of these kind that doesn't get much pleasure out of life in cloudy weather. His hat was the best; his boots was made to order, with extra long heels.

He rode a center-fire, full-stamped saddle, with twenty-eight-inch tapaderos; bearskin ancaroes, or saddle pockets; his chaparejos were of the same skin. He packed a sixty-five-foot rawhide. His spurs an' bit were silver inlaid, the last bein' a Spanish spade. But the gaudiest part of his regalia was his gun. It's a forty-five Colt's, silverplated an' chased with gold. Her handle is pearl, with a bull's head carved on.

"When the sun hits Mason with all this silver on, he blazes up like some big piece of jewelry. You could see him for miles when he's ridin' high country. Barrin' Mexicans, he's the fanciest cow dog I ever see, an' don't think he don't savvy the cow. He knows what she says to her calf. Of course there wasn't many of his stripe. All punchers liked good rigs, but plainer; an' as most punchers 're fond of gamblin' an' spend their spare time at stud poker or monte, they can't tell what kind of a rig they'll be ridin' the next day. I've seen many a good rig lost over a blanket. It depends how lucky the cards fall what kind of a rig a man's ridin'.

"I'm talkin' about old times, when cowmen were in their glory. They lived different, talked different, an' had different ways. No matter where you met him, or how he's rigged, if you'd watch him close he'd do something that would tip his hand. I had a little experience back in '83 that'll show what I'm gettin' at.

"I was winterin' in Cheyenne. One night a stranger stakes me to buck the bank. I got off lucky an' cash in fifteen hundred dollars. Of course I cut the money in two with my friend, but it leaves me with the biggest roll I ever packed. All this wealth makes Cheyenne look small, an' I begin longin' for bigger camps, so I drift for Chicago. The minute I hit the burg, I shed my cow garments an' get into white man's harness. A hard hat, boiled shirt, laced shoes—all the gearin' known to civilized man. When I put on all this rig, I sure look human; that is, I think so. But them shorthorns know me, an' by the way they trim that roll, it looks like somebody 's pinned a card on my back with the word 'EASY' in big letters. I ain't been there a week till my roll don't need no string around it,

an' I start thinkin' about home. One evenin' I throw in with
the friendliest feller I ever met. It was at the bar of the hotel
where I'm camped. I don't just remember how we got acquainted, but after about fifteen drinks we start holdin' hands
an' seein' who could buy the most and fastest. I remember him
tellin' the barslave not to take my money, 'cause I'm his friend.
Afterwards, I find out the reason for this goodheartedness; he
wants it all an' hates to see me waste it. Finally, he starts to
show me the town an' says it won't cost me a cent. Maybe
he did, but I was unconscious, an' wasn't in shape to remember.
Next day, when I come to, my hair's sore an' I didn't know
the days of the week, month, or what year it was.

"The first thing I do when I open my eyes is to look at the
winders. There's no bars on 'em, an' I feel easier. I'm in a small
room with two bunks. The one opposite me holds a feller that's
smokin' a cigarette an' sizin' me up between whiffs while I'm
dressin'. I go through myself but I'm too late. Somebody beat
me to it. I'm lacin' my shoes an' thinkin' hard, when the
stranger speaks:

" 'Neighbor, you're a long way from your range.'

" 'You call the turn,' says I, 'but how did you read my iron?'

" 'I didn't see a burn on you,' says he, 'an' from looks, you'll
go as a slick-ear. It's your ways, while I'm layin' here, watchin'
you get into your garments. Now, humans dress up an' punchers dress down. When you raised, the first thing you put on is
your hat. Another thing that shows you up is you don't shed
your shirt when you bed down. So next comes your vest an'
coat, keepin' your hindquarters covered till you slide into your
pants, an' now you're lacin' your shoes. I notice you done all
of it without quittin' the blankets, like the ground's cold. I
don't know what state or territory you hail from, but you've
smelt sagebrush an' drank alkali. I heap savvy you. You've
slept a whole lot with nothin' but sky over your head, an'
there's times when that old roof leaks, but judgin' from appearances, you wouldn't mind a little open air right now.'

"This feller's my kind, an' he stakes me with enough to get
back to the cow country."

CHARLES A. SIRINGO

Roping Wild Steers*

❨ CHARLES A. SIRINGO comes as near being the archetype of the old-time Texas cowboy as can be found, at least
in his best book, excerpted here, A Texas Cowboy, or
Fifteen Years on the Hurricane Deck of a Spanish Cow
Pony. Like McCoy, Siringo was one of the first in the field,
and his Texas Cowboy is the first of the cowpuncher autobiographies, as it has remained about the most pepperish
and flavorsome.

AFTER ARRIVING in Matagorda I hired out to a Mr. Tom
Nie, who was over there, from Rancho Grande, hiring some
Cow Boys.

"Rancho Grande" was owned by "Shanghai" Pierce and Allen
and at that time was considered one of the largest ranches in
the whole state of Texas. To give you an idea of its size, will
state, that the next year after I went to work we branded
twenty-five thousand calves—that is, just in one season.

Altogether there were five of us started to Rancho Grande to
work—all boys about my own age; we went in a sail boat to
Palacious Point, where the firm had an outside ranch and
where they were feeding a large lot of cow ponies for spring
work.

* From A Texas Cowboy, or Fifteen Years on the Hurricane Deck of a
Spanish Cow Pony (Chicago: M. Umbdenstock, 1885).

84

It was about the middle of April, 1871, that we all, about twenty of us, pulled out for the headquarter ranch at the head of Tresspalacious creek. It took us several days to make the trip as we had to brand calves and Mavricks on the way up.

A few days after arriving at the ranch Mr. or "Old Shang" Pierce as he was commonly called, arrived from Old Mexico with about three hundred head of wild spanish ponies, therefore we kids had a high old time learning the art of riding a "pitching" horse.

We put in several days at the ranch making preparations to start out on a two months trip. Being a store there we rigged up in good shape; I spent two or three months' wages for an outfit, spurs, etc., trying to make myself look like a thoroughbred Cow Boy from Bitter Creek.

There were three crowds of us started at the same time; one to work up the Colorado river, the other around home and the third which was ours, to work west in Jackson and Lavaca counties.

Our crowd consisted of fifteen men, one hundred head of ponies—mostly wild ones—and a chuck wagon loaded down with coffee, flour, molasses and salt. Tom Nie was our boss.

Arriving on the Navadad river, we went to work gathering a herd of "trail" beeves and also branding Mavricks at the same time. Some days we would brand as high as three or four hundred Mavricks—none under two years old.

After about a month's hard work we had the herd of eleven hundred ready to turn over to Mr. Black who had bought them, delivered to him at the Snodgrass ranch. They were all old mossy horn fellows, from seven to twenty-seven years old.

Mr. Black was a Kansas "short horn" and he had brought his outfit of "short horn" men and horses, to drive the herd "up the trail."

Some of the men had never seen a Texas steer, consequently they crossed Red river into the Indian territory with nothing left but the "grub" wagon and horses. They had lost every steer and Mr. Black landed in Kansas flat broke.

Lots of the steers came back to their old ranges and Mr. "Shanghai" had the fun of selling them over again, to some other greeny, may be.

"Shanghai" Pierce went to Kansas the next year and when he returned he told of having met Mr. Black up there, working at his old trade—blacksmithing. He said Mr. Black cursed Texas shamefully and swore that he never would, even if he should live to be as old as Isaac, son of Jacob, dabble in long horns again.

After getting rid of Mr. Black's herd we turned our whole attention to branding Mavricks.

About the first of August we went back to the ranch and found that it had changed hands in our absence. "Shanghai" Pierce and his brother Jonathan had sold out their interests to Allen, Pool & Co. for the snug little sum of one hundred and ten thousand dollars.

That shows what could be done in those days, with no capital, but lots of cheek and a branding iron. The two Pierce's had come out there from Yankeedom a few years before poorer than skimmed milk.

Everything had taken a change—even to the ranch. It had been moved down the river four miles to Mr. John Moore's place. Mr. Moore had been appointed "big chief," hence the ranch being moved to his place.

About the middle of August we pulled out again with a fresh supply of horses, six to the man and a bran new boss, Mr. Wiley Kuykendall.

Some of the boys hated to part with Mr. Nie, but I was glad of the change, for he wouldn't allow me to rope large steers nor fight when I got on the war-path. I remember one time he gave me fits for laying a Negro out with a four-year old club; and another time he laid me out with his open hand for trying to carve one of the boys up with a butcher knife.

We commenced work about the first of September on "Big Sandy" in Lavaca county, a place noted for wild "brush" cattle. Very few people lived in that section, hence so many wild unbranded cattle.

To illustrate the class of people who lived on Big Sandy, will relate a little picnic a Negro and I had a few days after our arrival there.

While herding a bunch of cattle, gathered the day before, on a small prairie, we noticed a footman emerge from the

Charles A. Siringo, "in Cow Boy Uniform"
From *A Texas Cowboy* (1885)

thick timber on the opposite side from where we were and make straight for a spotted pony that was "hobbled" and grazing out in the open space.

He was indeed a rough looking customer, being half naked. He had nothing on his head but a thick mat of almost gray hair; and his feet and legs were bare.

We concluded to "rope" him and take him to camp, so taking down our ropes and putting spurs to our tired horses we struck out.

He saw us coming and only being about a hundred yards from the spotted pony, he ran to him and cutting the "hobbles," which held his two front legs together, jumped aboard of him and was off in the direction he had just come, like a flash. The pony must have been well trained for he had nothing to guide him with.

A four hundred yard race for dear life brought him to the "brush"—that is timber, thickly covered with an underbrush of live-oak "runners." He shot out of sight like an arrow. He was not a minute too soon, for we were right at his heels.

We gave up the chase after losing sight of him, for we couldn't handle our ropes in the "brush."

The next day the camp was located close to the spot where he disappeared at, and several of us followed up his trail. We found him and his three grown daughters, his wife having died a short while before, occupying a little one room log shanty in a lonely spot about two miles from the little prairie in which we first saw him. The whole outfit were tough looking citizens. The girls had never seen a town, so they said. They had about two acres in cultivation and from that they made their living. Their nearest neighbor was a Mr. Penny, who lived ten miles west, and the nearest town was Columbus, on the Colorado river, fifty miles east.

As the cattle remained hidden out in the "brush" during the day-time, only venturing out on the small prairies at night, we had to do most of our work early in the morning, commencing an hour or two before daylight. As you might wish to know exactly how we did, will try and explain:—About two hours before daylight the cook would holloa "chuck," and then Mr. Wiley would go around and yell "breakfast, boys; d——n you get up!" two or three times in our ears.

Breakfast being over we would saddle up our ponies, which had been staked out the night before, and strike out for a certain prairie may be three or four miles off—that is all but two or three men, just enough to bring the herd, previously gathered, on as soon as it became light enough to see.

Arriving at the edge of the prairie we would dismount and wait for daylight.

At the first peep of day the cattle, which would be out in the prairie, quite a distance from the timber, would all turn their heads and commence grazing at a lively rate towards the nearest point of timber. Then we would ride around through the brush, so as not to be seen, until we got to the point of timber that they were steering for.

When it became light enough to see good, we would ride out, rope in hand, to meet them and apt as not one of the old-timers, may be a fifteen or twenty-year old steer, which were continuously on the lookout, would spy us before we got twenty yards from the timber. Then the fun would begin— the whole bunch, may be a thousand head, would stampede and come right towards us. They never were known to run in the opposite direction from the nearest point of timber. But with cattle raised on the prairies, it's the reverse, they will always leave the timber.

After coming in contact, every man would rope and tie down one of the finest animals in the bunch. Once in awhile some fellow would get more beef than he could manage; under those circumstances he would have to worry along until some other fellow got through with his job and came to his rescue.

If there was another prairie close by we would go to it and tie down a few more, but we would have to get there before sunup or they would all be in the brush. It was their habit to graze out into the little prairies at night-fall and go back to the brush by sunrise next morning.

Finally the herd which we had gathered before and which was already "broke in," would arrive from camp, where we had been night-herding them and then we would drive it around to each one of the tied-down animals, letting him up so he couldn't help from running right into the herd, where he would generally stay contented. Once in awhile though, we would strike an old steer that couldn't be made to stay in the herd. Just as soon as he was untied and let up he would go right through the herd and strike for the brush, fighting his way. Under those circumstances we would have to sew up their eyes with a needle and thread. That would bring them to their milk, as they couldn't see the timber.

I got into several scrapes on this trip, by being a new hand at the business. One time I was going at full speed and threw my rope onto a steer just as he got to the edge of the timber; I couldn't stop my horse in time, therefore the steer went on one side of a tree and my horse on the other and the consequence was, my rope being tied hard and fast to the saddle-horn, we all landed up against the tree in a heap.

At another time, on the same day, I roped a large animal and got my horse jerked over backwards on top of me and in the horse getting up he got me all wound up in the rope, so that I couldn't free myself until relieved by "Jack" a Negro man who was near at hand. I was certainly in a ticklish predicament that time; the pony was wild and there I hung fast to his side with my head down while the steer, which was still fastened to the rope, was making every effort to gore us.

Just before Christmas Moore selected our outfit to do the shipping at Palacious Point, where a Morgan steamship landed twice a week to take on cattle for the New Orleans market.

We used to ship about five hundred head at each shipping. After getting rid of one bunch we would strike right back, to meet one of the gathering outfits, after another herd. There were three different outfits to do the gathering for us.

We kept that up all winter and had a tough time of it, too, as it happened to be an unusually cold and wet winter.

Towards spring the cattle began to get terribly poor, so that during the cold nights while night-herding them a great many would get down in the mud and freeze to death. Have seen as high as fifty head of dead ones scattered over the ground where the herd had drifted during the night. It's a pity if such nights as those didn't try our nerves.

Sometimes it would be twelve o'clock at night before we

would get the cattle loaded aboard of the ship. But when we did get through we would surely have a picnic—filling up on Mr. Geo. Burkheart's red eye. Mr. Burkheart kept a store at the "Point" well filled with Cow Boys delight—in fact he made a specialty of the stuff.

Our camping ground was three miles from the Point, and some mornings the cook would get up and find several saddled horses standing around camp waiting for their corn—their riders having fallen by the wayside.

When spring opened, our outfit, under the leadership of Mr. Robert Partin, Mr. Wiley having quit, struck out up the Colorado river in Whorton and Colorado counties to brand Mavricks.

About the last of July we went to the "home" ranch, where Mr. Wiley was put in charge of us again. We were sent right out on another trip, west, to Jackson county.

It was on this trip that I owned my first cattle. Mr. Wiley concluded it would look more business like if he would brand a few Mavricks for himself instead of branding them all for Allen, Pool & Co., so he began putting his own brand on all the finest looking ones. To keep us boys from giving him away, he gave us a nest egg apiece—that is a few head to draw to. My nest eggs were a couple of two-year olds, and my brand was A. T. connected—the T. on top of the A. Of course after that I always carried a piece of iron tied to my saddle so in case I got off on the prairie by myself I could brand a few Mavricks for myself, without Mr. Wiley being any the wiser of it. The way I would go about it would be to rope and tie down one of the long-eared fellows and after heating the straight piece of round, iron bolt, in the brush or "cow-chip" fire, "run" my brand on his hip or ribs. He was then my property.

Everything ran along as smooth as if on greased wheels for about two months, when somehow or another, Mr. Moore, our big chief, heard of our little private racket and sent for us to come home.

Mr. Wiley got the "G.B." at once and a Mr. Logan was put in his place. Now this man Logan was a very good man but he was out of his latitude, he should have been a second mate on a Mississippi steamboat.

I worked with Logan one trip, until we got back to the ranch and then I settled up for the first time since going to work, nearly two years before.

An old irishman by the name of "Hunky-dorey" Brown kept the store and did the settling up with the men. When he settled with me he laid all the money, in silver dollars, that I had earned since commencing work, which amounted to a few hundred dollars, out on the counter and then after eyeing me awhile, said: "Allen, Pool & Co. owe you three hundred dollars," or whatever the amount was, "and you owe Allen, Pool & Co. two hundred ninety-nine dollars and a quarter, which leaves you seventy-five cents." He then raked all but six bits into the money drawer.

To say that I felt mortified wouldn't near express my feelings. I thought the whole pile was mine and therefore had been figuring on the many purchases that I intended making. My intentions were to buy a herd of ponies and go to speculating. I had a dozen or two ponies, that I knew were for sale, already picked out in my mind. But my fond expectations were soon trampled under foot. You see I had never kept an account, consequently never knew how I stood with the company.

After pocketing my six bits, I mounted "Fannie" a little mare that I had bought not long before and struck out for W. B. Grimes' ranch, a few miles up the river. I succeeded in getting a job from the old gentleman at fifteen dollars per month.

Mr. Grimes had a slaughter house on his ranch where he killed cattle for their hides and tallow—the meat he threw to the hogs. About two hundred head per day was an average killing. Did you ask, kind reader, if those were all his own cattle that he butchered? If so, will have to say that I never tell tales out of school.

OWEN WISTER

In a State of Sin*

⟦ OWEN WISTER and his celebrated novel, *The Virginian*, get only grudging acceptance from many cowboy and cattle experts, but Wister was in his own right an extremely interesting and gifted personality, turned into an artist by the magnetic pull the West exercised on him. Friend of Teddy Roosevelt, Yankee-bred in a distinguished family, an aristocrat by taste and training, he was mesmerized by a first casual visit to the Old West. In *The Virginian*, a still fabulously successful novel, he fixed for most of the nation's readers the image of the cowboy, however glamorized. The hero here is exceptional; the picture of the code of the range is faithful.

THUNDER SAT imminent upon the missionary's brow. Many were to be at his mercy soon. But for us he had sunshine still. "I am truly sorry to be turning you upside down," he said importantly. "But it seems the best place for my service." He spoke of the tables pushed back and the chairs gathered in the hall, where the storm would presently break upon the congregation. "Eight-thirty?" he inquired.

This was the hour appointed, and it was only twenty minutes off. We threw the unsmoked fractions of our cigars away, and returned to offer our services to the ladies. This amused the

* From *The Virginian* (New York: Macmillan Co., 1902).

ladies. They had done without us. All was ready in the hall.

"We got the cook to help us," Mrs. Ogden told me, "so as not to disturb your cigars. In spite of the cow-boys, I still recognize my own country."

"In the cook?" I rather densely asked.

"Oh, no! I don't have a Chinaman. It's in the length of after-dinner cigars."

"Had you been smoking," I returned, "you would have found them short this evening."

"You make it worse," said the lady; "we have had nothing but Dr. MacBride."

"We'll share him with you now," I exclaimed.

"Has he announced his text? I've got one for him," said Molly Wood, joining us. She stood on tiptoe and spoke it comically in our ears. " 'I said in my haste, All men are liars.' " This made us merry as we stood among the chairs in the congested hall.

I left the ladies, and sought the bunk house. I had heard the cheers, but I was curious also to see the men, and how they were taking it. There was but little for the eye. There was much noise in the room. They were getting ready to come to church—brushing their hair, shaving, and making themselves clean, amid talk occasionally profane and continuously diverting.

"Well, I'm a Christian, anyway," one declared.

"I'm a Mormon, I guess," said another.

"I belong to the Knights of Pythias," said a third.

"I'm a Mohammedist," said a fourth; "I hope I ain't goin' to hear nothin' to shock me."

And they went on with their joking. . . .

Our missionary did not choose Miss Wood's text. He made his selection from another of the Psalms, and when it came, I did not dare to look at anybody. I was much nearer unseemly conduct than the cow-boys. Dr. MacBride gave us his text sonorously, " 'They are altogether become filthy; There is none of them that doeth good, no, not one.' " His eye showed us plainly that present company was not excepted from this.

He repeated the text once more, then, launching upon his discourse, gave none of us a ray of hope.

I had heard it all often before; but preached to cow-boys it took on a new glare of untimeliness, of grotesque obsoleteness—as if some one should say, "Let me persuade you to admire woman," and forthwith hold out her bleached bones to you. The cow-boys were told that not only they could do no good, but that if they did contrive to, it would not help them. Nay, more; not only honest deeds availed them nothing, but even if they accepted this especial creed which was being explained to them as necessary for salvation, still it might not save them. Their sin was indeed the cause of their damnation, yet, keeping from sin, they might nevertheless be lost. It had all been settled for them not only before they were born, but before Adam was shaped. Having told them this, he invited them to glorify the Creator of the scheme. Even if damned, they must praise the person who had made them expressly for damnation. That is what I heard him prove by logic to these cow-boys. Stone upon stone he built the black cellar of his theology, leaving out its beautiful park and the sunshine of its garden. He did not tell them the splendor of its past, the noble fortress for good that it had been, how its tonic had strengthened generations of their fathers. No; wrath he spoke of, and never once of love. It was the bishop's way, I knew well, to hold cow-boys by homely talk of their special hardships and temptations. And when they fell he spoke to them of forgiveness and brought them encouragement. But Dr. MacBride never thought once of the lives of these waifs. Like himself, like all mankind, they were invisible dots in creation; like him, they were to feel as nothing, to be swept up in the potent heat of his faith. So he thrust out to them none of the sweet but all the bitter of his creed, naked and stern as iron. Dogma was his all in all, and poor humanity was nothing but flesh for its canons.

Thus to kill what chance he had for being of use seemed to me more deplorable than it did evidently to them. Their attention merely wandered. Three hundred years ago they would have been frightened; but not in this electric day. I saw Scipio stifling a smile when it came to the doctrine of original sin. "We know of its truth," said Dr. MacBride, "from the severe troubles and distresses to which infants are liable, and from death passing upon them before they are capable of sinning." Yet I knew he was a good man; and I also knew that if a missionary is to be tactless, he might almost as well be bad.

I said their attention wandered, but I forgot the Virginian. At first his attitude might have been mere propriety. One can look respectfully at a preacher and be internally breaking all the commandments. But even with the text I saw real attention light in the Virginian's eye. And keeping track of the concentration that grew on him with each minute made the sermon short for me. He missed nothing. Before the end his gaze at the preacher had become swerveless. Was he convert or critic? Convert was incredible. Thus was an hour passed before I had thought of time.

When it was over we took it variously. The preacher was genial and spoke of having now broken ground for the lessons that he hoped to instil. He discoursed for a while about trout-fishing and about the rumored uneasiness of the Indians north-ward where he was going. It was plain that his personal safety never gave him a thought. He soon bade us good night. The Ogdens shrugged their shoulders and were amused. That was their way of taking it. Dr. MacBride sat too heavily on the Judge's shoulders for him to shrug them. As a leading citizen in the Territory he kept open house for all comers. Policy and good nature made him bid welcome a wide variety of travellers. The cow-boy out of employment found bed and a meal for himself and his horse, and missionaries had before now been well received at Sunk Creek Ranch.

"I suppose I'll have to take him fishing," said the Judge, ruefully.

"Yes, my dear," said his wife, "you will. And I shall have to make his tea for six days."

"Otherwise," Ogden suggested, "it might be reported that you were enemies of religion."

"That's about it," said the Judge. "I can get on with most people. But elephants depress me."

So we named the Doctor "Jumbo," and I departed to my quarters.

At the bunk house, the comments were similar but more highly salted. The men were going to bed. In spite of their outward decorum at the service, they had not liked to be told that they were "altogether become filthy." It was easy to call names; they could do that themselves. And they appealed to me, several speaking at once, like a concerted piece at the opera: "Say, do you believe babies go to hell?"—"Ah, of course he don't."—"There ain't no hereafter, anyway."—"Ain't there?"—"Who told yu'?"—"Same man as told the preacher we were all a sifted set of sons-of-guns."—"Well, I'm going to stay a Mormon."—"Well, I'm going to quit fleeing from temptation."—"That's so! Better get it in the neck after a good time than a poor one." And so forth. Their wit was not extreme, yet I should like Dr. MacBride to have heard it. One fellow put his natural soul pretty well into words, "If I happened to learn what they had predestinated me to do, I'd do the other thing, just to show 'em!"

And Trampas? And the Virginian? They were out of it. The Virginian had gone straight to his new abode. Trampas lay in his bed, not asleep, and sullen as ever.

"He ain't got religion this trip," said Scipio to me.

"Did his new foreman get it?" I asked.

"Huh! It would spoil him. You keep around, that's all. Keep around."

Scipio was not to be probed; and I went, still baffled, to my repose.

No light burned in the cabin as I approached its door.

The Virginian's room was quiet and dark; and that Dr. Mac-Bride slumbered was plainly audible to me, even before I entered. Go fishing with him! I thought, as I undressed. And I selfishly decided that the Judge might have this privilege entirely to himself. Sleep came to me fairly soon, in spite of the Doctor. I was wakened from it by my bed's being jolted—

not a pleasant thing that night. I must have started. And it was the quiet voice of the Virginian that told me he was sorry to have accidentally disturbed me. This disturbed me a good deal more. But his steps did not go to the bunk house, as my sensational mind had suggested. He was not wearing much, and in the dimness he seemed taller than common. I next made out that he was bending over Dr. MacBride. The divine at last sprang upright.

"I am armed," he said. "Take care. Who are you?"

"You can lay down your gun, seh. I feel like my spirit was going to bear witness. I feel like I might get an enlightening."

He was using some of the missionary's own language. The baffling I had been treated to by Scipio melted to nothing in this. Did living men petrify, I should have changed to mineral between the sheets. The Doctor got out of bed, lighted his lamp, and found a book; and the two retired into the Virginian's room, where I could hear the exhortations as I lay amazed. In time the Doctor returned, blew out his lamp, and settled himself. I had been very much awake but was nearly gone to sleep again, when the door creaked and the Virginian stood by the Doctor's side.

"Are you awake, seh?"

"What? What's that? What is it?"

"Excuse me, seh. The enemy is winning on me. I'm feeling less inward opposition to sin."

The lamp was lighted, and I listened to some further exhortations. They must have taken half an hour. When the Doctor was in bed again, I thought that I heard him sigh. This upset my composure in the dark; but I lay face downward in the pillow, and the Doctor was soon again snoring. I envied him for a while his faculty of easy sleep. But I must have dropped off myself; for it was the lamp in my eyes that now waked me as he came back for the third time from the Virginian's room. Before blowing the light out he looked at his watch, and thereupon I inquired the hour of him.

"Three," said he.

I could not sleep any more now, and I lay watching the darkness.

"I'm afeared to be alone!" said the Virginian's voice presently in the next room. "I'm afeared." There was a short pause, and then he shouted very loud, "I'm losin' my desire afteh the sincere milk of the Word!"

"What? What's that? What?" The Doctor's cot gave a great crack as he started up listening, and I put my face deep in the pillow.

"I'm afeared! I'm afeared! Sin has quit being bitter in my belly."

"Courage, my good man." The Doctor was out of bed with his lamp again, and the door shut behind him. Between them they made it long this time. I saw the window become gray; then the corners of the furniture grow visible; and outside, the dry chorus of the blackbirds began to fill the dawn. To these the sounds of chickens and impatient hoofs in the stable were added, and some cow wandered by loudly calling for her calf. Next, some one whistling passed near and grew distant. But although the cold hue that I lay staring at through the window warmed and changed, the Doctor continued working hard over his patient in the next room. Only a word here and there was distinct; but it was plain from the Virginian's fewer remarks that the sin in his belly was alarming him less. Yes, they made this time long. But it proved, indeed, the last one. And though some sort of catastrophe was bound to fall upon us, it was myself who precipitated the thing that did happen.

Day was wholly come. I looked at my own watch, and it was six. I had been about seven hours in my bed, and the Doctor had been about seven hours out of his. The door opened, and he came in with his book and lamp. He seemed to be shivering a little, and I saw him cast a longing eye at his couch. But the Virginian followed him even as he blew out the now quite superfluous light. They made a noticeable couple in their underclothes: the Virginian with his lean racehorse shanks running to a point at his ankle, and the Doctor with his stomach and his fat sedentary calves.

"You'll be going to breakfast and the ladies, seh, pretty soon," said the Virginian, with a chastened voice. "But I'll worry through the day somehow without yu'. And to-night you can turn your wolf loose on me again."

Once more it was no use. My face was deep in the pillow, but I made sounds as of a hen who has laid an egg. It broke on the Doctor with a total instantaneous smash, quite like an egg.

He tried to speak calmly. "This is a disgrace. An infamous disgrace. Never in my life have I—" Words forsook him, and his face grew redder. "Never in my life—" He stopped again, because, at the sight of him being dignified in his red drawers, I was making the noise of a dozen hens. It was suddenly too much for the Virginian. He hastened into his room, and there sank on the floor with his head in his hands. The Doctor immediately slammed the door upon him, and this rendered me easily fit for a lunatic asylum. I cried into my pillow, and wondered if the Doctor would come and kill me. But he took no notice of me whatever. I could hear the Virginian's convulsions through the door, and also the Doctor furiously making his toilet within three feet of my head; and I lay quite still with my face the other way, for I was really afraid to look at him. When I heard him walk to the door in his boots, I ventured to peep; and there he was, going out with his bag in his hand. As I still continued to lie, weak and sore, and with a mind that had ceased all operation, the Virginian's door opened. He was clean and dressed and decent, but the devil still sported in his eye. I have never seen a creature more irresistibly handsome.

Then my mind worked again. "You've gone and done it," said I. "He's packed his valise. He'll not sleep here."

The Virginian looked quickly out of the door. "Why, he's leavin' us!" he exclaimed. "Drivin' away right now in his little old buggy!" He turned to me, and our eyes met solemnly over this large fact. I thought that I perceived the faintest tincture of dismay in the features of Judge Henry's new, responsible, trusty foreman. This was the first act of his administration. Once again he looked out at the departing missionary.

"Well," he vindictively stated, "I cert'nly ain't goin' to run afteh him." And he looked at me again.

"Do you suppose the Judge knows?" I inquired.

He shook his head. "The windo' shades is all down still oveh yondeh." He paused. "I don't care," he stated, quite as if he had been ten years old. Then he grinned guiltily. "I was mighty respectful to him all night."

"Oh, yes, respectful! Especially when you invited him to turn his wolf loose."

The Virginian gave a joyous gulp. He now came and sat down on the edge of my bed. "I spoke awful good English to him most of the time," said he. "I can, yu' know, when I cinch my attention tight on to it. Yes, I cert'nly spoke a lot o' good English. I didn't understand some of it myself!"

EMERSON HOUGH

The Rustler*

⟦ EMERSON HOUGH, who reached his widest audience
with two novels of pioneer life published in the 1920's,
North of 36 and *The Covered Wagon*, had factually surveyed the ways of the range decades earlier in *The Story
of the Cowboy*. More than sixty years later this book still
retains the validity of realistic exposition. Hough knew he
was writing in "the sunset of the range," and he insisted on
looking at the cowboy "not as a curiosity, but as a product;
not as an eccentric driver of horned cattle, but as a man
suited to his times."

AS IN THE Southern cattle country the nester was an
enemy to the interests of the cattle trade, so on the Northern range was the man who represented his exaggerated coun-
terpart, that somewhat famous Western character known as
the rustler. There has never been upon the range a character
more fully discussed or less fully understood. Many persons
are familiar with the curious Western verb "to rustle," and
know what is meant when one is asked to "rustle a little wood"
for the camp in the mountains, or when it is announced that
the horses should be turned out to "rustle a little grass," etc.;
but they would be unable, as indeed perhaps many resident
cattle men might be unable, to give the original derivation of
the term "rustler."

* From *The Story of the Cowboy* (New York: D. Appleton and Co., 1897).

102

Any one acquainted with the cattle country of the North would soon come to hear much of the rustler, and that in stories of the most confusing character. Thus he might hear of the murder of some dweller in an outlying camp, and be informed that the crime was attributed to "rustlers." A stagecoach might be held up, or a mountain treasure train robbed, and the act would be laid at the door of this same mysterious being, the rustler. He might hear that a number of men had been the victims of a lynching bee, and be advised that the men hung were rustlers. Thus in time he might come to believe that any and all bad characters of the West were to be called rustlers. In this he would be inaccurate and unjust. The real rustler was an operator in a more restricted field, and although it would be impossible to induce a cattle man to believe there was ever any such thing as a good rustler, it is at least true that there were sometimes two sides to the rustler's case, as there were two sides in that of the nester. In the later or acquired sense of the term, all rustlers were criminals. In the original sense of the word, no rustler was a criminal. He was simply a hard-working man, paid a little gratuity for a little extra exertion on his part. He got his name in the early Maverick days, before the present strict laws governing the handling of that inviting range product. He was then a cowboy pure and simple, and sometimes his employer gave him two, three, or five dollars for each Maverick he found and branded to the home brand. Then the cattle associations for a time paid any cowboy five dollars a head for any Maverick he found for the association. It behooved the cowboys of those days to "get out and rustle" for calves, the word being something of a synonym for the city slang word "hustle," and with no evil meaning attached to it. The term passed through some years of evolution before it gained its proper modern significance, or the improper and inaccurate use which is sometimes given it.

Under the system of Maverick gratuities the cowboy prospered on the Northern range. Those were his palmy days. Any cowpuncher of active habits and a saving disposition could easily lay up considerable sums of money each year. As he was bred upon the range and understood nothing but the cow business, it was the most natural thing in the world for him to buy a few cows and start in business for himself, sometimes while still under pay of his former employer, and sometimes quite "on his own hook." He gradually began his herd, and had his brand registered as those of the cowmen of the district. Thus he ceased to be cowboy and became cowman; or rather he remained as he really always was, both cowboy and cowman, both herder and owner. In this way many young men who went on the range "broke" began in a short time to "get ahead" very rapidly. There were few better avenues to quick fortunes than those offered by the cattle business at this stage of its growth. The logical sequel followed very rapidly. From all parts of the country all sorts of men pressed into the business. There appeared upon the range a great many men of the sort known to the old-time cowmen as "bootblack cowpunchers," men who came from the Eastern country to go into the cattle business for what money there was in it, and who were not slow to see where the quick ways of making money might be made still a little quicker. There also came into the business a great many Eastern men of wealth and standing, who were wise enough to see that the cattle business offered profits fairly Midaslike compared to the possibilities of capital in the older country. The West was now settling up rapidly along all the railroads with a good class of citizens, men of culture and refinement among them, all pressing into the new West to "grow up with the country," and to take advantage of the great opportunities of that promised land.

Under this influx of mixed population and this access of new business methods there appeared a factor never before known on the great cattle ranges—that of competition. Heretofore there had always been enough for all. Now there came the stress of the multitude, and with it the dog in the manger which belongs with the ways of modern business life. By this time there began to be hundreds of new brands upon the range, and the wealthy cattle men saw some of their cowboys building up herds in competition with their own. It always grieves the heart of capital to behold a poorer man begin to make too much money. In time there was inaugurated upon the cow range the good old game of the settlements, of dog-eat-dog, and the big dog began to eat the little one. The big men met and combined against the little ones. They agreed that no more Maverick commissions should be paid, and that the cowpuncher need "rustle" no more calves for himself, but should rustle them for his employer only. Moreover, it was agreed that no cowboy should be allowed to own a brand of his own. This all happened just at the period of the passing away of the good old times of the West. It was at the beginning of the West of to-day—the humdrum, commonplace, exact, businesslike, dog-eat-dog West—which is precisely like any other part of the country now, with as much competition as any, and with as few special opportunities in business.

This blow at the welfare of the cowboy had a curious effect. It was intended to stop "rustling," but it increased it a thousandfold. It was intended to protect the herds of the big ranchers, but it came near to ruining them. It was intended to stop an honest business system, and it resulted in establishing a dishonest one. It arrayed the written law against the unwritten law which had in all the past been the governing principle of the free West. It threw down the gauntlet for that inevitable war which must be waged between society and the individual; a conflict which can have but one end. In this case that end meant the destruction of all that free and wild character which had for a glorious generation been the distinguishing trait of a great and heroic country. Let us admit that the rustler—who now began to brand calves where he found them, Maverick or no Maverick—was a sinner against the written law, that he was a criminal, that he was the burglar, the bounds-breaker of the range; but let us not forget that he acted in many ways under the stern upholding of what seemed to him the justice of the old West. At any rate, we shall not be asked to forget him as the man who watched out the flickering breath of that dying West which not all our lamentations can now ever again bring back to life.

The rustler was a cowpuncher, and one of the best. He understood the wild trade of the range to its last detail. Among cowpunchers there were men naturally dishonest, and these turned to illegal rustling as matter of course. They were joined by the loose men of the upper country, who "were not there for their health," and who found the possibilities of the cattle system very gratifying. These took in with them, sometimes almost perforce and against their will, often at least against their convictions, some cowpunchers who were naturally as honest and loyal men as ever lived. To understand their actions one must endeavour to comprehend clearly what was really the moral code of that time and that country. This code was utterly different from that of the old communities. Under it the man who branded a few calves for himself as an act of "getting even" with the unjust rules of the large cow outfits and the big Eastern syndicates was not lowered in the least in the esteem of his fellow-men, but, to the contrary, was regarded as a man of spirit, and therefore entitled to the rough Western respect which had no eye for him who submitted to be "imposed upon." In some portions of the upper country, notably in a few counties of Wyoming, the rustlers, or men who took beef cattle or calves not their own, far outnumbered the men opposed to them. They were called thieves and cutthroats and outlaws, and so perhaps they were from one standpoint. From their own standpoint they were not, and there were so many of them that they really made the "sovereign people," which is supposed to be the ultimate court of appeal in this country. They elected all the officers and chose the judges in some counties, and they—the people—ran things to suit themselves. It was of no use for a syndicate man to try to get in one of those courts what he called justice, because he was sure to get what the people called justice, and the two were very different things.

To this organized rallying of the "little fellows," as the small cattle owners were called, there came all sorts of hard and dissolute characters out of the chaotic population of the West. The wild frontier life had attracted men of bold nature, who had taken on all the restless and unsettled habits of the country and were irked by restraint or law of any kind. Out of such population came many of the guides and scouts, who actually were such, as well as a deplorable number of a class contemptuously called "long-hair men" by the genuine Westerner. The man who lived on the "front" had to make his living as best he could. In the time of the buffalo a large class of men went regularly into the miserable occupation of "skin hunting," and it is due to their efforts that the innumerable hosts of the American bison were destroyed from the face of the earth. At the close of the rapid season of butchery which was thus set on foot, there were thrown upon the settlements and outlying country of the cattle range a large number of these ex-skin hunters, men of hardy nature and of exact knowledge of the wildest parts of the country. These men scattered over the country and fell into such occupations as they could find. Some of them went to punching cows, and some went to the Legislature. Some lived in out of the way corners of the land, dwelling in the dugout or cabin which was their old-time home, and making a living no one just knew how. There was a little wild game left in the country, but not in the old abundance. After awhile there swept over the country, all around the dugout of the hunter, the great herds of cattle which inundated the Northern range. Was it likely that this old hunting man would go without beef?

Thus it was that the cult of the rustler grew. The ranks were filled by cowpunchers wholly bad and only partly bad, by old-time cowpunchers and new-time ones, by ex-skin hunters and drifters of the range; in short, by all sorts of men who saw in the possibilities of the cow trade a chance to make a living in a way which to them seemed either excusable, expedient, or easily capable of concealment. The qualifications for the new calling, no matter what or who the man who filled them, were simply the best ones demanded by the calling of the cowpuncher. The rustler must without fail be a rider, a roper, a sure shot, and fully posted in all the intricacies of marks and brands. He must, moreover, be a man of "nerve."

In viewing him we view the criminal of the range, but an open and unaffected criminal, and we are less than broad if we fail to see the extenuating circumstances for his crime which existed in the conditions which then obtained. Of course, if we can not claim acquaintance with those conditions, and know only those of the old civilizations, we must call him a renegade, a thief, and often a murderer. Under those names no one can be admired.

The rustlers of the upper country rapidly joined their forces and arrived at an understanding with one another. The true story of their operations has never been written, and would make stirring reading, as indeed would a description of many of the scenes and incidents of the cowboy's life. They had in a way a creed and a dialect of their own. A genuine rustler was called a "waddy," a name difficult to trace to its origin. He might also, when spoken of in terms of admiration, be called a "pure," meaning that he was a thoroughbred, a reliable man, with "sand" and ability in his chosen profession. He was sure to be a good plainsman, and probably a "straight-up" rider— i.e., one who could ride any bucking horse without a "bucking strap" to hang on to. The rustler, and indeed pretty much everybody in his country, lived on "slow elk," which is to say that they ate yearling beef belonging to some one else, probably some big cow outfit. It was held strictly a point of honor among these men never to touch an animal belonging to a poor man or a small owner. The big non-resident cattle companies were the chief sufferers through losses of their "slow elk." Sometimes the spring freshets would carry away from the little willow-covered creek valleys the skeletons or hideless carcasses of many "slow elk." Resident managers for Eastern companies were obliged to report a lessening yearly increase among their herds, which after a while became almost a decrease. The profit was nearly taken out of non-resident cattle ranching by the operations of the rustlers in certain unfortunate parts of the range. Sometimes the foreman of a ranch was in open or concealed sympathy with the rustlers, and very often some of the cowpunchers were friendly to them. Perhaps some of the cowboys were a "little on the rustle" themselves in a quiet way. Sometimes such a cowboy would rope and tie out at some convenient place during the day a number of calves, and would then slip out at night and brand them with his own iron or that of some confederate.

Local sympathy was all with the rustlers and against the Eastern syndicate men, and it was unpopular to be too outspoken in condemnation of the rustling operations. The small homesteader or squatter who had made an attempt at a farm on some water way out in the dry and inhospitable country might not be much of a cowman, and might not wish to mix up in any of these crooked operations of the pseudo-cowman; but if a man came into his house some morning and made him a present of a quarter of beef, or sold it to him for half a dollar, who was to be the wiser? It was difficult, and not always safe, for the small settler to refuse. If he accepted, and did so again a few times, he became tacitly recognised as bound to secrecy, and practically a friend of the rustlers. After a time another man might come along and ask permission to leave a few calves in his pasture for a few weeks, and as he did not know where the calves came from, he was perhaps not averse to accepting the pay for this, unconscious of the fact that the calves were only being made into artificial Mavericks by being weaned away from their mothers, so that no discrepancy of brands might be noticeable between the mother and her calf. Thus also sometimes the corral of a sympathizer might be used at night to hold a few calves which were being run out of the country, or a bunch of horses which were going the same way. The very corral of the ranch from which the stock was taken might serve this same purpose. It was covertly understood by the majority of the population resident upon the cattle range of this section of the country that it was not well to watch things too closely. In this sentiment many cowboys joined who did not openly join the rustlers. The honest cowboys who remained steadfast in their endeavour to protect the interests of their employers were spoken of with contempt, and were referred to as being *"peoned* out" to their employers, and were accused of "living on bacon rinds, like so many jackasses." Sometimes they were called "pliers men," or "bucket men" by ex-cowboys who would have scorned to carry a "bucket of sheep dip," or to bother too much about mending a gap in a wire fence. Thus we see an entire perversion of the original cowpuncher love of justice, and his wish to give each man his own property. Instead of being ready to hang a cow thief or shoot a horse thief, we find our cowboys over a great strip of country sympathizing or conniving with such men. Such a pronounced change of principles surely requires a pronounced reason. In point of fact, this was not a change of principles, but a change of conditions. The cowboy remained true to the West, but he felt no loyalty for the East. He was true to his old code, but he maintained that the application of that code had changed in its conditions. Slowly he was to learn the new codes, and to become the cowboy of to-day.

THEODORE ROOSEVELT

Frontier Types*

⟦ THEODORE ROOSEVELT did not merely observe range life, he lived it—on a Dakota ranch in the 1880's. These years are recorded in two books from the busy pen of the strenuous future president, *Hunting Trips of a Ranchman* and the one from which this excerpt is taken, *Ranch Life and the Hunting Trail.* This book, Roosevelt's friend Owen Wister has pointed out, "is to be classed as the product of a hobby, energetically ridden as usual. . . . He was perfectly aware that the epoch of the range was but a brief episode in the history of the United States, and that its doom was already at hand. . . . After Dakota . . . the middle years set in, the trail leads away from birds and forests to the White House."

COWBOYS RESEMBLE one another much more and out-siders much less than is the case even with their employers, the ranchmen. A town in the cattle country, when for some cause it is thronged with men from the neighborhood, always presents a picturesque sight. On the wooden sidewalks of the broad, dusty streets the men who ply the various industries known only to frontier existence jostle one another as they saunter to and fro or lounge lazily in front of the straggling, cheap-looking board houses. Hunters come in from the plains and the mountains, clad in buckskin shirts and fur caps, greasy

* From *Ranch Life and the Hunting Trail* (New York: Century Co., 1888).

and unkempt, but with resolute faces and sullen, watchful eyes, that are ever on the alert. The teamsters, surly and self-contained, wear slouch-hats and great cowhide boots; while the stage-drivers, their faces seamed by the hardship and exposure of their long drives with every kind of team, through every kind of country, and in every kind of weather, proud of their really wonderful skill as reinsmen and conscious of their high standing in any frontier community, look down on and sneer at the "skin-hunters" and the plodding drivers of the white-topped prairie-schooners. Besides these there are trappers, and wolfers whose business is to poison wolves, with shaggy, knock-kneed ponies to carry their small bales and bundles of furs—beaver, wolf, fox, and occasionally otter; and silent sheep-herders, with cast-down faces, never able to forget the absolute solitude and monotony of their dreary lives, nor to rid their minds of the thought of the woolly idiots they pass all their days in tending. Such are the men who have come to town, either on business or else to frequent the flaunting saloons and gaudy hells of all kinds in search of the coarse, vicious excitement that in the minds of many of them does duty as pleasure—the only form of pleasure they have ever had a chance to know. Indians too, wrapped in blankets, with stolid, emotionless faces, stalk silently round among the whites, or join in the gambling and horse-racing. If the town is on the borders of the mountain country, there will also be sinewy lumbermen, rough-looking miners, and packers whose business it is to guide the long mule and pony trains that go where wagons cannot and whose work in packing needs special and peculiar skill; and mingled with and drawn from all these classes are desperadoes of every grade, from the gambler up through the horse-thief to the murderous professional bully, or, as he is locally called, "bad man"—now, however, a much less conspicuous object than formerly.

But everywhere among these plainsmen and mountain men, and more important than any are the cowboys—the men who follow the calling that has brought such towns into being. Singly, or in twos or threes, they gallop their wiry little horses down the street, their lithe, supple figures erect or swaying slightly as they sit loosely in the saddle; while their stirrups are so long that their knees are hardly bent, the bridles not taut enough to keep the chains from clanking. They are smaller and less muscular than the wielders of axe and pick; but they are as hardy and self-reliant as any men who ever breathed—with bronzed, set faces, and keen eyes that look all the world straight in the face without flinching as they flash out from under the broad-brimmed hats. Peril and hardship, and years of long toil broken by weeks of brutal dissipation, draw haggard lines across their eager faces, but never dim their reckless eyes nor break their bearing of defiant self-confidence. They do not walk well, partly because they so rarely do any work out of the saddle, partly because their *chaparejos* or leather overalls hamper them when on the ground; but their appearance is striking for all that, and picturesque too, with their jingling spurs, the big revolvers stuck in their belts, and

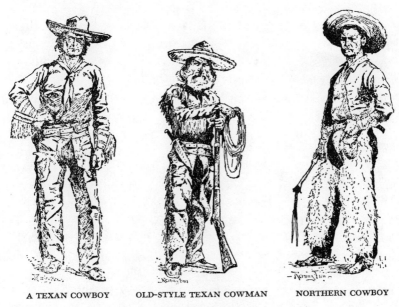

A TEXAN COWBOY   OLD-STYLE TEXAN COWMAN   NORTHERN COWBOY

Cowboy Types
Drawings by Frederic Remington

bright silk handkerchiefs knotted loosely round their necks over the open collars of the flannel shirts. When drunk on the villainous whiskey of the frontier towns, they cut mad antics, riding their horses into the saloons, firing their pistols right and left, from boisterous light-heartedness rather than from any viciousness, and indulging too often in deadly shooting affrays, brought on either by the accidental contact of the moment or on account of some long-standing grudge, or perhaps because of bad blood between two ranches or localities; but except while on such sprees they are quiet, rather self-contained men, perfectly frank and simple, and on their own ground treat a stranger with the most whole-souled hospitality, doing all in their power for him and scorning to take any reward in return. Although prompt to resent an injury, they are not at all apt to be rude to outsiders, treating them with what can almost be called a grave courtesy. They are much better fellows and pleasanter companions than small farmers or agricultural laborers; nor are the mechanics and workmen of a great city to be mentioned in the same breath.

The bulk of the cowboys themselves are Southwesterners; but there are also many from the Eastern and the Northern States, who, if they begin young, do quite as well as the Southerners. The best hands are fairly bred to the work and follow it from their youth up. Nothing can be more foolish than for an Easterner to think he can become a cowboy in a few months' time. Many a young fellow comes out hot with enthusiasm for life on the plains, only to learn that his clumsiness is greater than he could have believed possible; that the cowboy business is like any other and has to be learned by serving a painful apprenticeship; and that this apprenticeship implies the endurance of rough fare, hard living, dirt, exposure of every kind, no little toil, and month after month of the dullest monotony. For cowboy work there is need of special traits and special training, and young Easterners should be sure of themselves before trying it; the struggle for existence is very keen in the far West, and it is no place for men who lack the ruder, coarser virtues and physical qualities, no

matter how intellectual or how refined and delicate their sen-
sibilities. Such are more likely to fail there than in older communities. Probably during the past few years more than half
of the young Easterners who have come West with a little
money to learn the cattle business have failed signally and lost
what they had in the beginning. The West, especially the far
West, needs men who have been bred on the farm or in the
workshop far more than it does clerks or college graduates.

Some of the cowboys are Mexicans, who generally do the
actual work well enough, but are not trustworthy; moreover,
they are always regarded with extreme disfavor by the Texans
in an outfit, among whom the intolerant caste spirit is very
strong. Southern-born whites will never work under them,
and look down upon all colored or half-caste races. One
spring I had with my wagon a Pueblo Indian, an excellent
rider and roper, but a drunken, worthless, lazy devil; and in
the summer of 1886 there were with us a Sioux half-breed, a
quiet, hard-working, faithful fellow, and a mulatto, who was
one of the best cow-hands in the whole roundup.

Cowboys, like most Westerners, occasionally show remarkable versatility in their tastes and pursuits. One whom I know
has abandoned his regular occupation for the past nine months,
during which time he has been in succession a bartender, a
school-teacher, and a probate judge! Another, whom I once
employed for a short while, had passed through even more
varied experiences, including those of a barber, a sailor, an
apothecary, and a buffalo-hunter.

As a rule the cowboys are known to each other only by their
first names, with, perhaps as a prefix, the title of the brand
for which they are working. Thus I remember once overhear-
ing a casual remark to the effect that "Bar Y Harry" had
married "the Seven Open A girl," the latter being the daughter
of a neighboring ranchman. Often they receive nicknames, as,
for instance, Dutch Wannigan, Windy Jack, and Kid Williams,
all of whom are on the list of my personal acquaintances.

No man travelling through or living in the country need
fear molestation from the cowboys unless he himself accom-

panies them on their drinking-bouts, or in other ways plays the fool, for they are, with us at any rate, very good fellows, and the most determined and effective foes of real law-breakers, such as horse and cattle thieves, murderers, etc. Few of the outrages quoted in Eastern papers as their handiwork are such in reality, the average Easterner apparently considering every individual who wears a broad hat and carries a six-shooter a cowboy. These outrages are, as a rule, the work of the roughs and criminals who always gather on the outskirts of civilization, and who infest every frontier town until the decent citizens become sufficiently numerous and determined to take the law into their own hands and drive them out. . . .

The moral tone of a cow camp, indeed, is rather high than otherwise. Meanness, cowardice, and dishonesty are not tolerated. There is a high regard for truthfulness and keeping one's word, intense contempt for any kind of hypocrisy, and a hearty dislike for a man who shirks his work. Many of the men gamble and drink, but many do neither; and the conversation is not worse than in most bodies composed wholly of male human beings. A cowboy will not submit tamely to an insult, and is ever ready to avenge his own wrongs; nor has he an overwrought fear of shedding blood. He possesses, in fact, few of the emasculated, milk-and-water moralities admired by the pseudo-philanthropists; but he does possess, to a very high degree, the stern, manly qualities that are necessary to a nation.

.   .   .   .

Cowboys lose much of their money to gamblers; it is with them hard come and light go, for they exchange the wages of six months' grinding toil and lonely peril for three days' whooping carousal, spending their money on poisonous whiskey or losing it over greasy cards in the vile dance-houses. As already explained, they are in the main good men; and the disturbance they cause in a town is done from sheer rough light-heartedness. They shoot off boot-heels or tall hats occasionally, or make some obnoxious butt "dance" by shooting round his feet; but they rarely meddle in this way with men who have not themselves played the fool. A fight in the streets is almost always a duel between two men who bear each other malice; it is only in a general mêlée in a saloon that outsiders often get hurt, and then it is their own fault, for they have no business to be there. One evening at Medora a cowboy spurred his horse up the steps of a rickety "hotel" piazza into the barroom, where he began firing at the clock, the decanters, etc., the bartender meanwhile taking one shot at him, which missed. When he had emptied his revolver he threw down a roll of bank-notes on the counter, to pay for the damage he had done, and galloped his horse out through the door, disappearing in the darkness with loud yells to a rattling accompaniment of pistol-shots interchanged between himself and some passer-by who apparently began firing out of pure desire to enter into the spirit of the occasion—for it was the night of the Fourth of July, and all the country round about had come into town for a spree.

All this is mere horse-play; it is the cowboy's method of "painting the town red," as an interlude in his harsh, monotonous life. Of course there are plenty of hard characters among cowboys, but no more than among lumbermen and the like; only the cowboys are so ready with their weapons that a bully in one of their camps is apt to be a murderer instead of merely a bruiser. Often, moreover, on a long trail, or in a far-off camp, where the men are for many months alone, feuds spring up that are in the end sure to be slaked in blood. As a rule, however, cowboys who become desperadoes soon perforce drop their original business, and are no longer employed on ranches, unless in counties or territories where there is very little heed paid to the law, and where, in consequence, a cattle-owner needs a certain number of hired bravos. Until within two or three years this was the case in parts of Arizona and New Mexico, where land claims were "jumped" and cattle stolen all the while, one effect being to insure high wages to every individual who combined murderous proclivities with skill in the use of the six-shooter.

Even in much more quiet regions different outfits vary

greatly as regards the character of their employees: I know one or two where the men are good ropers and riders, but a gambling, brawling, hard-drinking set, always shooting each other or strangers. Generally, in such a case, the boss is himself as objectionable as his men; he is one of those who have risen by unblushing rascality, and is always sharply watched by his neighbors, because he is sure to try to shift calves on to his own cows, to brand any blurred animal with his own mark, and perhaps to attempt the alteration of perfectly plain brands. The last operation, however, has become very risky since the organization of the cattle country and the appointment of trained brand-readers as inspectors. These inspectors examine the hide of every animal slain, sold, or driven off, and it is wonderful to see how quickly one of them will detect any signs of a brand having been tampered with. Now there is, in consequence, very little of this kind of dishonesty; whereas formerly herds were occasionally stolen almost bodily. . . .

But all these things are merely incidents in the cowboy's life. It is utterly unfair to judge the whole class by what a few individuals do in the course of two or three days spent in town, instead of by the long months of weary, honest toil common to all alike. To appreciate properly his fine, manly qualities, the wild roughrider of the plains should be seen in his own home. There he passes his days, there he does his life-work, there, when he meets death, he faces it as he has faced many other evils, with quiet, uncomplaining fortitude. Brave, hospitable, hardy, and adventurous, he is the grim pioneer of our race; he prepares the way for the civilization from before whose face he must himself disappear. Hard and dangerous though his existence is, it has yet a wild attraction that strongly draws to it his bold, free spirit. He lives in the lonely lands where mighty rivers twist in long reaches between the barren bluffs; where the prairies stretch out into billowy plains of waving grass, girt only by the blue horizon—plains across whose endless breadth he can steer his course for days and weeks and see neither man to speak to nor hill to break the level; where the glory and the burning splendor of the sunset kindle the blue vault of heaven and the level brown earth till they merge together in an ocean of flaming fire. . . .

The best days of ranching are over. . . . The great free ranches, with their barbarous, picturesque, and curiously fascinating surroundings, mark a primitive stage of existence as surely as do the great tracts of primeval forests and, like the latter, must pass away before the onward march of our people; and we who have felt the charm of the life, and have exulted in its abounding vigor and its bold, restless freedom, will not only regret its passing for our own sakes, but must also feel real sorrow that those who come after us are not to see, as we have seen, what is perhaps the pleasantest, healthiest, and most exciting phase of American existence.

LEWIS NORDYKE

Boss of the Plains: The Story behind the "Stetson"*

⟨[LEWIS NORDYKE supplements his work as a news-paperman in Amarillo, Texas, with extensive studies in western history. Two of his books are on range subjects—*Cattle Empire*, a history of the vast XIT Ranch, and *Great Roundup: The Story of Texas and Southwestern Cowmen*. A third volume is a contemporary view, *The Truth about Texas.* "Boss of the Plains" is reprinted from the *Saturday Review* for May 16, 1942, a special regional issue devoted to a "cultural inventory" of the Southwest under guest editorship of John H. McGinnis and Lon Tinkle.

T HERE ARE thousands of cattle brands, many of them famous in the history of the cattle industry and in literature, but there is only one all-inclusive symbol of the West—the ten-gallon hat. There are famous boots, of course, but many brands and types; there are distinctive leather britches, saddles and horses of many varieties. But there's only one hat. In the West, throughout the whole cattle country, it's the "Stetson."

No other commercial article has had such a lasting effect on the habits and taste of the Westerner. And no other specific

* From *Saturday Review* (May 16, 1942).

trade brand, with the possible exception of the Colt's six-shooter, has been so much a character in the literature of the region. The John B. Stetson hat is the Westerner's trade mark, his crowning glory.

The notion for a distinctive Western hat started struggling in the mind of John B. Stetson one day on a Colorado prairie. Stetson, son of a Philadelphia hatter, was going West in the 1860's to seek a cure for tuberculosis, the plague of hatters. He and a small group of companions, in a trek from St. Joseph, Missouri, to the Pike's Peak region, camped in the cold. Talk

naturally turned to the subject of shelter, particularly the immediate need of a tent. Tents made of untanned animal skins were exceptionally unpleasant, and Stetson, being a hatter, happened to mention that a fur could be processed without tanning and that cloth could be made without weaving. His companions contested the statement and challenged Stetson to prove it.

With hatchet and improvised tools, Stetson used an age-old process of felting and converted fur from a rabbit skin into felt. The little square of soft fur felt amazed Stetson's companions. For amusement, he fashioned a hat which he considered the best head protector for the rigors of Western weather. It was a big hat, one that would protect a man from rain, sun, cold, wind, and even hail.

Stetson wore the hat and was the talk of the mining camps. Most of the talk was good-natured ridicule—but Stetson had his moment. A rough but handsome horseman rode about the camps one day. He saw the hat and wanted to try it on. Stetson handed over the hat and the horseman placed it on his head. The ex-hatter surveyed the picture. Here was a giant of a man—the Western type—in a silver-ornamented saddle on a spirited horse. Stetson liked the effect. The horseman did, too. He gave Stetson five dollars.

About a year later, after Stetson regained his health, he returned to Philadelphia and started making hats—just ordinary hats—which he peddled to the dealers. But the hatted horseman kept riding in Stetson's mind, and he groped for the reason. He looked at the horseman from stirrup to the big hat. For months the hatter fought poverty and worried about the hatted horseman. One night the whip cracked. The horseman looked like a cattle king, the boss of the plains.

Stetson knew the cattle business was gaining headway; he knew, too, that cattlemen didn't wear hats, at least any one particular kind of hat. The cattlemen were from every walk of life. Captain Richard King, founder of the King Ranch, which is still the nation's greatest land and cattle empire, was a steamboat captain and had spent his time during the Civil War running the federal blockade. There were no born cattlemen; the industry wasn't old enough. So Stetson reasoned that the cattle kings might be receptive to something new.

The hatter sat in his dark little upstairs shop at Seventh and Callowhill Street, and mulled over the idea of a hat for the cattle kings. He determined to gamble everything, including his credit and health, on the notion.

Stetson fashioned a big, natural-colored felt hat. The new hat pleased him, and he made a number of them. He named the hat "The Boss of the Plains." Then he sent out the hats as samples to dealers in the Southwest and West and invited orders.

Within three weeks the orders poured in; Stetson's big job became that of making enough hats. The Boss of the Plains caught the eye of the cattlemen; they need in a hat the very things Stetson had needed when he made the hat for Colorado weather. Besides that, the hat looked good; it had a distinctive appearance. The Texas Rangers quickly adopted it. Dealers rushed orders and repeat orders, some of them sending cash and requesting preference. Within a year Stetson abandoned his Eastern trade and made only the Western hat. He built a 30 by 100 foot, three-story factory. And the big hats rolled out of Philadelphia.

About the time Stetson got his business going, the longhorns were plodding over the trail to the Northern markets, and within a short time the big hat was the one distinguishing thing about the cowman's dress. Moreover, it was the utility piece of the cowboy's wearing apparel. In case of emergency the cowboy carried oats or corn in the crown for his horse; many a cowboy climbed into almost inaccessible places, dipped up water in his hat, and carried it out to his horse; or cupped the brim and used it as his own drinking vessel. A prospector caught in the desert with a leaky canteen conserved his water by pouring it in his Stetson; a ranger caught in a forest fire buried himself in the ground, leaving only his face exposed. He covered his face with his Stetson; when rescuers found him, he was uninjured, but his hat was badly charred.

The Stetson was handy for fanning campfires into life, for blindfolding or whipping stubborn horses, for slapping ornery steers in the face, for fighting grass fires, for replacing broken window panes, for dummy, or actual, targets in gun fights. Then the cowboy brushed it with his elbow and wore it to town or to the Saturday night dance. A Stetson with a bullet hole in it has always been a prize possession with Westerners, and there's a common expression: "You can put a dozen bullet holes in a Stetson and it won't ravel." When you own a big

Stetson you don't brag about how new it is but about how old it is. Many a Stetson has been in service twenty to thirty years, and a hat that old is a prized family heirloom. A Stetson will take on weight and it will get to the point where you can smell it across the room, but you can't wear it out.

When he died at the age of 76 in 1906, Stetson was making hundreds of thousands of hats each year. Since that time the big 30-acre factory in Philadelphia has increased production to almost 4,000,000 John B. Stetsons annually, but the Boss of the Plains remains much the same as the first one. Saddles have changed. Methods of ranching have changed. Cowmen got out of the saddle and stepped into automobiles; now many a ranch has at least one airplane. Everything in the West of the 1870's and 1880's has changed—that is, except the J.B. and perhaps a few cuss-words.

The Stetson is perhaps the most popular character of Western fiction, and has appeared by trade name alone in much of the general literature of the country. A Western story would not be complete, or even plausible, without a few Stetsons every several pages. Will James rarely mentioned the hats of his cowboy characters because, he explained, he figured that everyone interested in reading a Western story knew that a big Stetson was just part of the cowboy.

JAMES EMMIT McCAULEY

Tough Hombres, Tougher Pudding*

⟦ JAMES EMMIT McCAULEY set down in A *Stove-Up Cowboy's Story* one of the most flavorful accounts of life on the range ever published; "God pity the wight for whom this vivid, honest story has no interest," John A. Lomax wrote in an introduction. While in one mood McCauley could declare "I wish I had have never saw a cow ranch," he could also praise "the wild free life whare you have to feel if your closest friend is still on your hip and wonder whare you are going to get your next water, and if your old horse will make it in, and to make the Mexico line and get back without any holes in your hide—that is real living, that is sport, but 'tis the violant kind and lots of people love it beyond a doubt."

ONE WINTER when I was working on the XT Ranch in the Animas Valley in Arizona, it fell to my lot to do the cooking, or most of it.

Christmas I concluded I'd try to cook up something extra. We had plenty of most everything you could find to eat in a grocery store, for, having a large store, the XT outfit furnished plenty at the ranch. First I tried to make some apple pies.

* From *A Stove-Up Cowboy's Story* (Austin and Dallas, Tex.: Texas Folklore Society and Southern Methodist University Press, 1943).

In the place of using lard for shortning, I put in tallow and I put in plenty, too. When I rolled out the crust, the tallow it hardened until it was lumpy, but I made the pies just the same. They ought to have been very good as I put in all the kinds of flavorings they had at the ranch. All the cowboys from the neighboring ranches who visited us while they lasted said they was hard to beat. But you can fix up any sort of stuff and call it pie, sink it in the Rio Grande River, and every cowboy in New Mexico would be drowned diving after it. Anything a cowboy likes is pie and 'tis something hardly ever crosses their path.

After the pie racket old John Cummins, he got after me to cook an outfit after his prescription which was called English pudding. I put very near everything they was in from a latago strap to bear marrow, such as squad berries, yellow currants, dried mescal, rice, dried grapes, but I never put in any baking powder. The consequence was it didn't swell any, and I had cooked enough to know that anything that has flour in it has to swell or 'tis no good. Anyhow, I got it mixed up and ready after while. Then I didn't have any sack to put her in, so tied her up in a piece of deer skin and biled her for two whole days. That ought to have been enough. She certainly had all the chance any fairminded pudding could ask for swelling and showing her strength. But she didn't seem to come up none, not a bit. I got sick of seeing and smelling after the second day and took her out of the pot.

Cummins said she ought to be sort of cured before she was ready to be eaten. I laid her out on top of the dobe ranch house where she could enjoy the sun. She sure got cured. I reckon she was not used to being in the sun of a day and cold wind of a night and it must to have been kindly hard on her. I forgot all about her, and when I did think of her and went for to bring her in she had fell off of the house and was laying in a snow drift. I had to peel the hide off with a chizel.

Then Cummins said we ought to have the right kind of sause to bathe her in to cheer her up and get her in the right shape to eat; but we didn't have anything only some Mescal—

that's a kind of Mexican whiskey. I put her in that and let
her soak over night but the stuff didn't seem to soften in the
least bit and she was about the darkest complected pudding
you ever put your two eyes on. I kindly mistrusted her a whole
lot when I got a square look at her. She looked like she had
a mean disposition and meant murder. While I was getting
dinner I worried a little chunk loose from her to get a taste
and I liked to a never got it off my teeth. Even Cummins
could not eat any of it and nobody that come along could bear
to eat it.

We kept the thing for a kind of an ornament after that until
one day it rolled off the table and liked to a broke my foot.
I throwed her out in the yard and she kindly knocked around
for herself for a while. They was an old magpie around the
ranch, a fine old fellow. We had made a pet of him and
learned him lots of tricks. The day the pudding was throwed
out he found it and pecked a little piece off. We never sus-
pected he could talk but when he got that taste in his mouth,
he screamed, "Holy Moses, what have I done!" The next
morning we found him dead. That summer a fellow come
down by the ranch a-hunting Indian relics for some museum
back east. He worked around for two whole days digging in
some ruins out by the corral, getting old jugs and things. One
day he come across that old pudding laying out in the yard.

"My, my!" he says, "how fortunate I must be."

"What is it?" I asked him, and what do you think—he told
me it was one of those stones the Aztecs had used to pound
their corn with to make bread. He told me he would give me
$5 for it and I was taking him up when old Cummins had to
put in and tell him 'twas no stone but a pudding. The fellow
asked me if I would have took the money. I told him yes,
for didn't every man have to take the consequence of his
ignorance. I've paid good money for things I would not have
wanted at all if I had knowed better. Anyway, that ain't the
point. I never could see the use of spoiling a good joke just
for nothing and besides I had never got no pay for building
that pudding. If Cummins had a kept his mouth shut that

pudding would a had a nice, easy job right now in some big museum back east where people would see it and imagine she had a beat up hundreds of bushels of corn for Indians before Columbus discovered America.

After the professor left, as he had brought the wonderful pudding in and used it for a footstool we put it against the door and used it to keep the door open. After we had peeled her with a chizel and could not eat her we named her old Rough and Ready. One day she got too close to the fire and when I went in the room she had melted and had run all over the hearth and was the stickiest outfit I ever set my two peepers on. Gus de Cordova, he come in with an old tobacco box and took her up with a shovel and took it out and buried the remains. One day I happened around and he had put up a board with this inscription on it:

HERE LAYS OLD IRONSIDES
BY HER HAND SIX MEN WAS SAVED FROM DEATH
(that was when we could not eat her, Gus explained)
ALSO KILLED ONE MAGPIE
ALSO FOOLED ONE PROFESSOR
AND SHE DONE HER DUTY AND LIES HERE

I laughed until I was sick, but from then until this very now I never built another pudding.

. . . .

Another time I was shipping with trains of cattle to Bakersfield, California, out of Deming, New Mexico, for the Diamond A outfit. Thought I would see San Francisco. It was all kindly new to a Texas cowpuncher.

Saw the sign *CAFE* in big letters. I knew this was some kind of an eating house. I went in. I saw 'twas a fine place, just a bit too good for a common cowpuncher. I was shown to a table by a very nice dude called a waiter. I saw I had overjumped my pile but thought maybe I could stand one dinner with them, as I always when I got caught in a trap made the best of a bad bargain. The waiter asked me what I wished for dinner. I asked him what they had. He named over things for a while that I had never heard of in my life. He had me kindly bested. I was afraid to tell him some of the things for fear I could not eat it after it was brought to me. I looked wise, told him to bring me a steak about the size of a mule's lip from the ear down, and to put in a few more things that he thought would fill up, like fried eggs with the sunny side up and some good coffee. He asked me if would like some fried oysters. Told him yes, put in some of them too.

Well, directly he come in with a load and run back and brought in some more. I had more stuff than a four-year-old mule could have jumped. He brought me a bottle of wine. I took a smile. 'Twas as sour as vinegar. I flew at the dinner and did the best I could to get on the outside of all of it I could. I got done, asked what I owed them. Said $2.50. I asked if they charged that much for every meal. Said 'twas owing to what I ordered. I told them I never ordered one-fourth of what they brought me—said when I ordered one thing those others was put in with it. I told them if I had ordered a box of 45 caliber cartridges they would have brought me a battleship to go along with them. They called the proprietor. He come in with a spike-tailed coat and a pair of one-eyed specks, with his hair parted in the middle, a collar on so high he had to set down quick or it would have cut his ears off. He come in, asked what on earth could be the matter. They told him a great long tale and said I kicked at the price. I told them I had lived over a quarter of a century and had never been charged $2.50 for one dinner before. The gentleman said that was the price. I forked over the money. They asked me to come back. I asked if supper cost as much as dinner. I told them that down in Texas I could get all I could eat for 25 cents but if I found I had more money than I could carry around very well I'd probably come round and donate to them again, but as long as the court knows herself I'd eat some place else. I asked them if every other eating house in the town was the same price. They didn't know any thing about any other. I thought they would throw me out of the place but I felt for my old standby, and they didn't lay their hands on me and they wouldn't call the police either. They had just robbed me and I knew they dared not to call the police. I passed along there several times and if I ever saw any of them I always asked the price of bull beef in that joint.

.   .   .   .

All in all I got out of cowpunching is the experience. I paid a good price for that. I wouldn't take anything for what I have saw but I wouldn't care to travel the same road again, and my advice to any young man or boy is to stay at home and not be a rambler, as it won't buy you anything. And above every-thing stay away from a cow ranch, as not many cowpunchers ever save any money and 'tis a dangerous life to live.

My warning will have to be heeded to some extent, but the ranch is fast playing out in the west and the man with the hoe is taking his place. It looks strange to see the country now and what it was twenty-five years ago. Could ride for days and days then and hardly ever see a house. Now a house on lots of eighty and one hundred and sixty acres of land, and a small town where then they was not even a ranch house. I have enough to live on and a place to sleep at night, and when it rains I don't have to hurry to get my slicker on and get to my night horse to go hold a herd of wild, stampeded cattle, but just sleep on. And I don't have to ride horses that it takes three or four men to hold while I put the saddle on and while I crawl up in the saddle. All in all, I'll just as soon to farm. But every cowboy has his day, and I've had mine, and 'tis up to the younger generations to see after the longhorns and to ride the broncoes. I've stepped down and out—

> For a cowboy's life is a weary, dreary life,
> So I've oft been told.
> A cowboy's life is a weary, dreary life,
> For he rides through the heat and the cold.

MALCOLM S. MacKAY

...>...━━━━▶>●<◀━━━...◀...

Some Cow Ponies of
Personality*

¶ MALCOLM MacKAY is one of a surprising number of range writers with a philosophical turn of mind. His *Cow Range and Hunting Trail* reveals a man whose natural affinity was with the outdoor life of the West, not only for its ruggedness and challenge but also because it satisfied some deep yearning inside him for harmony with the natural world.

O F THE MANY cow ponies that we rode, a few seemed to have had real personalities; and their traits have stayed in my memory. They were Captain, Baldy, Crockett, Coyote, Prince, Fox, Ginger, Texas and Five Dollars.

Captain was a small, chunky sorrel, with long mane and tail. He took life easy whenever possible, but was full of devilment, and would "crow-hop" pretty nearly every time you crawled on him. He was a good rope pony, and good at all cow work. We used him almost all the time as a picket pony, because he kept so fat on a picket rope.

Baldy was a thickset, big-boned pinto with a bald face, a good, strong, upstanding pony for riding the circle in that

---

* From *Cow Range and Hunting Trail* (New York: G. P. Putnam's Sons, 1925).

steep, rocky foothill country. He was not very fast, but he was there for all day, and he could climb hills like a bull-moose.

Crockett was a nice trim-built sorrel with a blazed face. He was one of the best cow ponies I ever straddled. He had seen lots of work on the open range, and knew the game by heart. I remember well how one day I was holding herd on him, and it was long towards sundown. I was tired and sleepy —in fact was asleep, when like a bolt of lightning, of his own initiative, he tore out after a cow that had broken out of the herd. He nearly left me standing on my head, but I couldn't get sore at a pony that worked while you slept.

Coyote was a big, upstanding chestnut full of high life, and of them all stood nearest my heart. He was so full of zest and courage. He was good at all kinds of cow work—roping, cutting out, holding herd or riding the circle. I rode him more than any other pony. In the hot summer suns and cold blasts of winter I could always depend on getting back on Coyote. He and I swam icy rivers, crossed treacherous quicksands of the bad-land streams, sweated and thirsted on the alkali plains, enjoyed the beauty of sweet water and tall grass on the mountain meadows, and through it all we always loved each other, always trusted each other. I hope to meet him again on the starry ranges.

Prince was a large, big-boned grey with the strength of a moose, very easy-gaited, somewhat headstrong, but a good "all-round" cow pony. Even yet, I can feel his beautifully muscled body climbing up the steep slants of our foothills, and remember the zest with which he would bring the ponies down from the hillsides to the corral gate. I rode him on our trip to and through Yellowstone Park and he was "up and a-coming" all the way. Later on he got blind in his left eye. I remember how he loved to try and dodge out of the corral if he had half a chance, and believe me, you did not want to try and head him off, for he would not turn for anybody. All of which I learned by being spun around and nearly killed when old Prince decided to go out one time.

Fox was a heavy-boned, thickset sorrel and his name suited

him well, for he was sure foxy. One morning I put a new
saddle on him that had attached to it a beautiful pair of white
Angora saddle pockets. Fox did not seem to notice the new rig
until I got up on the flat behind our barn and hit into a lope,
then the Angora flaps began to flap. Fox took one look, and lost
his head, and started, high, wide and handsome, straight for
a cut bank, twenty feet down to the creek bottom. I stuck
him for three or four jumps, and then I saw he really was
going over the bank, and I would sure be killed if I went along,
so I threw my left leg over his head and tried to land on my
feet, but didn't quite get the right slant to it, and lit on
my right hip, which laid me up for about ten days. Fox went
on over, turned a somersault or two, and lit in the creek with
a grunt. He finally got to his feet, and staggered up on the
flat again. As I was out of the play for a while, George caught
him and led him back to the barn. The next time I was able to
get on him, we let Fox smell the flaps, flapped them up and
down a few times and after a bit he got so he wouldn't pitch
at sight of them, but I never took very many chances with that
little gentleman, for he was liable to "go to it" any time that
things didn't just suit him. . . . You couldn't ride Fox down.
I've seen him go fifty and sixty miles a day right along, and
come in high-headed and foxy as ever.

Ginger was a dark chestnut Cayuse that I bought as a three-
year-old. He was only about half broken and I sure had a time
making a good horse out of him. I remember one cold morning
I wanted to ride down to the stage station after our mail, and
I ran in the horse bunch and put my string on Ginger. I put
the saddle on nice and easy, and led him out to a level spot,
and started to crawl on him. Before I got half on, he had lost
his head, and started pitching straight for the brush and the
creek. I ducked my head, held the horn, and managed to
hang on as he tore through the willows. Then I straightened
up, got mad and went to riding, and I was all in when the
battle was over. For over an hour, off and on, we had it, all
the way down to the stage station; then, he, too, seemed to
have had enough, and came home like a gentleman.

Ginger was a mighty good pony, tough as nails, could run like a deer and was very easy riding. He got to be a good all-round cow pony, and also did well on hunting trips in the mountains.

Little Old Texas I bought as a four-year-old from John Weaver at Red Lodge. He was a bay, quite small, with a mean look in his eye. He *was* a little devil for a while, and stubborn as a mule. Morning after morning, when I would start out on the circle, he would refuse to go. He'd balk and turn around and rear and try to roll. I made up my mind that it was either he or me, and I'd get out my quirt and we'd have a battle royal for a half hour or so. Then he'd straighten out and do his thirty, forty or fifty miles like an old-timer.

I remember one time my old hunting pard, Horace Mullendore, was riding "Tex," and wanted to bring his bed roll from the wagon up to my cabin so he laid it in front of him on Tex, and started for the cabin. Well, all went well for a spell, until my horse broke out in a trot, and Tex wanted to stay along. Right *pronto* he decided to shed the bed; and lowering his head between his legs, lit into the prettiest piece of "sun-fishing" you ever put your eyes on. Horace was a game old scout, and he tried to stay, bed and all, but about the fourth jump he decided that if he wanted to stay on himself, he had to shed the bed, and so he let the bed roll off, and buckled down to do some real riding. He rode him out and then we went back and got the bed and I took it up on my horse and we came in all right. Horace and I always have a good laugh when we think of little old "Tex," and the bedding race.

Tex acted a little balky toward men who rode him, but was kind and safe for the kiddies. They all took a ride on him in all ways and manners, even to standing up on him bareback, and he always played square with them.

Old "Five Dollars" was a big flea-bitten grey. I bought him on the road to Red Lodge from a fellow I met coming out that was broke, and had to have some cash right away. He said he wanted sixty dollars for him, and he and I argued for an hour before I got him to come down five dollars. But I finally bought him for fifty-five, put my rope on him and led him along in, leaving my friend sitting on the roadside with his saddle and bridle and blanket waiting for the mail stage to carry him on out. I forgot to ask the fellow the name of the horse, and so took the Indian method of naming him after the first thing that occurred after I got him. Talking so long for a reduction of five dollars stuck in my mind, and I called him "Five Dollars."

Old Five was the best horse I ever rode in the mountains. He was sure-footed and strong, with a very fast walk. I could shoot off his back, and even pack a bear on him.

FRED GIPSON

A Working Cowhand's Day*

⟨ FRED GIPSON of Mason, Texas, is perhaps best known for those evocative novels of universal appeal, *Old Yeller* and *Hound-dog Man;* but the same writing skill, the same knowledge of region and a way of life, went into the nonfiction work from which this selection is taken, *Cowhand: The Story of a Working Cowboy.* In contrast with historic or nostalgic views of the cowboy's vocation, Gipson's emphasis is on the way the West is now—and his "hero" is a bull-necked, potbellied hand who couldn't "hire on as a Hollywood extra in the quickest of quickie Westerns." But Ed ("Fat") Alford knows cattle and he knows horses, and he knows how to work them both.

IN THOSE DAYS, the Elsinore was about an average-size ranch for West Texas. The owners had around five hundred sections of land under control. In good years, when the rains fell right and the grama grass stood tall and green as a wheat field, the outfit ran around fifteen thousand head of cattle. A part of this herd were big three- and four-year-old steers, but most of it was she-stuff, grazed for the calf crop they'd produce.

The herds browsed over the same range the year round, and nobody ever thought of winterfeeding. That was back when the grass was still so good that winterfeeding wasn't necessary.

The cows started dropping calves in March, and generally the wagon for the spring roundup rolled about the first of April. Unless, of course, the big steers were to be sent to the blue-grass country of Oklahoma and Kansas for priming. Then the spring roundup started early enough to get the steer gather out of the way before the calf work started.

The wagon boss was in charge of the roundup. With a crew of some fifteen cowhands, he would generally wind up the spring work on the Elsinore in about three months. During the summer, ranch work slacked off, with nothing much for the hands to do except hunt and doctor "wormies," and make certain the windmills were producing water. Then, around the first of September, the fall roundup began, when the calves, now weighing some four hundred pounds, were gathered and trailed to the nearest shipping point and sent to market.

Of it all, Fat [Alford] liked the spring roundup best. He liked the coming of warm weather after a long winter of blizzards. He liked to see the green tips of the young grass pushing up through the gray of the winter-dead turf. He liked the fun and excitement of working out in the open with a crew of young bloods who lived free and easy and were inclined to damn the consequences of most any act they took a notion to perform. He liked to lie out under the stars of a night and listen to one coyote making enough yap for a dozen and watch a spring moon climb high, bathing the rolling prairies with its pale light.

The day's work began early. Around four o'clock in the morning, the cook built up the campfire and started rattling pots and pans as he dragged them from the chuckbox. This was the signal for the horse wrangler to roll out, saddle his night horse, and ride in search of the grazing *remuda*.

The cowhands had it easy. They didn't stir till the coffee started boiling, sending out its tantalizing aroma. Then out they'd come, and that's when the swearing started.

Some of the swearing might be on account of stiff, sore muscles from the previous day's work. Most of it, however, had to do with tight-fitting boots that wouldn't slip on over dew-damp socks. It is well worth a man's time to study the sight of several half-dressed cowhands bent over to hang to their boot-straps while they crow-hop around their bedrolls on one bare foot. The swearing is as colorful and original as men living free of women can make it, and Fat claims the only thing he ever heard to beat it was the praying that one cowhand did every morning—calling for divine help to get his boot on.

They dressed—in boots with heels high enough to keep a man's foot from running through a stirrup; spurs heavy enough to knock the fight out of a bad horse in a hurry and help a man keep his balance on him; Levi britches because they're tough; bullhide batwing chaps to shed brush and rain and cold; neckerchiefs to keep the sun off a man's neck; and in wide-brimmed hats that'll shed sun and rain, fan a branding fire, dip water, or whip a fighting cow in the face.

The cowhand's next move was to tie up his bedroll and pitch it on the ground beside the wagon. Failure to perform this little chore was just asking the camp cook to leave it when he moved the wagon later on.

If it was a shivery-cold morning, the cook would allow a rider to pour himself a cup of coffee before breakfast was ready —but only if the man backed off away from the fire to squat and drink it. Cow camp cooks were notoriously cranky indi-viduals, and the greenhorn who didn't have sense enough to keep out of the cook's way while he prepared a meal soon got set straight on that matter.

Breakfast generally consisted of beefsteak and sourdough biscuits baked in a Dutch oven, with a little black molasses thrown in for sweetening. Sometimes there'd be oatmeal, but no milk for it. Who ever heard of milk in a cow camp?

About the time the crew was sopping the last of the molasses out of their tin plates, here'd come the wrangler, bringing in the *remuda* at a gallop. A man might not be quite through eating, but it didn't matter. Right then, it was time to pitch his eating tools into the washtub set out for that purpose, and grab himself a rope.

The wrangler needed a place to corral his horses, and that corral had to be built in a hurry—out of men and ropes. It was built on the order of a kid's merry-go-round, the main difference being that there were some thirty feet of rope held between each of the men, and the circle wasn't closed till the horses had been run through the gap.

Into this corral would come the stamping, snorting *remuda,* each horse crowding and kicking, looking for an escape hole but seldom finding it before the corral was drawn shut behind him.

The wagon boss did the roping. There were fifteen men, each with his special string of ten horses and each calling for the particular mount he'd ride that day. One would call for old "Peewee," another for "Cannon Ball." There'd be "Hell's Angel," and "Redbird," and "Liverpill," and "Screwtail," and "Stump Sucker," and "Pearly Gates," and "Leaping Lena," and "Darling Jill." A hundred and fifty, maybe two hundred head of horses. And yet, with day just barely breaking and no real light to see by, the wagon boss recognized each horse called for, reached into the milling herd with his loop and brought it out—and was embarrassed as all hell on those rare occasions when he made a mistake.

With the horses caught, the saddling and mounting started, and with it started the fun. Always, even in the best sort of *remuda,* there'd be a good number of horses still determined not to pack men on their backs. Trying to change those horses' minds quite often resulted in rough and unexpected doings.

By the time this early-morning show was over, every cowhand in the crew was wide awake and ready for work; so the boss led them out for a swing drive over country they hadn't worked the day before. He'd drop one man off here and one a little further along till the last man, riding the outside swing, had such a big circle to cover that he sometimes had to hunt and drive cattle at a gallop in order to reach the designated water hole or holding ground by the time the rest got there.

Thev'd pull in to the holding grounds around dinner-time or a little past, each man driving before him his morning gather of bawling cows and calves. They'd throw the cattle together, around three hundred head, and the cattle would mill and bawl and churn up dust with their hoofs.

The cook, who'd already moved his four-mule wagon to this new camp site, would start beating on a dishpan with an iron spoon.

Dinner on the Range

Drawing by William Alexander Bowie, from "The Cow Walks Neatly: Texas in 1876," by William Alexander Bowie, edited by Ellen Bowie Holland (*Southwest Review*, Winter, 1959)

"Come an' git it!" he'd bawl out, touching off an immediate horse race from the holding grounds to camp, with every man spurring for the first plate of beans. Three or four unlucky ones were left to hold the herd bunched till the others had eaten.

There was no time for rest at noon. A man ate, swapped his saddle to the back of a fresh horse, and rode out to the herd to start the real work of the day.

Branding fires were started and fanned till the blaze heated the running irons to glowing cherry red. The ropers went to work—generally two of them—catching calves out of the herd, heeling the biggest ones, catching the little ones around the neck. The ropers dragged their catches toward the branding fires, and the flankers fell on them, wrestling them to the ground.

When everything came off right, a flanker could get hold of a calf, reach across his back, grab a handhold in his flank, give a yank as the calf jumped, roll him in the air, and bust him against the ground hard enough that the calf would lie there till the flanker could get on him, using his weight to hold the calf down.

But when something slipped, and it quite often did, then it was sometimes a hard matter to figure out which one was throwing which. Calf and man would get locked up, leg in arm, and around and around they'd go, with the calf bawling and the man swearing, and the iron man trying to fight them away from his branding fire.

Every cowhand knows that a calf is born with only four feet. But there are flankers who'll take a solemn cowhand oath that the minute you start to throw some calves, the animals sprout eight or ten extras. They claim that nothing with only four feet could kick so hard and so fast and from so many different directions at once.

So many flankers have lost front teeth before this whirlwind of flailing hoofs that a gapped mouth has become a sort of trademark of the cowhand profession. In fact, some riders claim that a full set of front teeth is a distinct handicap in getting work at a new place. The wagon boss figures that a cowhand who's never had a tooth kicked out of his head is either short of experience or is a deadhead who won't step in and really take hold of a job.

When finally the calf was stretched out, here came one man with a branding iron and another with a knife. And what those two did to the calf in the next couple of minutes proved to the calf that he ought to have fought harder. When finally released to go in search of his mother, the calf had been marked, dehorned, branded, and castrated.

The knife man generally kept a sack handy, into which he

tossed the bloody cods he'd removed from the bull calves.
These were termed "mountain oysters," and were to be fried
for supper.

Among the cowhands Fat worked with, it was a common
belief that the consumption of "mountain oysters" greatly increased a man's potency, and any time one expected to do
some heavy courting, he made a point of eating plenty of
them.

Throughout the afternoon, the work went on, hot and heavy.
The churned-up dust fogged thicker and higher above the
bawling clamor, carrying with it the mingled odors of horse
sweat, man sweat, blood, wood smoke, and scorched hair.

Sometimes the heavy work grew monotonous; but generally,
before that happened, a rider would let an angry cow charge
between the holdup men. A flanker or iron man would glance
up, and there that old mad sister would be, coming right at
him with her horns drooped and blood in her eye. The man
would let out a yell and whip her in the face with his hat till
he could get to his feet; then he'd make a fast run for cover.

He'd duck around the first horse he came to and let the cow
go by, then come back, swearing at all the whooping and
jeering cowhands who had stopped to watch the show. Sometimes he'd get mad and offer to fist-whip the holdup man who'd
allowed the cow to charge him; but usually he let it go. At
least, the incident had put a little variety into the afternoon's
work.

Finally, along about sundown, a roper waved a hand as a
signal that the last calf had been through the mill. Then the
riders holding the herd rode away from it, giving the cattle a
chance to scatter. The lost calves located their mothers, who
sniffed at the burned and bloody wounds of their offspring and
lifted their heads to bawl in outraged protest.

For the men, it was strip the gear from tired and sweaty
horses, wash up, eat a leisurely supper, swap a few lies about
their experiences with bad horses, good liquor, and reluctant
women, then heave their hotrolls from the wagon and bed
down for the night.

Some might stay up an hour later, playing poker on a saddle blanket spread out in the campfire light, but these games seldom amounted to much. Money was scarce, the men bone-tired, and, by daylight next morning, they'd be back in the saddle, riding out to comb a new part of the range.

GRANVILLE STUART

The Cattle Business*

⟨ GRANVILLE STUART was a leading Montana ranchman before and after his most active days in the 1880's;
according to his son-in-law, "Teddy Blue" Abbott, he *was*
the history of Montana from the time he made the first
discovery of gold in Montana Territory in 1857. In 1884 he
won fame as leader of a band of vigilantes who cleaned out
a gang of horse thieves at the mouth of the Musselshell;
something like thirty outlaws wound up hanged or shot.
There is much about Stuart in Abbott's *We Pointed Them
North;* he told his own story, however, in *Forty Years on
the Frontier,* edited by Paul C. Phillips. "Nothing better
on the cowboy has ever been written," says Frank Dobie,
"than the chapter entitled 'Cattle Business' in Volume II."

ISOLATED FROM EVERYTHING but cattle, the cowboys
came to know and understand the habits and customs of
range cattle as no one else could know them. Always on the
frontier beyond organized society or law, they formulated
laws of their own that met their requirements, and they enforced them, if necessary, at the point of the six shooter.
They were reluctant to obey any law but their own and
chafed under restraint. They were loyal to their outfit and to

* Reprinted by permission of the publishers, The Arthur H. Clark Company,
from *Forty Years on the Frontier* by Granville Stuart, pp. 182–84, 188–90.
Copyright, 1925, by The Arthur H. Clark Company.

one another. A man that was not square could not long remain with an outfit.

A herd was perfectly safe in the hands of a "boss" and his outfit. Every man would sacrifice his life to protect the herd. If personal quarrels or disputes arose while on a roundup or on a drive, the settlement of the same was left until the roundup was over and the men released from duty, and then they settled their differences man to man and without interference from their comrades. They often paid the penalty with their lives.

Cowpunchers were strictly honest as they reckoned honesty but they did not consider it stealing to take anything they could lay hands on from the government or from Indians. There was always a bitter enmity between them and soldiers.

A shooting scrape that resulted in the death of one or both of the combatants was not considered a murder but an affair between themselves. If a sheriff from Texas or Arizona arrived on one of our northern ranges to arrest a man for murder, the other cowpunchers would invariably help him make his escape.

They were chivalrous and held women in high esteem and were always gentlemen in their presence. They wore the best clothes that they could buy and took a great pride in their personal appearance and in their trapping. The men of our outfit used to pay $25.00 a pair for made-to-order riding boots when the best store boots in Helena were $10.00 a pair.

Their trappings consisted of a fine saddle, silver mounted bridle, pearl-handled six shooter, latest model cartridge belt with silver buckle, silver spurs, a fancy quirt with silver mountings, a fine riata sometimes made of rawhide, a pair of leather chaps, and a fancy hatband often made from the dressed skin of a diamond-backed rattlesnake. They wore expensive stiff-brimmed light felt hats, with brilliantly colored silk handkerchiefs knotted about their necks, light colored shirts and exquisitely fitted very high heeled riding boots.

Each cowpuncher owned one or more fine saddle horses, often a thoroughbred, on which he lavished his affections, and the highest compliments he could pay you was to allow you to ride his favorite horse. Horse racing was one of his favorite sports.

There were men among them who were lightning to draw a gun, and the best shots that I ever saw; others that could do all the fancy turns with a rope and others that could ride any horse that could be saddled or bridled; but the best and most reliable men were those who did all these things reasonably well.

On the range or the trail their work was steady, hard, and hazardous and with a good deal of responsibility. They were out from three to six months at a time, so when they did get to town it is not to be wondered at if they did do a little celebrating in their own way. Few of them drank to excess, some of them gambled, they all liked a good show and a dance and they always patronized the best restaurant or eating place in town and ice cream and fresh oysters were never omitted from their menu.

When on night herd it was necessary to sing to the cattle to keep them quiet. The sound of the boys' voices made the cattle know that their protectors were there guarding them and this gave them a sense of security. There were two songs that seemed to be favorites. The tunes were similar and all their tunes were monotonous and pitched to a certain key. I suppose they learned just the tune that was most soothing to the cattle. I know that their songs always made me drowsy and feel at peace with the world.

The first place they struck for in a town was the livery stable where they saw to it that their horses were properly cared for, and the barber shop was their next objective. The noisy fellow in exaggerated costume that rode up and down the streets whooping and shooting in the air was never a cowpuncher from any outfit. He was usually some "would be" bad man from the East decked out in paraphernalia from Montgomery, Ward's of Chicago.

As the country settled up and the range business became a thing of the past most of the old reliable cowboys engaged in other business. Their natural love of animals and an out of doors life led many of them to settle on ranches, and they are today among our most successful ranchers and cattle growers.

. . . .

In the fall of 1883 there was not one buffalo remaining on the range and the antelope, elk, and deer were indeed scarce. In 1880 no one had heard tell of a cowboy in "this niche of the woods" and Charlie Russell had made no pictures of them; but in the fall of 1883 there were six hundred thousand head of cattle on the range. The cowboy, with leather chaps, wide hat, gay handkerchiefs, clanking silver spurs, and skin fitting high heeled boots was no longer a novelty but had become an institution. Small ranches were being taken by squatters along all the streams and there were neat and comfortable log school houses in all the settlements.

The story of the Montana cattle ranges would not be complete without a brief description of the Texas trail, as more than one half of the Montana range cattle were driven over that trail and almost every cowboy that worked on the ranges made one or more drives up the trail.

The trail started at the Rio Grande, crossing the Colorado river at San Angelo, then across the Llanos Estacado, or Staked Plains to the Red river about where Amarillo now is. From there it ran due north to the Canadian river and on to Dodge City where it crossed the Arkansas river and then on to Ogalalla, crossing the North Platte at Camp Clark. From Ogalalla it followed the Sidney and Black hills stage road north to Cottonwood creek, then to Hat creek and across to Belle Fourche, then over to Little Powder river and down that stream to its mouth where it crossed Tongue river to the Yellowstone, crossing that stream just above Fort Keogh. From here it ran up Sunday creek across the Little Dry, following up the Big Dry to the divide, then down Lodge Pole creek to the Musselshell river which was the end of the trail. Texas cattle were sometimes driven clear up into Canada but never in any considerable numbers. Ogalalla was a great trading center in the range days. Many herds were driven up from Texas, sold, and turned over to northern buyers, at that place.

There were usually from two to three thousand cattle in a trail herd, and the outfit consisted of a trail boss, eight cowpunchers, a cook, a horse wrangler, about sixty-five cow horses, and a four-horse chuck wagon that carried provisions and the men's blankets. The food provided was corn meal, sorghum molasses, beans, salt, sugar, and coffee.

The cattle were as wild as buffalo and difficult to handle for the first week or ten days, until they had gained confidence in the cowpunchers and accustomed themselves to the daily routine. By that time some old range steer had established himself leader of the herd and everything settled down to a regular system.

The daily program was breakfast at daylight and allow the herd to graze awhile. The horse herd and mess wagon pulled out and then the herd started, with two cowpunchers in the lead or "point." The man on the left point was next, in command, to the "trail boss," two on the swing, two on the flank, and two drag drivers whose business it was to look after the calves that played out, the footsore and the laggards. In this order they grazed along until noon. The mess wagon would camp; one-half the crew would go in, eat dinner, change horses and go back to the herd as quickly as possible and the other half would eat, change horses and the herd would be started forward again. It would be kept moving until the sun was low and sufficient water for the cattle would be found. Camp would then be made, one half the men would go in to supper, catch up night horses and return to the herd when the remaining half would do the same. The herd would be grazing on bed ground and by dark would all be down.

The nights were divided into four periods. The first watch stood until 10 o'clock, the second until 12 o'clock, the third until 2 A.M. and the fourth until morning. In case of storms or a stampede, the entire crew was on duty and remained with the herd until it was back on the trail again, no matter how long that might be. It was no unusual thing for cowpunchers to remain in the saddle thirty-six hours at a stretch but they never complained and not one of them ever left a herd until relieved.

Of all the thousands of herds driven over the Texas trail, there was never one lost or abandoned by the cowpunchers.

When the first herds started north, Indians and Mexican outlaws tried the experiment of slipping up to the herd on a dark night, popping a blanket to stampede it, with the hope of

Night Camp

Drawing by William Alexander Bowie from "The Cow Walks Neatly: Texas in 1876," by William Alexander Bowie, edited by Ellen Bowie Holland (*Southwest Review*, Winter, 1959)

cutting off some of the lead cattle and driving them east to a market. The practice did not last long. The dead bodies of a few Indians and Mexicans found on the plains, told the story and was sufficient warning to others similarly minded. The cowpunchers were loyal to their outfit and would fight for it quicker than they would for themselves.

FREDERIC REMINGTON

A Rodeo at Los Ojos*

❨ FREDERIC REMINGTON came to the close of a too-brief life (he died in 1909 at forty-eight) with a suggestion for his own epitaph: "He knew the horse." He did; and in some three thousand works of art—drawings, paintings, bronzes—he showed that he knew all facets of the Old West: cowboys, Indians, military life, nesters, mountain men, and all the rest. To him perhaps more than to any other single artist, says Harold McCracken, "we owe a great debt of gratitude for so successfully perpetuating that colorful and important era of American history." Skilled with words as well as with pen, Remington wrote five books. "A Rodeo at Los Ojos" is from *Pony Tracks*, which describes the travels of the author in the Sierra Madre of Old Mexico among other places.

THE SUN BEAT DOWN on the dry grass, and the punchers were squatting about in groups in front of the straggling log and *adobe* buildings which constituted the outlying ranch of Los Ojos.

Mr. Johnnie Bell, the *capitan* in charge, was walking about in his heavy *chaparras*, a slouch hat, and a white "biled" shirt. He was chewing his long yellow mustache, and gazing across the great plain of Bavicora with set and squinting eyes. He

---

* From *Pony Tracks* (New York: Harper & Brothers, 1895).

150

passed us and repassed us, still gazing out, and in his long Texas drawl said, "Thar's them San Miguel fellers."

I looked, but I could not see any San Miguel fellows in the wide expanse of land.

"Hyar, crawl some horses, and we'll go out and meet 'em," continued Mr. Bell; and, suiting the action, we mounted our horses and followed him. After a time I made out tiny specks in the atmospheric wave which rises from the heated land, and in half an hour could plainly make out a cavalcade of horsemen. Presently breaking into a gallop, which movement was imitated by the other party, we bore down upon each other, and only stopped when near enough to shake hands, the half-wild ponies darting about and rearing under the excitement. Greetings were exchanged in Spanish, and the peculiar shoulder tap, or abbreviated embrace, was indulged in. Doubtless a part of our outfit was as strange to Governor Terraza's men—for he is the *patron* of San Miguel—as they were to us.

My imagination had never before pictured anything so wild as these leather-clad *vaqueros*. As they removed their hats to greet Jack, their unkempt locks blew over their faces, back off their foreheads, in the greatest disorder. They were clad in terra-cotta buckskin, elaborately trimmed with white leather, and around their lower legs wore heavy cowhide as a sort of legging. They were fully armed, and with their jingling spurs, their flapping ropes and buckskin strings, and with their gay *serapes* tied behind their saddles, they were as impressive a cavalcade of desert-scamperers as it has been my fortune to see. Slowly we rode back to the corrals, where they dismounted.

Shortly, and unobserved by us until at hand, we heard the clatter of hoofs, and, leaving in their wake a cloud of dust, a dozen punchers from another outfit bore down upon us as we stood under the *ramada* of the ranch-house, and pulling up with a jerk, which threw the ponies on their haunches, the men dismounted and approached, to be welcomed by the master of the *rodeo*.

A few short orders were given, and three mounted men started down to the springs, and, after charging about, we could see that they had roped a steer, which they led, bawling and resisting, to the ranch, where it was quickly thrown and slaughtered. Turning it on its back, after the manner of the old buffalo-hunters, it was quickly disrobed and cut up into hundreds of small pieces, which is the method practised by the Mexican butchers, and distributed to the men.

In Mexico it is the custom for the man who gives the "round-up" to supply fresh beef to the visiting cow-men; and on this occasion it seemed that the pigs, chickens, and dogs were also embraced in the bounty of the *patron,* for I noticed one piece which hung immediately in front of my quarters had two chickens roosting on the top of it, and a pig and a dog tugging vigorously at the bottom.

The horse herds were moved in from the *llano* and rounded up in the corral, from which the punchers selected their mounts by roping, and as the sun was westering they disappeared, in obedience to orders, to all points of the compass. The men took positions back in the hills and far out on the plain; there, building a little fire, they cook their beef, and, enveloped in their *serapes,* spend the night. At early dawn they converge on the ranch, driving before them such stock as they may.

In the morning we could see from the ranch-house a great semicircle of gray on the yellow plains. It was the thousands of cattle coming to the *rodeo.* In an hour more we could plainly see the cattle, and behind them the *vaqueros* dashing about, waving their *serapes.* Gradually they converged on the *rodeo* ground, and, enveloped in a great cloud of dust and with hollow bellowings, like the low pedals of a great organ, they begin to mill, or turn about a common centre, until gradually quieted by the enveloping cloud of horsemen. The *patron* and the captains of the neighboring ranches, after an exchange of long-winded Spanish formalities, and accompanied by ourselves, rode slowly from the ranch to the herd, and, entering it, passed through and through and around in solemn procession. The cattle part before the horsemen, and the dust rises so as to obscure to unaccustomed eyes all but the silhouettes of the moving thousands. This is an important function in a cow country, since it enables the owners or their men to estimate what numbers of the stock belong to them, to observe the brands, and to inquire as to the condition of the animals and the numbers of calves and "mavericks," and to settle any dispute which may arise therefrom.

All controversy, if there be any, having been adjusted, a part of the punchers move slowly into the herd, while the rest patrol the outside, and hold it. Then a movement soon begins. You see a figure dash at about full speed through an apparently impenetrable mass of cattle; the stock becomes uneasy and moves about, gradually beginning the milling process, but the men select the cattle bearing their brand, and course them through the herd; all becomes confusion, and the cattle simply seek to escape from the ever-recurring horsemen. Here one sees the matchless horsemanship of the punchers. Their little ponies, trained to the business, respond to the slightest pressure. The cattle make every attempt to escape, dodging in and out and crowding among their kind; but right on their quarter, gradually forcing them to the edge of the herd, keeps the puncher, until finally, as a last effort, the cow and the calf rush through the supporting line, when, after a terrific race, she is turned into another herd, and is called "the cut."

One who finds pleasure in action can here see the most surprising manifestations of it. A huge bull, wild with fright, breaks from the herd, with lowered head and whitened eye, and goes charging off indifferent to what or whom he may encounter, with the little pony pattering in his wake. The cattle run at times with nearly the intensity of action of a deer, and whip and spur are applied mercilessly to the little horse. The process of "tailing" is indulged in, although it is a dangerous practice for the man, and reprehensible from its brutality to the cattle. A man will pursue a bull at top speed, will reach over and grasp the tail of the animal, bring it to his saddle, throw his right leg over the tail, and swing his horse suddenly to the left, which throws the bull rolling over and over. That this method has its value I have seen in the case of pursuing "mavericks," where an unsuccessful throw was made with the rope, and the animal was about to enter the thick timber; it would be impossible to coil the rope again, and an escape would follow but for the wonderful dexterity of these men in this accomplishment. The little calves become separated from their mothers, and go bleating about; their mothers respond by bellows, until pandemonium seems to reign. The dust is blinding, and the puncher becomes grimy and soiled; the horses lather; and in the excitement the desperate men do deeds which convince you of their faith that "a man can't die till his time comes." At times a bull is found so skilled in these contests that he cannot be displaced from the herd; it is then necessary to rope him and drag him to the point desired; and I noticed punchers ride behind recalcitrant bulls and, reaching over, spur them. I also saw two men throw simultaneously for an immense creature, when, to my great astonishment, he turned tail over head and rolled on the ground. They had both sat back on their ropes together.

The whole scene was inspiring to a degree, and well merited Mr. Yorick's observation that "it is the sport of kings; the image of war, with twenty-five per cent of its danger."

Fresh horses are saddled from time to time, but before high noon the work is done, and the various "cut-offs" are herded in different directions. By this time the dust had risen until lost in the sky above, and as the various bands of cowboys rode slowly back to the ranch, I observed their demoralized condition. The economy *per force* of the Mexican people prompts them to put no more cotton into a shirt than is absolutely necessary, with the consequence that, in these cases, their shirts had pulled out from their belts and their *serapes*, and were flapping in the wind; their mustaches and their hair were perfectly solid with dust, and one could not tell a bay horse from a black.

Now come the cigarettes and the broiling of beef. The bosses were invited to sit at our table, and as the work of cutting and branding had yet to be done, no time was taken for ablutions. Opposite me sat a certain individual who, as he engulfed his food, presented a grimy waste of visage only broken by the rolling of his eyes and the snapping of his teeth.

We then proceeded to the corrals, which were made in stockaded form from gnarled and many-shaped posts set on an end. The cows and calves were bunched on one side in fearful expectancy. A fire was built just outside of the bars, and the branding-irons set on. Into the corrals went the punchers, with their ropes coiled in their hands. Selecting their victims, they threw their ropes, and, after pulling and tugging, a bull calf would come out of the bunch, whereat two men would set upon him and "rastle" him to the ground. It is a strange mixture of humor and pathos, this mutilation of calves—humorous when the calf throws the man, and pathetic when the man throws the calf. Occasionally an old cow takes an unusual interest in her offspring, and charges boldly into their midst. Those men who cannot escape soon enough throw dust in her eyes, or put their hats over her horns. And in this case there were some big steers which had been "cut out" for purposes of work at the plough and turned in with the young stock; one old grizzled veteran manifested an interest in the proceedings, and walked boldly from the bunch, with his head in the air and bellowing; a wild scurry ensued, and hats and *serapes* were thrown to confuse him. But over all this the punchers only laugh, and go at it again. In corral roping they try to catch the calf by the front feet, and in this they become so expert that they rarely miss. As I sat on the fence, one of the foremen, in play, threw and caught my legs as they dangled.

When the work is done and the cattle are again turned into the herd, the men repair to the *casa* and indulge in games and pranks. We had shooting-matches and hundred-yard dashes; but I think no records were broken, since punchers on foot are odd fish. They walk as though they expected every moment to sit down. Their knees work outward, and they have a decided "hitch" in their gait; but once let them get a foot in a stirrup and a grasp on the horn of the saddle, and a dynamite cartridge alone could expel them from their seat. When loping

over the plain the puncher is the epitome of equine grace, and
if he desires to look behind him he simply shifts his whole
body to one side and lets the horse go as he pleases. In the
pursuit of cattle at a *rodeo* he leans forward in his saddle,
and with his arms elevated to his shoulders he "plugs" in his
spurs and makes his pony fairly sail. While going at this tremendous speed he turns his pony almost in his stride, and no
matter how a bull may twist and swerve about, he is at his
tail as true as a magnet to the pole. The Mexican punchers
all use the "ring bit," and it is a fearful contrivance. Their
saddle-trees are very short, and as straight and quite as shape-
less as a "saw-buck pack-saddle." The horn is as big as a
dinner plate, and taken altogether it is inferior to the California
tree. It is very hard on horses' backs, and not at all comfortable
for a rider who is not accustomed to it.

They all use hemp ropes which are imported from some of
the southern states of the republic, and carry a lariat of hair
which they make themselves. They work for from eight to
twelve dollars a month in Mexican coin, and live on the most
simple diet imaginable. They are mostly *peoned,* or in hopeless
debt to their *patrons,* who go after any man who deserts the
range and bring him back by force. A puncher buys nothing but
his gorgeous buckskin clothes, and his big silver-mounted straw
hat, his spurs, his riata, and his *cincha* rings. He makes his
teguas or buckskin boots, his heavy leggings, his saddle, and
the *patron* furnishes his arms. On the round-up, which lasts
about half of the year, he is furnished beef, and also kills game.
The balance of the year he is kept in an outlying camp to
turn stock back on the range. These camps are often the most
simple things, consisting of a pack containing his "grub," his
saddle, and *serape,* all lying under a tree, which does duty
as a house. He carries a flint and steel, and has a piece of
sheet-iron for a stove, and a piece of pottery for boiling things
in. This part of their lives is passed in a long siesta, and a man
of the North who has a local reputation as a lazy man should
see a Mexican puncher loaf, in order to comprehend that he
could never achieve distinction in the land where *poco tiempo*

means forever. Such is the life of the *vaquero*, a brave fellow, a fatalist, with less wants than the pony he rides, a rather thoughtless man, who lacks many virtues, but when he mounts his horse or casts his riata all men must bow and call him master.

The *baile*, the song, the man with the guitar—and under all this *dolce far niente* are their little hates and bickerings, as thin as cigarette smoke and as enduring as time. They reverence their parents, they honor their *patron*, and love their *compadre*. They are grave, and grave even when gay; they eat little, they think less, they meet death calmly, and it's a terrible scoundrel who goes to hell from Mexico.

The Anglo-American foremen are another type entirely. They have all the rude virtues. The intelligence which is never lacking and the perfect courage which never fails are found in such men as Tom Bailey and Johnnie Bell—two Texans who are the superiors of any cow-men I have ever seen. I have seen them chase the "mavericks" at top speed over a country so difficult that a man could hardly pass on foot out of a walk. On one occasion Mr. Bailey, in hot pursuit of a bull, leaped a tremendous fallen log at top speed, and in the next instant "tailed" and threw the bull as it was about to enter the timber. Bell can ride a pony at a gallop while standing up on his saddle, and while Cossacks do this trick they are enabled to accomplish it easily from the superior adaptability of their saddles to the purpose. In my association with these men of the frontier I have come to greatly respect their moral fibre and their character. Modern civilization, in the process of educating men beyond their capacity, often succeeds in vulgarizing them; but these natural men possess minds which, though lacking all embellishment, are chaste and simple, and utterly devoid of a certain flippancy which passes for smartness in situations where life is not so real. The fact that a man bolts his food or uses his table-knife as though it were a deadly weapon counts very little in the game these men play in their lonely range life. They are not complicated, these children of nature, and they never think one thing and say another. Mr. Bell was wont to

squat against a fireplace—*à la* Indian—and dissect the peculiarities of the audience in a most ingenuous way. It never gave
offence either, because so guileless. Mr. Bailey, after listening
carefully to a theological tilt, observed that "he believed he'd
be religious if he knowed how."

The jokes and pleasantries of the American puncher are so
close to nature often, and so generously veneered with heart-
rending profanity, as to exclude their becoming classic. The
cow-men are good friends and virulent haters, and, if justified
in their own minds, would shoot a man instantly, and regret the
necessity, but not the shooting, afterwards.

CHARLES J. STEEDMAN

···✦···━━━❧►◄❦━━━···✦···

Handling a Trail Herd*

❴ CHARLES J. STEEDMAN gathered his recollections of
experiences on the Oregon Trail in the 1870's in *Bucking
the Sagebrush,* in which "Handling a Trail Herd" appears.
The book was illustrated by Charles M. Russell.

WE SOON DISCOVERED that our men were utterly ig-
norant of the proper way to work cattle on the trail. To
make matters worse the animals were all strange to each other,
with no previous trail experience, and were evidently all homesick and anxious to return to their own particular haunts. This
they were constantly striving to do at all times of night or
day, sometimes singly or in bunches, sometimes all together
in a solemn absent-minded walk, and then again in a determined gallop, but always with a dogged persistence against
which strong language had not the slightest effect, and even
clubs made but a temporary impression. It can easily be seen
that we did not have much time to give to lawn tennis and
afternoon teas.

We now began to have other worries added to our bundle.
When we started the cattle, having just come off the finest feed
in the world—bunch grass—many of them were in fine flesh.
In fact a great many of them could have been killed for beef.

* From *Bucking the Sagebrush* (New York: G. P. Putnam's Sons, 1904).

But we soon found that an excess of fat, at the start, anyhow, was not the thing to be desired.

It was now the end of June and the sun was getting very hot in the middle of the day. The country was rolling and the trail crossed a number of divides between the watercourses. Some of these hills, though not long, were steep, and we soon found that our overfat stock began to die from a sort of apoplexy, brought on by their exertions in climbing these steep slopes. For several days we lost from five to ten head from this cause, and that was another lesson, costly, but necessary.

For a beginner on the trail to see his finest steers lie down and die in the first month, when he knows he has several more months ahead of him, is like seeing a ship wrecked when just starting on a voyage, and it surrounds him with a gloom that can be cut with a dull axe. Visions of flowers for his best girl and trips to Europe fade, and the best he can see ahead of him is a cabin in the mountains with a milk cow to give him luxuries. Later on, however, the boot was on the other leg —fat cattle did not bother us. They got so thin that we had to wrap them with rawhide to keep them from falling apart.

To drive cattle on the trail is simple enough when you know how, but cows, like human beings, must be drilled before they can march. The proper way is as follows: At about sundown a "bed ground" is selected. It should be as level as possible, half a mile to a mile from water, on high ground and free from sagebrush. This, of course, is the ideal spot which is seldom found, but one tries to come as near to it as possible. It is also well to have it at least half a mile from camp.

If the grass and water have been plentiful, the herd is liable to be in a cheerful frame of mind and allows itself to be rounded into a bunch gradually. This is usually done by about four or five hands, the rest of the men being sent to camp for supper, among them those who go "on herd" the first part of the night. The latter get fresh horses, and about eight o'clock go out and send in the men who have bedded the herd.

When it becomes dark the animals lie down, and if nothing

happens to disturb them, they remain perfectly quiet until about twelve, when they get up, stretch and turn over, and then peace reigns until the first break of day. Some times a steer will create a commotion by horning another to make it give up its comfortable warm bed, but that amounts to little. Under these rose-colored conditions, two men can easily hold 2500 head of cattle.

The men ride around the herd in different directions, keeping about fifty yards from the edge of the bunch, and the real cowboy will sing to his herd as a mother sings to her baby, the music of the lullaby. There is no doubt that the sound of a human voice has a quieting effect on a dumb brute, and many a stampede has been avoided by this practice of singing. The length of the watches varies according to circumstances. If everything runs smooth, and the cattle hold easy, it is usual to have but two periods—from eight at night till four or five in the morning. But some times it is necessary to reduce the time to two hours per watch, and then every man takes a turn during the night. Some times all hands are up all night, so that there really is no hard and fast rule. Ordinarily when the period of the watch is up one of the men on herd comes into camp and wakens the relief, and woe to the man who cuts off any from his own time. There is always liable to be more than one watch in camp, and they are kept pretty well synchronized, so that the plea of the watch being wrong won't work, and the shirker has his life made very unhappy.

As soon as it is light enough to see, the cattle get on their legs and begin to look for breakfast. When the herd begins to graze the leaders naturally go in the direction in which they happen to be facing. It is then that the cowboy who knows his business comes in. With the help of one other he will "point" them in the direction in which the herd is being driven without fuss or noise.

The method is simple. One man keeps, we will say, to the north of the herd and the other works the head animals from the south until they reach him, when, like water meeting an obstacle, they will seek the spot of least resistance, which

in this case would be to the east, as otherwise they would face
back into the main bunch. Thus, a herd takes the shape of
a wedge, or of a flock of wild geese on the wing, if on the
open prairie; if in a narrow defile, they, of course, lengthen
out. The riders gradually take up their places on either flank
and the rear is brought up by four or five men "pounding 'em
on the back," as the term goes.

The Trail Herd
Drawing by Charles M. Russell, from *Bucking the Sagebrush,* by
Charles J. Steedman (Putnam, 1904)

In all herds there are a certain number of animals that are
always in the lead, unless disabled by lameness. These may
number a couple of hundred head, and of this number there
are half a dozen or so that are usually in the van. The "leaders"
are soon known, and it is necessary to be able to distinguish
them from the main herd, for the reason that if any of them
are missing after a night stampede, you can be sure that your
lead cattle have not been rounded up.

The tail end of a herd is called the "drag" and never was
a truer appellation given. Under the best of circumstances,
to push along the cripples and worn-out "critters," of which
there are always quite a number, is a task that I don't believe
old Job could handle with any degree of complacence. If the
wind is against you, the dust from four times two thousand

feet is coming directly into your face—and mind you, most of the soil on the trail has a good proportion of alkali. The sun comes down hot, and sometimes, if water is scarce and the drive is a long one, it may mean seven or eight hours without a drink. It is almost as trying as being marooned, to see the main body of the herd gradually disappearing ahead with the grub-wagon and the horse herd, and find yourself with two or three other unfortunates trying to hurry up, by all the means known to the profession, a couple of hundred laggards.

Even the camp has its routine. The cook gets up generally about 2.30 or 3 A.M., according to his nature, and proceeds to get breakfast. Just as soon as he can see to count his horses the "cavarango" or "horse wrangler" rounds up his bunch and brings them into camp.

I must here explain that in the evening, when all the horses have been turned loose, except those needed for night herding, the "wrangler" gathers them in a bunch and drives them off to wherever he thinks he will find good grass, and holds them there until morning.

The science of night herding horses is a difficult one for white men to learn. To Indians and Mexicans it is easy, as they have been brought up to it. The trouble generally lies in the fact that the herder is either too careful or not careful enough. A man who keeps his bunch too close because he is afraid some will get away will knock the flesh off his horses almost as much as hard riding. On the other hand, the careless or sleepy man will always be out several horses in the morning, and they are usually the best of the lot. An Indian or Mexican seems to have the faculty of sleeping with one eye open. They rarely lose an animal, and if the weather is of the average, they will stand all night, and yet, except for a nap of perhaps an hour at noon, they don't seem to need sleep; at all events, they don't regularly get into their blankets—if they have any.

Around the neck of one of the horses—preferably an old mare kept for the occasion and called the bell mare—a cowbell is strapped. After a week or so the horses become attached to the sound and will always keep within earshot unless something alarms them or they are thirsty and smell water, in which case nothing but a rope will hold them. The bell is also a great help to the cavarango, as by the sound he can tell the direction and distance the horses are from him, and he can also tell if they are grazing or moving away from him.

We left the cook preparing breakfast, and the horse herd coming toward camp; we will now see what the men are doing. In every cow camp you will find some one, who, either from a bad conscience, a lumpy bed, or vigorous appetite will get up when he hears the cook stirring. Sometimes he is a cheerful soul and begins to bellow at the top of his lungs. Again, he is a particular bird, and immediately puts on his spurs and chaps, rolls up his blankets, and cords the bundle, all with a running accompaniment of jingles, snorts, and oaths. Then he tramps right through the prostrate forms and dumps his bedding into the wagon.

It is a peculiar and disagreeable sensation, when lying with your ear close to the ground, to hear a man with a big spur tramping in your immediate neighborhood. I think the sound travels more clearly than it does higher up. At all events, with your senses only half aroused, you are dead sure that the next step the man takes is going to land his heel in your mouth and his spur in your eye. This has the necessary effect, and one by one the weary boys wake with a moan or an oath, stretch and get on their feet.

At one time on this trail we had a man who invariably yodled the following ditty as his greeting to the newborn day:

> "I'm ragged I know,
> But look at the rigging on Billy Barlow."

The last note was a prolonged falsetto howl. We got rid of him as soon as possible.

Dressing consists of pulling on your boots and trousers and chaps. Washing is usually postponed until the sun comes up. Each man, as he happens to be slovenly or neat in his habits, rolls and ties up his bed and takes it to the wagon to await loading.

By this time the horses are near at hand, a rope about fifty feet long is tied to the top of the front wagon wheel and another to the rear one, and the loose ends are held by two men standing off and pulling taut on them, thus making a V. This forms a corral.

One of the peculiarities of a bronco is that he doesn't like a loose rope, and he won't jump it unless he has to. It is also astonishing to the uninitiated, and I myself have often wondered at the impunity with which a man can walk in among a lot of broncos and push them about without getting kicked. I don't remember ever hearing of a man being hurt in that way. Yet I have frequently found myself at the business end of an unbroken pony in a crowded corral, even being shoved against him by another horse, and the only effect was to make him scramble to get farther away.

On the trail the horses soon get to know what is wanted, and generally it is an easy matter to catch your horse, but sometimes there is a "breacher" in the band, and he makes all kinds of trouble. In the first place he will dodge a rope, and every time he sees a chance to make a break for the prairie he will do so, always followed by all the rowdies. When a pony shows he is an artist in that line he is generally dropped out of the bunch and left to graze peacefully, unless it is his turn to be ridden, and then things are different. One day a horse with this trait, in his efforts to dodge through the lines, laid a course directly across the spot where the cook had piled his hot breakfast. The obituary notice and set of resolutions passed by the members of that camp, and placed near his carcass, would bring tears to your eyes, but I doubt if they could be published.

Each man catches and saddles the horse he wishes to ride that morning, and then eats his breakfast and skips for the herd. Horses are caught up for the men who may not yet have come in from night herd, and are tied to the wagon, as are also the work horses for the wagon.

Finally, when all hands have been fed, the cook proceeds to wash up his dishes and pack his wagon. The horse herder, unless he has lost some horses during the night, generally lends a hand, sometimes grudgingly, but usually the cook and he work well together. A good cook always has his eye on the wood supply. If he happens to be at a camp where it is plentiful, he will get the herder to "snake up" a log or two, and after he has loaded his outfit and blankets he will put the wood on top of the load. It is the same with his water barrel; if he comes to a good spring he will empty out the stale water and replenish his supply. I have had cooks, confound them, who did not have sense enough to think, but I must say, that, as a general rule, the camp cook, although belonging to an independent, drunken, disagreeable tribe, usually has more than average intelligence.

The horses are harnessed—most large outfits have four to the wagon—and when all is ready, the cook pulls out in the direction the herd has gone, and the horse herd falls in behind. In this way they proceed until they are halted for the midday rest and meal, by some one detailed to hunt up a camping spot.

The distance made in a day depends on circumstances over which you have absolutely no control. The conditions that govern are weather, topography, water, grass and behavior of cattle. With everything coming your way it is easy to make ten miles, or even twelve, and find your cattle, horses, and men full of food and good nature when bedding down time comes. Then again, you can work like a steam drill and starve like a Hindoo for food and drink for eighteen hours, and only make five or six miles.

I think, however, that taking the average for six months on the trail, a distance of seven or eight miles a day is fair, with three meals a day three fourths of the time. The other fourth is divided between afternoon teas and lying down where night finds you with nothing to feed on but the bawl of a hungry steer, and the hope that you'll find the main herd in the morning.

The object, of course, is to move the herd, and at the same time keep all the flesh on them that you can. For this reason undue haste is bad, and empty bellies are worse. A man with experience will not try to keep his cattle on the main-travelled trail, except when he has to in order to get through mountain passes, or where the valleys are narrow.

The best plan is to send two scouts ahead each day, or go yourself, and see what the prospects are for the next day's drive. We used to ride forward on the trail a distance of about fifteen miles, so as to know what direction the road took, then separate, going to the right and left from the trail a distance of five or six miles, and thence back to camp. In that way we knew exactly where the bad places were, and where water could be found, if at all, in sufficient quantities to water a big herd, and also where the best feed was for five miles on each side of the trail. At night we would compare notes and the man who could show the best country took charge of the herd next day.

It was great training for a young man, and to-day I am often surprised that I recognize a district I have only been over once, and that perhaps a long period back, and it is seldom that I lose my way either in a city or country. Unconsciously I make note of land-marks. As I write this there are many portions of the Oregon trail that stand out as clearly as a photograph, but I have not been there for twenty odd years.

We always tried to get the wagon to the place where we were to camp for the night, somewhere about five in the afternoon. We would get our supper at about sundown, and immediately after that, if things were normal, the men would hunt about for a smooth place, and unroll their beds.

I always think of Balch as he looked about for a depression in the ground to accommodate his hip bone. He contended that if that part of his anatomy was taken care of he did not care about the rest. Sand is the most uncomfortable bed because it packs so hard. When you find a thick growth of sagebrush, it takes a high order of intelligence so to arrange your couch that you can dove-tail in between the stumps— one in the small of your back, one back of your knees—always being careful not to get your head too near a clump, as there is the ever-present fear that a rattlesnake may be concealed in the bunch.

The last thing a man does before he turns in is to see that his saddle, bridle and rope are handy and ready to be thrown on a horse at a minute's notice, as, like a fireman, he never knows when all hands will be routed out by an alarm.

E. DOUGLAS BRANCH

Ranch Life*

❴ *The Cowboy and His Interpreters* by E. Douglas Branch
is a lively sort of encyclopedia or dictionary of cowboy life,
put together by a southwestern journalist of parts. Two
other similar works are *The Cowboy* by Philip Ashton Rollins (more pedestrian but more detailed and complete)
and *The American Cowboy: The Myth and the Reality* by
Joe B. Frantz and Julian Ernest Choate, Jr. (more reflec-
tive and critical).

IN THE NORTH the ranch-house was usually a large building, the timbers well chinked, perhaps hewn and squared.
The windows and the door were carefully fitted, for the cold of
winter was sure to find out every gaping joint. Inside was one
large unpartitioned room. Cowboys' bunks lined the walls;
where they ended began rows of pegs, for the saddles, spurs,
bridles, chaps, lariats, and other gear, to be used by those
cowpunchers who remembered not to throw their things on the
floor. A huge fireplace and a good sized stove were in the
room; if on a still summer's night the flavor of ancient bacon-
grease might linger in the bunks, in winter the warmth of the
cook's fire was a comfort that atoned. In the South, where the
warmth of nature was itself sufficient, the cook's house was
often a connecting building.

* From: *The Cowboy and His Interpreters* by Douglas Branch. Reprinted by
permission of the publishers Appleton-Century-Crofts, Inc.

Reginald Aldridge remembers a unique ranch-house he shared with his partner-cattleman in Kansas, where lumber was scarce—a small wooden house, ten feet by six, which could be placed upon an ordinary set of wagon-wheels and drawn about where it was wanted. At one end were the bunks, one over the other; on another side hung a flap-board on hinges, that could be propped up for a table. This portable head-quarters was probably better to live in than the little ranch-houses of the small stockmen in the country about Denver, poorly-jointed log affairs that the owners apologized for year after year as only temporary structures.

Simple equipment in ranch-houses was the rule. One long table, near the stove for the convenience of the cook as he dished out the meals, and a few chairs, were enough; perhaps there was also a small table used for card games. "We had lots of wood, a good supply of grub, a keg of whiskey, lots of robes, and one bed," writes John Clay of one of his first camps. This simplicity was as it should be; the range knew instances where the feminine touch, with a Montgomery Ward catalogue to inspire it, had added ornamentation saddening and devastating.

With the beginning of dawn "Miss Sally," the cook, was out of his bunk, grunted to rouse the horse-wrangler, and growled to encourage the coffee. As a coyote, emitting his last wail of the night, trotted off along the horizon line, and "near by in the cottonwoods, a mourning dove called softly to its mate, and from a fence-post a meadow-lark gave full voice in his glad, joyful way," the cowboy came out from his blankets for the morning's coffee and bacon.

The first faint smoke from the stove-chimney had warned the horses grazing outside the ranch-house that the working-day was about to begin; but by the time breakfast was over the horse-wrangler had the skittish herd shut in the corral, ready for the cowboys to pick the mounts they wanted for the day's riding.

Said Roosevelt of his outfit, "We worked under the scorching midsummer sun, when the wide plains simmered and

wavered in the heat; and we knew the freezing misery of riding
night-guard round the cattle in the late fall roundup. . . . We
knew toil and hardship and hunger and thirst, and we saw
men die violent deaths as they worked among the horses and
cattle, or fought in evil feuds with one another; but we felt
the beat of hardy life in our veins, and ours was the glory of
work and the joy of living."

The season's routine of "outriding," of making "sign camps,"
of horse-gentling, of branding, needed men who lived and
worked in the open by their own choice, who coupled cow-
craft and horsemanship with a faithfulness of work that carried
them through gamuts of physical ordeals. These men saw life
romantically—a wild, free existence, from the morning cup of
bitter, pleasant coffee to the night's rest under clear skies.

Groups of cowboys rode on inspection trips, "outridings,"
to locate the scattered groups of cattle, to note the condition
of grass and water, to move back cattle found wandering too
near the borders of the range, to watch for danger-signs of
men or wolves, to attend to the many details that arose naturally
in the course of a season's cowpunching.

Ready to Ride

Drawing by William Alexander Bowie, from "The Cow Walks
Neatly: Texas in 1876," by William Alexander Bowie, edited by
Ellen Bowie Holland (*Southwest Review*, Winter, 1959)

A party might discover a yearling with smooth sides and unmarked ears. To rope and brand him might provide some fun, for if the first lariat fell short, the yearling was away at his best pace. Once a rope was tight about the yearling's neck, the rider kept the rope taut while the animal bawled and jumped; but shortly a fire had been built, an iron was taken from its rawhide fastenings on the side of a saddle, and the yearling was branded. If the outriding group found a "maverick" steer, an old "mossback," one or two of the group would ride in pursuit. Once he was roped one or two cowboys dismounted and fastened the steer's feet with a "hog-tie" hitch. If there were no pieces of hobble-rope in the party, the steer might be tied down with his own tail, the hair divided into equal parts and knotted together at the ends, the loop stretched once or twice around the upper hind leg of the steer, keeping that leg drawn up so that the cow could not rise. In the handling of these animals the punchers seemed brave to recklessness. The artist Remington, well acquainted with the West though he was, marveled at the cowboys' "seeming to pay no attention to the imminent possibilities of a trip to the moon. . . . They toss their ropes and catch the bull's feet, they skilfully avoid his rush, and in a spirit of bravado they touch his horns, pat him on the back, or twist his tail." But the appearance of bravado was largely for the entertainment of spectators; behind their studied indifference was the knowledge of cows and their behavior included in the equipment of a genuine cowboy.

"Sign camps" were occasionally established about an entire range. There were two men to each camp; their work was to herd back all cattle that might have drifted across the "line." The ride of each man was from his "sign camp" half-way toward the next camp. The rides were generally timed so that at the half-way point two riders met, exchanged greetings, and rode back each to his own camp. In the morning the line-riders would search for the trail of any cattle that might have crossed the range boundary during the night; such cattle had seldom wandered far, and were quickly overtaken and driven back.

"Starting west of the Utah line, most all riding is done from camps, and very seldom is there a change of horses in one day," writes Will James. "There's no night guard, only maybe three or four nights a year, and that's when the cattle is took to the railroad."

"Style" in cowpunching varied with the locality. In the Far Western states the traditions in methods and outfitting that held from Texas to Montana did not always hold, with Mexican labor more common and the roughness of the country demanding different tactics. Texas tradition insisted that one end of the lariat should be tied to the saddle-horn, so that once roped an animal could not escape; a fine rawhide or hemp rope was costly, and an unlucky cowboy sorrowed to see forty feet of lariat trailing after a steer loping toward the horizon. But in the Far West the rope was "dallied," turned one or two times about the saddle-horn, so that if the roped animal should tumble into a gulch, or attempt to "wind up" the horse and rider, the rope could be turned loose. A cowboy on the northern range rose in his stirrups as he rode a high-tempered horse, while a cowboy farther West "rode close," bobbing up and down with his mount.

Breezy and pleasant days there were on the range, when the cowboy mused as he rode on "the breadth of things, the height of things, the magnificent distances," how fine a country was the West, how fortunate he was to be a part of it.

But there were summer days when the yellow plains were shimmering with heat, when the water the cowboys drank, the ground they slept on, the leather of their saddles were all comfortless and warm. The horses' bits had to be steeped in water before they were adjusted, or the iron would blister the flesh it touched. The water-starved ground, with its gaping cracks, was treacherous footing for haggard, restive cattle. When relief came after such a drouth it was usually a sharp, sudden rainstorm, with vicious flashings of lightning. . . .

In the spring of 1876 a great prairie fire was driven from the Staked Plains in the Panhandle into the Canadian River breaks. The fire was sighted at headquarters of the LX ranch late in the evening; saddle ponies were rounded up and dozens of cowboys set out at a swift gallop. A ride of about fifteen miles over rough country in darkness relieved only by the flames brought the party to the fire. Droves of cattle were running ahead of the advancing flames. Some of the largest animals were killed, and their carcasses split open. Then the cowboys paired off, two fastening their ropes to the hind legs of the dead animal, and dragging it to the blaze. If the fire was at the moment burning in an arroyo, where the blue-stem grass grew tall, it was allowed to burn its way to a flat covered with buffalo grass. Here the two cowboys would "straddle the blaze"—one on the burnt side, close up, and the other in the path of the smoke, with his rope played out to its knot on the saddle-horn. The wet carcass was dragged slowly along the line of the blaze, until the carcass was worn into ribbons; then another animal was killed and dragged in its place. What little spots of fire survived were thrashed out by cowboys who followed with pieces of wet cow-hide or with wet saddle-blankets. With only hastily broiled beef to eat in snatches, the cowboys worked on until three o'clock the following evening, when the fire was beaten, and the LX range was saved.

ANDY ADAMS

Dodge: Good Whiskey and Bad Women*

❨ ANDY ADAMS' *The Log of a Cowboy* is generally regarded as the one indispensable single volume for a true
picture of what the cowboy and his life were really like.
Andy Adams came to Texas from Indiana when he was
twenty-three, in 1882; he ranched for a decade, then turned
miner for another decade, then turned to writing. His *Log*
is cast in fiction form, but Dobie says: "If all other books
on trail driving were destroyed, a reader could still get a
just and authentic conception of trail men, trail work, range
cattle, cow horses and the cow country in general from
The Log of a Cowboy."

O N REACHING DODGE, we rode up to the Wright House,
where Jim Flood met us and directed our cavalcade across
the railroad to a livery stable, the proprietor of which was a
friend of Don Lovell's. We unsaddled and turned our horses
into a large corral, and while we were in the office of the
livery, surrendering our artillery, Flood came in and handed
each of us twenty-five dollars in gold, warning us that when
that was gone no more would be advanced. On receipt of the

* From *The Log of a Cowboy: A Narrative of the Old Trail Days* (Boston:
Houghton Mifflin Co., 1903).

money, we scattered like partridges before a gunner. Within an hour or two, we began to return to the stable by ones and twos, and were stowing into our saddle pockets our purchases, which ran from needles and thread to .45 cartridges, every mother's son reflecting the art of the barber, while John Officer had his blond mustaches blackened, waxed, and curled like a French dancing master. "If some of you boys will hold him," said Moss Strayhorn, commenting on Officer's appearance, "I'd like to take a good smell of him, just to see if he took oil up there where the end of his neck's haired over." As Officer already had several drinks comfortably stowed away under his belt, and stood up strong six feet two, none of us volunteered.

After packing away our plunder, we sauntered around town, drinking moderately, and visiting the various saloons and gambling houses. I clung to my bunkie, The Rebel, during the rounds, for I had learned to like him, and had confidence he would lead me into no indiscretions. At the Long Branch, we found Quince Forrest and Wyatt Roundtree playing the faro bank, the former keeping cases. They never recognized us, but were answering a great many questions, asked by the dealer and lookout, regarding the possible volume of the cattle drive that year. Down at another gambling house, The Rebel met Ben Thompson, a faro dealer not on duty and an old cavalry comrade, and the two cronied around for over an hour like long lost brothers, pledging anew their friendship over several social glasses, in which I was always included. There was no telling how long this reunion would have lasted, but happily for my sake, Lovell—who had been asleep all the morning—started out to round us up for dinner with him at the Wright House, which was at that day a famous hostelry, patronized almost exclusively by the Texas cowmen and cattle buyers.

We made the rounds of the gambling houses, looking for our crowd. We ran across three of the boys piking at a monte game, who came with us reluctantly; then, guided by Lovell, we started for the Long Branch, where we felt certain we would find Forrest and Roundtree, if they had any money left. Forrest was broke, which made him ready to come, and Roundtree, though quite a winner, out of deference to our employer's wishes, cashed in and joined us. Old man Don could hardly do enough for us; and before we could reach the Wright House, had lined us up against three different bars; and while I had confidence in my navigable capacity, I found they were coming just a little too fast and free, seeing I had scarcely drunk anything in three months but branch water. As we lined up at the Wright House bar for the final before dinner, The Rebel, who was standing next to me, entered a waiver and took a cigar, which I understood to be a hint, and I did likewise.

We had a splendid dinner. Our outfit, with McNulta, occupied a ten-chair table, while on the opposite side of the room was another large table, occupied principally by drovers who were waiting for their herds to arrive. Among those at the latter table, whom I now remember, was "Uncle" Henry Stevens, Jesse Ellison, "Lum" Slaughter, John Blocker, Ike Pryor, "Dun" Houston, and last but not least, Colonel "Shanghai" Pierce. The latter was possibly the most widely known cowman between the Rio Grande and the British possessions. He stood six feet four in his stockings, was gaunt and rawboned, and the possessor of a voice which, even in ordinary conversation, could be distinctly heard across the street.

"No, I'll not ship any more cattle to your town," said Pierce to a cattle solicitor during the dinner, his voice in righteous indignation resounding like a foghorn through the diningroom, "until you adjust your yardage charges. Listen! I can go right up into the heart of your city and get a room for myself, with a nice clean bed in it, plenty of soap, water, and towels, and I can occupy that room for twenty-four hours for two bits. And your stockyards, away out in the suburbs, want to charge me twenty cents a head and let my steer stand out in the weather."

After dinner, all the boys, with the exception of Priest and myself, returned to the gambling houses as though anxious to work overtime. Before leaving the hotel, Forrest effected the loan of ten from Roundtree, and the two returned to the Long Branch, while the others as eagerly sought out a monte game.

But I was fascinated with the conversation of these old cow-men, and sat around for several hours listening to their yarns and cattle talk.

"I was selling a thousand beef steers one time to some Yankee army contractors," Pierce was narrating to a circle of listeners, "and I got the idea that they were not up to snuff in receiving cattle out on the prairie. I was holding a herd of about three thousand, and they had agreed to take a running cut, which showed that they had the receiving agent fixed. Well, my foreman and I were counting the cattle as they came between us. But the steers were wild, long-legged coasters, and came through between us like scared wolves. I had lost the count several times, but guessed at them and started over, the cattle still coming like a whirlwind; and when I thought about nine hundred had passed us, I cut them off and sang out, 'Here they come and there they go; just an even thousand, by gatlins! What do you make it, Bill?'

"'Just an even thousand, Colonel,' replied my foreman. Of course the contractors were counting at the same time, and I suppose didn't like to admit they couldn't count a thousand cattle where anybody else could, and never asked for a re-count, but accepted and paid for them. They had hired an outfit, and held the cattle outside that night, but the next day, when they cut them into car lots and shipped them, they were a hundred and eighteen short. They wanted to come back on me to make them good, but, shucks! I wasn't responsible if their Jim Crow outfit lost the cattle."

Along early in the evening, Flood advised us boys to return to the herd with him, but all the crowd wanted to stay in town and see the sights. Lovell interceded in our behalf, and promised to see that we left town in good time to be in camp before the herd was ready to move the next morning. On this assurance, Flood saddled up and started for the Saw Log, having ample time to make the ride before dark. By this time most of the boys had worn off the wire edge for gambling and were comparing notes. Three of them were broke, but Quince Forrest had turned the tables and was over a clean hundred winner for the day. Those who had no money fortunately had good credit with those of us who had, for there was yet much to be seen, and in Dodge in '82 it took money to see the elephant. There were several variety theatres, a number of dance halls, and other resorts which, like the wicked, flourish best under darkness. After supper, just about dusk, we went over to the stable, caught our horses, saddled them, and tied them up for the night. We fully expected to leave town by ten o'clock, for it was a good twelve mile ride to the Saw Log. In making the rounds of the variety theatres and dance halls, we hung together. Lovell excused himself early in the evening, and at parting we assured him that the outfit would leave for camp before midnight. We were enjoying ourselves immensely over at the Lone Star dance hall, when an incident occurred in which we entirely neglected the good advice of McNulta, and had the sensation of hearing lead whistle and cry around our ears before we got away from town.

Quince Forrest was spending his winnings as well as drinking freely, and at the end of a quadrille gave vent to his hilarity in an old-fashioned Comanche yell. The bouncer of the dance hall of course had his eye on our crowd, and at the end of a change, took Quince to task. He was a surly brute, and instead of couching his request in appropriate language, threatened to throw him out of the house. Forrest stood like one absent-minded and took the abuse, for physically he was no match for the bouncer, who was armed, moreover, and wore an officer's star. I was dancing in the same set with a red-headed, freckled-faced girl, who clutched my arm and wished to know if my friend was armed. I assured her that he was not, or we would have had notice of it before the bouncer's invective was ended. At the conclusion of the dance, Quince and The Rebel passed out, giving the rest of us the word to remain as though nothing was wrong. In the course of half an hour, Priest returned and asked us to take our leave one at a time without attracting any attention, and meet at the stable. I remained until the last, and noticed The Rebel and the bouncer taking a drink together at the bar—the former apparently in a most amiable mood. We passed out together shortly afterward, and found the other boys mounted and awaiting our return, it being now about midnight. It took but a moment to secure our guns, and once in the saddle, we rode through the town in the direction of the herd. On the outskirts of the town, we halted. "I'm going back to that dance hall," said Forrest, "and have one round at least with that woman-herder. No man who walks this old earth can insult me, as he did, not if he has a hundred stars on him. If any of you don't want to go along, ride right on to camp, but I'd like to have you all go. And when I take his measure, it will be the signal to the rest of you to put out the lights. All that's going, come on."

There were no dissenters to the programme. I saw at a glance that my bunkie was heart and soul in the play, and took my cue and kept my mouth shut. We circled round the town to a vacant lot within a block of the rear of the dance hall. Honeyman was left to hold the horses; then, taking off our belts and hanging them on the pommels of our saddles, we secreted our six-shooters inside the waistbands of our trousers. The hall was still crowded with the revelers when we entered, a few at a time, Forrest and Priest being the last to arrive. Forrest had changed hats with The Rebel, who always wore a black one, and as the bouncer circulated around, Quince stepped squarely in front of him. There was no waste of words, but a gun-barrel flashed in the lamplight, and the bouncer, struck with the six-shooter, fell like a beef. Before the bewildered spectators could raise a hand, five six-shooters were turned into the ceiling. The lights went out at the first fire, and amidst the rush of men and the screaming of women, we reached the outside, and within a minute were in our saddles. All would have gone well had we returned by the same route and avoided the town; but after crossing the railroad track, anger and pride having not been properly satisfied, we must ride through the town.

On entering the main street, leading north and opposite the bridge on the river, somebody of our party in the rear turned his gun loose into the air. The Rebel and I were riding in the lead, and at the clattering of hoofs and shooting behind us, our horses started on the run, the shooting by this time having become general. At the second street crossing, I noticed a rope of fire belching from a Winchester in the doorway of a store building. There was no doubt in my mind but we were the object of the manipulator of that carbine, and as we reached the next cross street, a man kneeling in the shadow of a building opened fire on us with a six-shooter. Priest reined in his horse, and not having wasted cartridges in the open-air shooting, returned the compliment until he emptied his gun. By this time every officer in the town was throwing lead after us, some of which cried a little too close for comfort. When there was no longer any shooting on our flanks, we turned into a cross street and soon left the lead behind us. At the outskirts of the town we slowed up our horses and took it leisurely for a mile or so, when Quince Forrest halted us and said, "I'm going to drop out here and see if any one follows us. I want to be alone, so that if any officers try to follow us up, I can have it out with them."

As there was no time to lose in parleying, and as he had a good horse, we rode away and left him. On reaching camp, we secured a few hours' sleep, but the next morning, to our surprise, Forrest failed to appear. We explained the situation to Flood, who said if he did not show up by noon, he would go back and look for him. We all felt positive that he would not dare to go back to town; and if he was lost, as soon as the sun arose he would be able to get his bearings. While we were nooning about seven miles north of the Saw Log, some one noticed a buggy coming up the trail. As it came nearer we saw that there were two other occupants of the rig besides the driver. When it drew up old Quince, still wearing The Rebel's hat, stepped out of the rig, dragged out his saddle from under the seat, and invited his companions to dinner. They both declined, when Forrest, taking out his purse, handed a twenty-dollar gold piece to the driver with an oath. He then asked the other man what he owed him, but the latter very haughtily declined any recompense, and the conveyance drove away.

"I suppose you fellows don't know what all this means," said Quince, as he filled a plate and sat down in the shade of the wagon. "Well, that horse of mine got a bullet plugged into him last night as we were leaving town, and before I could get him to Duck Creek, he died on me. I carried my saddle and blankets until daylight, when I hid in a draw and waited for something to turn up. I thought some of you would come back and look for me sometime, for I knew you wouldn't understand it, when all of a sudden here comes this livery rig along with that drummer—going out to Jetmore, I believe he said. I explained what I wanted, but he decided that his business was more important than mine, and refused me. I referred the matter to Judge Colt, and the judge decided that it was more important that I overtake this herd. I'd have made him take pay, too, only he acted so mean about it."

After dinner, fearing arrest, Forrest took a horse and rode on ahead to the Solomon River. We were a glum outfit that afternoon, but after a good night's rest were again as fresh as daisies. When McCann started to get breakfast, he hung his coat on the end of the wagon rod, while he went for a bucket of water. During his absence, John Officer was noticed slipping something into Barney's coat pocket, and after breakfast when our cook went to his coat for his tobacco, he unearthed a lady's cambric handkerchief, nicely embroidered, and a silver mounted garter. He looked at the articles a moment, and, grasping the situation at a glance, ran his eye over the outfit for the culprit. But there was not a word or a smile. He walked over and threw the articles into the fire, remarking, "Good whiskey and bad women will be the ruin of you varmints yet."

JOSEPH G. McCOY

Abilene Frolics, 1868*

⟨ JOSEPH G. McCOY, the leading pioneer in the cattle trade, gets credit for the "landmark" book on range life with his *Historic Sketches of the Cattle Trade of the West and Southwest*. McCoy, against considerable township opposition, converted Abilene, Kansas, into the first dependable market at the end of the Chisholm Trail, in 1867. He went broke doing it, which may explain his granitic lack of warmth toward cowhands in general. But if some streak of reserve in him was repelled by the raw life around him, he did not flinch at setting down the exact details.

NO SOONER had it become a conceded fact that Abilene, as a cattle depot, was a success, than trades' people from all points came to the village and, after putting up temporary houses, went into business. Of course the saloon, the billiard table, the ten-pin alley, the gambling table—in short, every possible device for obtaining money in both an honest and dishonest manner, were abundant.

Fully seventy-five thousand cattle arrived at Abilene during the summer of 1868, and at the opening of the market in the spring fine prices were realized and snug fortunes were made by such drovers as were able to effect a sale of their herds. It was the custom to locate herds as near the village as good

* From *Historic Sketches of the Cattle Trade of the West and Southwest* (Kansas City: Ramsey, Millett and Hudson, 1874).

water and plenty of grass could be found. As soon as the herd is located upon its summer grounds a part of the help is discharged, as it requires less labor to hold than to travel. The camp was usually located near some living water or spring where sufficient wood for camp purposes could be easily obtained. After selecting the spot for the camp, the wagon would be drawn up. Then a hole dug in the ground in which to build a fire of limbs of trees or drift wood gathered to the spot, and a permanent camp instituted by unloading the contents of the wagon upon the ground. And such a motley lot of assets as come out of one of those camp carts would astonish one, and beggar minute description: a lot of saddles and horse-blankets, a camp-kettle, coffee-pot, bread pan, battered tin cups, a greasy mess chest, dirty soiled blankets, an ox yoke, a log chain, spurs and quirts, a coffee-mill, a broken-helved ax, bridles, picket-ropes, and last, but not least, a side or two of fat mast-fed bacon; to which add divers pieces of raw-hide in various stages of dryness. A score of other articles not to be thought of will come out of that exhaustless camp cart. But one naturally inquires what use would a drover have for a raw-hide, dry or fresh? Uses infinite; nothing breaks about a drover's outfit that he cannot mend with strips or thongs of raw-hide. He mends his bridle or saddle or picket-rope, or sews his ripping pants or shirt, or lashes a broken wagon tongue, or binds on a loose tire, with raw-hide. In short, a raw-hide is a concentrated and combined carpenter and blacksmith shop, not to say saddler's and tailor's shop, to the drover. Indeed, it is said that what a Texan cannot make or mend with a raw-hide is not worth having, or is irretrievably broken into undistinguishable fragments. It is asserted that the agricultural classes of that State fasten their plow points on with raw-hide, but we do not claim to be authority on Texan agriculture, therefore cannot vouch for this statement.

The herd is brought upon its herd ground and carefully watched during the day, but allowed to scatter out over sufficient territory to feed. At nightfall it is gathered to a spot selected near the tent, and there rounded up and held during the night. One or more cow-boys are on duty all the while, being relieved at regular hours by relays fresh aroused from slumber, and mounted on rested ponies, and for a given number of hours they ride slowly and quietly around the herd, which, soon as it is dusk, lies down to rest and ruminate. About midnight every animal will arise, turn about for a few moments, and then lie down again near where it arose, only changing sides so as to rest. But if no one should be watching to prevent straggling, it would be but a short time before the entire herd would be up and following off the leader, or some uneasy one that would rather travel than sleep or rest. All this is easily checked by the cow-boy on duty. But when storm is imminent, every man is required to have his horse saddled ready for an emergency. The ponies desired for use are picketed out, which is done by tying one end of a half inch rope, sixty or seventy feet long, around the neck of the pony and fastening the other end to a pointed iron or wooden stake, twelve or more inches long, which is driven in the firm ground. As all the strain is laterally and none upward, the picket pin will hold the strongest horse. The length of the rope is such as to permit the animal to graze over considerable space, and when he has all the grass eat off within his reach, it is only necessary to move the picket pin to give him fresh and abundant pasture. Such surplus ponies as are not in immediate use, are permitted to run with the cattle or herded to themselves, and when one becomes jaded by hard usage, he is turned loose and a rested one caught with the lasso and put to service. Nearly all cow-boys can throw the lasso well enough to capture a pony or a beef when they desire so to do. Day after day the cattle are held under herd and cared for by the cow-boys, whilst the drover is looking out for a purchaser for his herd, or a part thereof, especially if it be a mixed herd—which is a drove composed of beeves, three, two and one year old steers, heifers and cows. To those desiring any one or more classes of such stock as he may have, the drover seeks to sell, and if successful, has the herd rounded up and cuts out the class sold; and after counting carefully until all parties are satisfied, straightway delivers them to the purchaser. The counting of the cattle, like the separating or cutting out, is invariably done on horseback. Those who do the counting, take positions a score of paces apart, whilst the cow-boys cut off small detachments of cattle and force them between those counting, and when the bunch or cut is counted satisfactorily, the operation is repeated until all are counted. Another method is to start the herd off, and when it is well drawn out, to begin at the head and count back until the last are numbered. As a rule, stock cattle are sold by the herd, and often beeves are sold in the same manner, but in many instances sale is made by the pound, gross weight. The latter manner is much the safest for the inexperienced, for he then pays only for what he gets; but the Texan prefers to sell just as he buys at home, always by the head. However, in late years, it is becoming nearly the universal custom to weigh all beeves sold in Northern markets.

Whilst the herd is being held upon the same grazing grounds, often one or more of the cow-boys, not on duty, will mount their ponies and go to the village nearest camp and spend a few hours; learn all the items of news or gossip concerning other herds and the cow-boys belonging thereto. Besides seeing the sights, he gets such little articles as may be wanted by himself and comrades at camp; of these a supply of tobacco, both chewing and smoking, forms one of the principal, and often recurring wants. The cow-boy almost invariably smokes or chews tobacco—generally both; for the time drags dull at camp or herd ground. There is nothing new or exciting occurring to break the monotony of daily routine events. Sometimes the cow-boys off duty will go to town late in the evening and there join with some party of cow-boys—whose herd is sold and they preparing to start home—in having a jolly time. Often one or more of them will imbibe too much poison whisky and straightway go on the "war path." Then mounting his pony he is ready to shoot anybody or anything; or rather than not shoot at all, would fire up into the air, all the while yelling as only a semi-civilized being can. At such times it is not safe to be on the streets, or for that matter within a house, for the drunk cowboy would as soon shoot into a house as at anything else.

.   .   .   .

The life of the cow-boy in camp is routine and dull. His food is largely of the "regulation" order, but a feast of vegetables he wants and must have, or scurvy would ensue. Onions and potatoes are his favorites, but any kind of vegetables will disappear in haste when put within his reach. In camp, on the trail, on the ranch in Texas, with their countless thousands of cattle, milk and butter are almost unknown, not even milk or cream for the coffee is had. Pure shiftlessness and the lack of energy are the only reasons for this privation, and to the same reasons can be assigned much of the privations and hardships incident to ranching.

It would cost but little effort or expense to add a hundred comforts, not to say luxuries, to the life of a drover and his cow-boys. They sleep on the ground, with a pair of blankets for bed and cover. No tent is used, scarcely any cooking utensils, and such a thing as a camp cook-stove is unknown. The warm water of the branch or the standing pool is drank; often it is yellow with alkali and other poisons. No wonder the cow-boy gets sallow and unhealthy, and deteriorates in manhood until often he becomes capable of any contemptible thing; no wonder he should become half-civilized only, and take to whisky with a love excelled scarcely by the barbarous Indian.

When the herd is sold and delivered to the purchaser, a day of rejoicing to the cow-boy has come, for then he can go free and have a jolly time; and it is a jolly time they have. Straightway after settling with their employers the barber shop is visited, and three to six months' growth of hair is shorn off, their long-grown, sunburnt beard "set" in due shape, and properly blacked; next a clothing store of the Israelitish style is "gone through," and the cow-boy emerges a new man, in outward appearance, everything being new, not excepting the hat and boots, with star decorations about the tops, also a new——, well, in short everything new. Then for fun and frolic. The bar-

room, the theatre, the gambling-room, the bawdy house, the
dance house, each and all come in for their full share of attention. In any of these places an affront, or a slight, real or im-
aginary, is cause sufficient for him to unlimber one or more
"mountain howitzers," invariably found strapped to his person,
and proceed to deal out death in unbroken doses to such as
may be in range of his pistols, whether real friends or enemies,
no matter, his anger and bad whisky urge him on to deeds of
blood and death.

At frontier towns where are centered many cattle and, as a
natural result, considerable business is transacted, and many
strangers congregate, there are always to be found a number of
bad characters, both male and female; of the very worst class
in the universe, such as have fallen below the level of the
lowest type of the brute creation. Men who live a soulless, aimless life, dependent upon the turn of a card for the means of
living. They wear out a purposeless life, ever looking blear-
eyed and dissipated; to whom life, from various causes, has
long since become worse than a total blank; beings in the form
of man whose outward appearance would betoken gentlemen,
but whose heart-strings are but a wisp of base sounding chords,
upon which the touch of the higher and purer life have long
since ceased to be felt. Beings without whom the world would
be better, richer and more desirable. And with them are always
found their counterparts in the opposite sex; those who have
fallen low, alas! how low! They, too, are found in the frontier
cattle town; and that institution known in the West as a dance
house, is there found also. When the darkness of the night is
come to shroud their orgies from public gaze, these miserable
beings gather into the halls of the dance house, and "trip the
fantastic toe" to wretched music, ground out of dilapidated
instruments, by beings fully as degraded as the most vile. In
this vortex of dissipation the average cow-boy plunges with
great delight. Few more wild, reckless scenes of abandoned
debauchery can be seen on the civilized earth, than a dance
house in full blast in one of the many frontier towns. To say
they dance wildly or in an abandoned manner is putting it

mild. Their manner of practising the terpsichorean art would put the French "Can-Can" to shame.

The cow-boy enters the dance with a peculiar zest, not stopping to divest himself of his sombrero, spurs, or pistols, but just as he dismounts off of his cow-pony, so he goes into the dance. A more odd, not to say comical sight, is not often seen than the dancing cow-boy; with the front of his sombrero lifted at an angle of fully forty-five degrees; his huge spurs jingling at every step or motion; his revolvers flapping up and down like a retreating sheep's tail; his eyes lit up with excitement, liquor and lust; he plunges in and "hoes it down" at a terrible rate, in the most approved yet awkward country style; often swinging "his partner" clear off of the floor for an entire circle, then "balance all" with an occasional demoniacal yell, near akin to the war whoop of the savage Indian. All this he does, entirely oblivious to the whole world "and the balance of mankind." After dancing furiously, the entire "set" is called to "waltz to the bar," where the boy is required to treat his partner, and, of course, himself also, which he does not hesitate to do time and again, although it costs him fifty cents each time. Yet if it cost

Dance-House in Abilene

From *Historic Sketches of the Cattle Trade of the West and Southwest*, by Joseph G. McCoy (1874)

ten times that amount he would not hesitate, but the more he dances and drinks, the less common sense he will have, and the more completely his animal passions will control him. Such is the manner in which the cow-boy spends his hard earned dollars. And such is the entertainment that many young men— from the North and the South, of superior parentage and youthful advantages in life—give themselves up to, and often more, their lives are made to pay the forfeit of their sinful foolishness.

After a few days of frolic and debauchery, the cow-boy is ready, in company with his comrades, to start back to Texas, often not having one dollar left of his summer's wages. To this rather hard drawn picture of the cow-boy, there are many creditable exceptions—young men who respect themselves and save their money, and are worthy young gentlemen—but it is idle to deny the fact that the wild, reckless conduct of the cowboys while drunk, in connection with that of the worthless Northern renegades, have brought the *personnel* of the Texan cattle trade into great disrepute, and filled many graves with victims, bad men and good men, at Abilene, Newton, Wichita, and Ellsworth. But by far the larger portion of those killed are of that class that can be spared without detriment to the good morals and respectability of humanity.

It often occurs when the cow-boys fail to get up a melee and kill each other by the half dozen, that the keepers of those "hell's half acres" find some pretext arising from "business jealousies" or other causes, to suddenly become belligerent, and stop not to declare war, but begin hostilities at once. It is generally effective work they do with their revolvers and shot guns, for they are the most desperate men on earth. Either some of the principals or their subordinates are generally "done for" in a thorough manner, or wounded so as to be miserable cripples for life. On such occasions there are few tears shed, or even inquiries made, by the respectable people, but an expression of sorrow is common that, active hostilities did not continue until every rough was stone dead.

. . . .

In concluding we offer a few reflections on the general character of Southwestern cattle men. In doing so we are not ani-
mated by other motives than a desire to convey a correct impression of that numerous class as a whole; reflections and
impressions based upon close observation and a varied experience of seven or eight years spent in business contact and
relation with them.

They are, as a class, not public spirited in matters pertaining
to the general good, but may justly be called selfish, or at least
indifferent to the public welfare. They are prodigal to a fault
with their money, when opportunity offers to gratify their
appetites or passions, but it is extremely difficult to induce
them to expend even a small sum in forwarding a project or
enterprise that has other than a purely selfish end in view. In
general they entertain strong suspicions of Northern men, and
do not have the profoundest confidence in each other. They
are disposed to measure every man's action and prompting
motives by the rule of selfishness, and they are slow indeed to
believe that other than purely selfish motives could or ever do
prompt a man to do an act or develop an enterprise. If anything happens to a man, especially a Northern man, so that he
cannot do or perform all that they expect or require of him, no
explanation or reasons are sufficient to dispel the deep and instant conviction formed in their breasts, that he is deliberately
trying to swindle them, and they can suddenly see a thousand
evidences of his villainy, in short, instantly vote such an one a
double dyed villain.

Their reputation is wide spread for honorably abiding their
verbal contracts. For the very nature of their business, and
the circumstances under which it is conducted, renders an
honorable course imperative; and, as a rule, where agreements
or contracts are put into writing, they will stand to them un-
flinchingly, no matter how great the sacrifice; but when the
contract or understanding is verbal only, and not of the most
definite nature, their consciences are full as pliant as are those
of any other section. A promise made as to some future trans-
action is kept or broken, as their future interests may dictate.

Nor are they any more brave, or more fond of facing death's cold pillets on an equal footing with their adversaries, than are men in general from other sections of the country. True, their habits of life and the necessities and exposed nature of their business, renders the daily use and carrying of firearms imperative; hence their habitual use of the pistol renders them fair to good shots. Besides the habit of settling their disputes, often very trifling, with the revolver—which with some is considered the first and only legitimate law, argument or reason—has given to the denizens of the Lone Star State a name and reputation abroad for universal, genuine bravery, not warranted by the facts. They are just as brave, but no more so, than are the men of other sections.

They are almost invariably convivial in habit, preferring as a rule the strongest liquors, and take them "straight." Nevertheless, it is rare indeed that a drover is a confirmed drunkard or sot.

They think, act, and conduct their business in an independent, self-reliant manner, seldom seeking or following the advice of others.

Each man seems to feel himself an independent sovereign, and as such capable of conducting his affairs in his own way, subject to nobody or nothing save the wishes, tastes and necessities of himself.

They are in common with all stock-men universal lovers of the ladies, and as a class present a discouraging field for a Shaker Missionary. Indeed they are specially noteworthy as being obedient to the first commandment.

Sanguine and speculative in temperament; impulsively generous in free sentiment; warm and cordial in their friendships; hot and hasty in anger; with a strong innate sense of right and wrong; with a keen sense for the ridiculous and a general intention to do that that is right and honorable in their dealings; they are, as would naturally be supposed, when the manner of their life is considered, a hardy, self-reliant, free and independent class, acknowledging no superior or master in the wide universe.

E. C. ("TEDDY BLUE") ABBOTT

and

HELENA HUNTINGTON SMITH

Cowboy Annie of Miles City*

❨ "TEDDY BLUE" ABBOTT, a great favorite with the
Wyoming and Montana cowboys, saltily and bluntly re-
lated his life story to the ideal recorder, journalist Helena
Huntington Smith, who seems only a faithful and flawless
loud speaker in the captivatingly frank *We Pointed Them
North* (Farrar & Rinehart, 1939; University of Oklahoma
Press, 1955). Abbott married the daughter of Granville
Stuart, who married a remarkable Indian woman. The wives
seem to have been as remarkable as their men.

MILES CITY was the cow town then for the north end of
the range. The first Texas herds got up there in '80, and
the Northern Pacific reached it in the fall of '81. There were
plenty of places along the line where Montana and Wyoming
cattle could have been shipped, but Miles City had the best
stockyards and, besides that, it appealed to Wyoming cowmen
because they could follow Tongue River in and have good grass
and water all the way. . . .

The cowpunchers was a totally different class from the other
fellows on the frontier. We was the salt of the earth, anyway

---

* From *We Pointed Them North: Recollections of a Cowpuncher* (Norman,
Okla.: University of Oklahoma Press, 1955).

in our own estimation, and we had the pride that went with it. That was why Miles City changed so much after the trail herds got there; even the women changed. Because buffalo hunters and that kind of people would sleep with women that cowpunchers wouldn't even look at, and it was on our account that they started bringing in girls from eastern cities, young girls and pretty ones. Those girls followed us up, like I told you, and we would meet old pals in new places.

.   .   .   .

Cowboy Annie lived at Mag Burns' house. She was the N Bar outfit's girl. They were all stuck on her except the book-keeper, the nigger cook, and me. Her pal was my sweetheart. But Cowboy Annie surely had the rest of them on her string, and that was true as long as the N Bar outfit in that part of the country held together. She used to tickle me to death. She had a little book, with all her fellows' names written down in it, and she would say to me: "Now just make all the brands in it, Teddy." The boys wouldn't all get to town at once as a rule, but when they did there was hell apopping.

Burgess was really gone on her. I introduced them that fall in Miles City, and it lasted until she got played out and went to Fort Assiniboine, on Milk River, to a soldier dive. She took to drinking and bad acting before that—rode her horse up and down the street and got arrested, and went on downhill from there. The soldiers was at the bottom. They used to say out in this country that when a woman left the dogs she'd go to the soldiers. But all that was quite a few years later. She was at her height in Miles City, an awful pretty girl, with dark eyes and hair. And she could work Burgess for anything.

One day she said to him, kind of coaxing, "Oh, Johnny, I've got a sealskin coat and cap coming from Chicago, and there's still $150 against it at the express office. Won't you get it out for me?"

He made some excuse—said he didn't have $150. She pouted. "I don't care. Jim Green [1] will get it out for me." He was fore-

_____
[1] Fictitious name.

man of the S T outfit. And Johnny fell like a ton of bricks. He
said: "I've got just as much money as any S T son of a gun
in Montana." And he went down to the express office and
got it for her.

I believe he'd have married her if she'd have had him. She
could have had her pick of a dozen fellows, but she didn't want
any of them. I guess after the life she'd led she couldn't see
living on a homestead, getting up early in the morning, working
hard, having a lot of kids. The girls like her that quit and
settled down was usually worn out and half dead before they
did it.

There was a lot of fellows in the eighties who were glad
enough to marry them, but I never would have married that
kind. I always secretly had in my heart the hopes of meeting
a nice girl. I always wanted a cow ranch and a wife, and I got
them both. And it was hard going at times, but believe me it
was worth it.

I got to talking to one of those chippies out in this country
about thirty years back, about the life, and the different places
she had been, and so forth. Her name was Myrtle, and her
and her sister came up here to Gilt Edge for payday. I was
riding into town, and she had knocked the heel off her shoe
and I got a nail and fixed it for her. Afterwards when she had
more or less reformed and was running a decent rooming house
in Lewistown, I stayed there one time and got to talking with
her. I said: "Before I was married, I used to hop around among
you folks a good deal and I don't see how you stand it. It
looks like a hell of a life to me."

She said: "Well, you know there's a kind of a fascination
about it. Most of the girls that are in it wouldn't leave it if they
could."

Some of those girls in Miles City were famous, like Cowboy
Annie and Connie the Cowboy Queen. Connie had a $250 dress
embroidered with all the different brands—they said there
wasn't an outfit from the Yellowstone down to the Platte, and
over in the Dakotas too, that couldn't find its brand on that
dress.

We all had our favorites after we got acquainted. We'd go
in town and marry a girl for a week, take her to breakfast and
dinner and supper, be with her all the time. You couldn't do
that in other places. There was two girls I knew in Lincoln—
it was Lily Davis and her pal—that I wanted to take to a show
one night. I had to take them in a hack, because if they had
walked down the street they would have been arrested. But
Lincoln had a very religious mayor and was getting civilized.
You couldn't walk around with those girls in the daytime like
you could in Miles City.

Things were different down South, too, from what they were
up North. In Texas men couldn't be open and public about
their feelings towards those women, the way we were. There
was a fellow who fell in love with a madam in Miles City, and
he was a prominent man. He used to take her everywhere.
She had another lover at the same time, a deputy sheriff, and
they came near having a fight over it. Everybody was looking
for it. They was just dodging one another. But finally the
second fellow died, and the first one married her and they went
to Mexico.

I suppose those things would shock a lot of respectable
people. But we wasn't respectable and we didn't pretend to
be, which was the only way we was different from some others.
I've heard a lot about the double standard, and seen a lot
of it, too, and it don't make any sense for the man to get off
so easy. If I'd have been a woman and done what I done, I'd
have ended up in a sporting house.

I used to talk to those girls, and they would tell me a lot
of stuff, about how they got started, and how in Chicago and
those eastern cities they wasn't allowed on the streets, how
their clothes would be taken away from them, only what they
needed in the house, so it was like being in prison. They could
do as they pleased out here. And they were human, too. They
always had money and they would lend it to fellows that were
broke. The wagon bosses would come around looking for men
in the spring, and when a fellow was hired he would go to his
girl and say: "I've got a job, but my bed's in soak." Or his

saddle or his six-shooter or his horse. And she would lend
him the money to get it back and he would pay her at the end
of the month. Cowboy Annie was the kind who would always
dig down and help the boys out, and so were a lot of them.
They always got it back. I never knew of but one case where
a fellow cheated one of those girls, and I'll bet he never tried
it again. He come up the trail for one of the N Bar outfits—
not ours, but the one on the Niobrara—and he went with Cowboy Annie for a week. Then he got on his horse and rode away,
owing her seventy dollars. First he went back to the Niobrara,
but the foreman of the outfit heard of it and fired him, then
he went down in Texas, but they heard of it down there and
fired him again. And the N Bar fellows took up a collection and
paid her what he owed, because they wouldn't have a thing like
that standing against the name of the outfit.

That shows you how we were about those things. As Mag
Burns used to say, the cowpunchers treated them sporting
women better than some men treat their wives.

Well, they were women. We didn't know any others. And
any man that would abuse one of them was a son of a gun. I
remember one time when a pimp beat up on his girl for not
coming through with enough money or something like that,
and a fellow I knew jumped on him and half-killed him. The
man hadn't done nothing to him. It was none of his business.
It was just the idea of mistreating a woman.

I can tell you about something that happened to me one
time, and the close shave I had, all because of these notions of
chivalry toward women, no matter who they were. I was with
a girl at a house one night—Omaha, I called her, because she
said that was where she came from. This happened in Miles
City, the winter I was with the F U F, and I was just twenty-
three years old.

In the middle of the night we heard this fracas downstairs—
a woman's screams and then something that sounded like a
body falling. I thought, "Somebody's been killed, sure." And
then I heard footsteps coming up the stairs. I got up and got
my six-shooter and went and stood at the head of the stairs,

and there was a woman coming up, slowly. She had on a white nightgown, and the front of it was all covered with blood. I found out later that it just came from a cut on her forehead. But it looked terrible. I heard someone coming behind her, and I called down: "If you take one more step, I'll shoot you." And I would have, because I thought I couldn't do less.

Well, the woman was Willie Johnson, who ran the house. She was about two years older than I was. She came into the room, and I helped her to get fixed up. She was in an awful mess, with blood all over her from that cut on her forehead, and a black eye that he gave her, this man who was her sweetheart.

"I don't care for the black eye, Teddy," she whimpered, "but he called me a whore."

Can you beat that? It was what she was. I was never so disgusted in my life. I was such a damn fool. I might have killed that man and got into a peck of trouble. Knight of the plains. Had to protect all females. Lord!

After I got older and got more sense I got onto some of it, and I got so at least I wouldn't believe all the things they told me about myself. After I had heard it all a hundred times I got so I would just laugh when they flattered me up and told me I was so wonderfully this, that, and the other. And they would say, "What are you laughing at?" I never told them.

But the black-eye story was another one of the things that were repeated all around, and got to be a by-word with the cowpunchers. So that when I was on herd, somebody would yell across in a high-pitched voice: "Oh, Ted-dee! I don't mind the black eye . . ." and so forth. But just the same it shows the way I felt about those women at that time.

If you were good to them, they'd appreciate it, and believe me, they had ways of repaying a kindness, as I ought to know. One time a few years after this I was shipping beef at a station on the N. P., and I went to a honky-tonk, and there was a girl there that I had knowed in Miles City. We were drinking and fooling around, and after awhile I said: "Come on, let's go back to your room." She said: "No, Teddy. Not with you."

A few minutes later I saw her going back there with another fellow. Well, she had to live.

And before that in Lincoln there was a girl called Eddie, that I took on after my pal Lily Davis left and went to Cheyenne. She was a newcomer in the same house, and while I don't know whether she was new to the game or not, she had just landed in Lincoln and she didn't have any good clothes. She told me about it, and told me she couldn't compete with the other girls. I wasn't much more than a kid then, but I had money, and I staked her to an outfit. She paid it all back eventually. And in return she told me a lot of things that stood me in good stead.

I always had money because I didn't gamble—only a little, now and then. I couldn't see giving it to them tinhorns. You knew they were going to take it away from you. And besides, I never had time to gamble; I couldn't sit still long enough; I always had to be up, talking, singing, drinking at the bar. I was so happy and full of life, I used to feel, when I got a little whisky inside me, that I could jump twenty feet in the air. I'd like to go back and feel that way once more. If I could go back I wouldn't change any part of it.

A night or two before we left town that fall, we were all together with the girls, drinking and having a good time, and I got dressed up. Cowboy Annie put her gold chain around my neck, and wound her scarf around the crown of my Stetson, and this dressing up in a woman's clothes started us talking about the stunt that Jake Des Rosses pulled at Ogallala the year before. There was a dance going on and not enough women to go around, which was the usual way of it in that country, and a couple of fellows got left without a partner. So one of them said: "I'll fix that." And he went in a back room—this was in a honky-tonk, of course—and he came out with a pair of woman's white ruffled drawers pulled on over his pants. He and the other fellows danced around, and it brought down the house. We'd all heard the story. It went all over the range, and it even got into books.[2]

[2] Edgar Beecher Bronson's *Reminiscences of a Ranchman*.

So we were talking about it and Cowboy Annie turned to me. "Would you do that?" she says.

I said yes, naturally. So she pulled them off, and I put them on over my pants. And we all paraded down the street, me with my gold necklace and the trimming on my hat and Cowboy Annie's drawers on. The whole town turned out to see us. It turned the place upside down.

Well, that was the kind of wild, crazy stunt that gave me my reputation. They'd tell about a thing like that clear down to Texas, especially anything that came up that was funny. The reps would ride around to the roundups and carry it along, and in the winter time the grub line riders would carry it. We had to talk about something. It was all the fun we had.

Next day, or the day after that, we all left for the mouth of the Musselshell. In the morning when we was ready Burgess wasn't there. Somebody had seen his horse, with the reins dropped, standing in front of the parlor house, and I went up there to get him. He was in Cowboy Annie's room. He had been to the bank and got the money and gone back there to pay her, for the week. And when I came in—because I was a friend of them both—she flipped back the pillow cover and showed me the yellow pile nested there—seventy dollars in gold.

After that, going back to the mouth of the Musselshell, I made up a song about Cowboy Annie, that went:

> *Cowboy Annie was her name,*
> *And the N Bar outfit was her game.*

and ended up:

> *And when the beef is four years old,*
> *We'll fill her pillow slips with gold.*

I still had Cowboy Annie's ruffled drawers that she gave me that night, and I put them on a forked stick and carried them that way to the mouth of the Musselshell, like a flag. And before we left, my girl took one of her stockings off and tied it around my arm, you know, like the knights of old, and I wore *that* to the mouth of the Musselshell.

After we got up there, I had the flag hanging on the wall of the cabin, until Harry Rutter got sore one day and tore it down and throwed it in the stove. He said it wasn't decent. And no more it was.

RAMON F. ADAMS

Cowboys Bendin' an Elbow*

⟨ RAMON F. ADAMS of Dallas has devoted half a century
to gathering the lore and the lingo of the American cowboy, presenting his findings in three volumes, *Cowboy
Lingo, Western Words,* and *Come an' Get It.* An assiduous
collector of rare Americana, he is also author of two standard bibliographies—one on western outlaws, *Six-Guns and
Saddle Leather,* and *The Rampaging Herd* covering the
cattle industry—as well as editor of an anthology, *The Best
of the American Cowboy.*

DURING MY MANY YEARS of collecting the cowman's
language as a hobby, my association with the cowboy had
chiefly been confined to ranches and "the wagon" during roundups, with an occasional visit to a cowman's convention or a
rodeo.

It was Dusty Lynch, a cowboy of New Mexico, who suggested broader fields. Dusty once said I was "crazy as a parrot
eatin' sticky candy" to be spending good time collecting such
stuff, and insisted that cow hands talked just like any other
plain, everyday human. For a long time no one could convince
him that I wasn't "plumb weak north o' the ears," but he finally
became interested enough—mostly through curiosity—to sug-
gest that we ride to the little near-by cow town on payday

* From *Southwest Review,* Vol. XXX, No. 4 (Summer, 1945).

where I could meet the boys from other ranches who would be "ridin' in to spill a pot o' paint."

"If you'll calf round any saloon while the boys're gatherin' a talkin' load," he confided, "you'll maybe collect some remarks to put in your little tally book. Ketch 'em 'fore their tongues git so thick they have to resort to the sign language, and you'll hear some real verbal lather. It's the first few cow swallers o' that conversation fluid that brings out the tongue oil."

When that anxious day arrived, we and a number of the other hands went out early to "throw leather on our hosses" and were soon on our joyous way to "bend an elbow" with the boys.

Upon our arrival in town we found the hitch racks crowded with horses. It looked like every man in the county was there, all suffering from a disease known as *bottle fever*.

"We'll lean our hosses in the livery stable," said Dusty. "No man that thinks anything of his hoss will let 'im fight flies at a snortin' post while he fights booze at a bar."

Pretty good philosophy, I thought.

This town was of the typical, false-front variety where most of the doors swung both ways, and, as one cow hand said, it was a town "with the hair on." The first place we entered seemed to be the popular saloon of the town. It was crowded and already becoming boisterous with loud-mouthed conversation and the friendly back-slapping of new arrivals. The man in the once white apron on the *sober side* of the bar was eyeing the crowd with growing apprehension.

"I'm a-thinkin' you'll soon be hearin' some chin music you can use," said Dusty, as we paused near the door to consider this motley crowd through a stratified layer of tobacco smoke. He then moved forward quickly to slap a friend on the back with, "Hiyah, Zeb, you ole catawampus. Whatcha doin' here lappin' up likker like a fired cow hand?"

"Thish is barg'in night," answered his friend Zeb Fisher drunkenly. "The ole bar-dog here's shervin' a free shnake with ever' drink."

"Yeah," said a fellow next to Zeb, raking his spurs ruthlessly

on the once varnished bar front, "this t'rantula juice'd draw
blood blisters on a rawhide boot."

"How the hell do they keep such stuff corked?" put in a third
drinker. "It'd shore grow horns on a muley cow."

"Oh, I guess it ain't so bad," grinned Dusty. "You fellers are
soakin' it up like a dry sponge."

"It's done took the firsh layer off my tonshils," complained
Zeb.

About that time a young red-headed puncher started to
leave, "reelin' round like a pup tryin' to find a soft spot to lie

"Reelin' round like a pup tryin' to find
a soft spot to lie down in"

Drawing by Harold D. Bugbee, from *Son-of-a-Gun Stew: A Sampling of the Southwest*, edited by Elizabeth Matchett Stover
(Southern Methodist University Press, 1945)

down in" until he could get his sense of direction. When he
finally discovered the door and zigzagged toward it, someone
yelled, "Hey, Red, somebody done stole yo' rudder!" Then
everyone laughed, and I found Dusty's predictions coming
true. I had discovered a new fountainhead for many rich ex-
amples of the cowboy's lusty speech.

When it comes to drinking, the cowman "don't belong to the
garden variety." He doesn't have an "educated thirst that calls
for bottles with pretty labels and silver-foiled bonnets on 'em."
He seldom wastes his time on wine and fancy mixtures, and
has little appetite for beer because in the old days he could
seldom get it cold. Whisky is his drink, and he takes it straight,
occasionally with a small chaser. Like the cowboy accused of
being "water-shy"—meaning bodily unclean—who answered
promptly: "I ain't afraid o' water. In fact, I like a little for a
chaser once in a while." Usually the chaser is ignored because
the drinker "don't want to put the fire out."

Right here let me correct the impression left by early dime
novelists that the cowboy had nothing to do but wear his boot
soles out on a brass rail and make calluses on his elbows leaning
on a bar. These yellow journalists only saw him when he hit
town at the end of months on the trail fighting dust, loneliness,
swollen rivers, stampedes, and general bovine cussedness.
When the drive was over, he was relieved of an exacting responsibility; and, being young and full of vinegar, he *cut his
wolf loose.*

His noisy exuberance was but an expression of a young, free
spirit and healthy body. I have seen college students after a
victorious football game just as drunk and their back-firing
jalopies noisier than the popping of pistols. And who wouldn't
rather meet a drunk on a horse than one behind a wheel? At
least, the horse has some sense.

The pulps continue to follow this perverse pattern of making
the cowboy a savage in chaps. Yet cards and whisky are strictly
forbidden on all well-managed ranches. This ban is not based
upon religious principles. Cow work is dangerous even for
sober men, and for one befogged with booze it would likely

be fatal. Card playing leads to quarrels and hard feelings among men young and reckless, and at best keeps them up late. Since the cowboy is limited in his drinking to his infrequent visits to town, he doesn't drink as much as the town inhabitant.

Yet fiction persists in filling his life with booze, bullets, and badmen and making his existence one round of gambling, guzzling, and gore. Pardon my wandering from the trail in his defense, but such misrepresentation of this lovable American character is my pet peeve.

I'm glad I have been privileged to mingle with his kind when his "crop was freighted" with *scamper juice,* for then he possesses "more lip than a muley cow" and has added pages to my notebook.

When a cow hand goes into town to make a night of it, it is said that he "rides in to hear the owl hoot," "gets on a high lonesome," "stays out with the dry cattle," or "lets his weakness for booze run wild." Jug Jeter acquired his nickname because it was said he "never went to town till his jug needed fillin'."

I've heard the cowboy give many descriptions of his drunken companions, none of them being what you would call elegant, but apt nevertheless. Alkali Upton spoke of one having a "full-grown case o' booze blind"; Hunk Bowden declared that another "never knowed he had a twin brother till he looked in the mirror behind the bar."

Shanks Malloy spoke of a staggering drunk "knockin' round like a blind dog in a meat shop." Rawhide Pryor referred to an habitual drunkard as a "walkin' whisky vat." "Drunk as a b'iled owl," "drunk as a fiddler's clerk," and "drunk as a Mexican opal" are common cowboy expressions.

Some men just take on enough *tonsil varnish* to loosen their tongues. In time, they get what the cowman calls "diarrhea of the jaw bone," and their prattle "sounds like rain on a tin roof." If you keep them well supplied with small doses of *neck oil,* they can run a long time and have so much to say it "gets in their way." Yet they stay as "peaceful as a church," seemingly contented to stand with a hand curled lovingly around a glass and just *talk.*

Others are primed for *cow swallers* of the "stuff that cures
snake bites," and they can't stop until they get floored or
frenzied. One of this breed usually has a "bronc" disposition,
and by the time his hide is full of *red disturbance* he's also full
of peevishness and starts "haulin' hell out of its shuck." In the
words of Pieface Bender, "Hell goes on a holiday when he hits
town," and Cal Grose once said of such a man, "He's givin' the
town hell with the hide off." When a man of this type gets
drunk, he wants everybody to know it—and they usually do if
they're in the same county.

The quality of liquor served in some of the frontier saloons
would "eat its way plumb to your boot soles." Hoot Gilroy,
complaining of such liquor, told the barkeep that he "forgot to
strain this stuff to get out the tobaccer leaves." Muley Metcalf
once stated to a barkeep in Silver City that "you should a-been
a snake charmer, judgin' from the likker you're shovin' across
the mahogany," and Bill Pitman told another in Cheyenne that
he "might be the best bar-dog that ever waved a bar-rag, but I
don't want you spittin' tobaccer juice in the barrel to make it
pleasant to the taste." At another time Stormy Morse described
such whisky as "a brand o' booze that a man could git drunk
on and be shot through the brain and it wouldn't kill 'im till he
sobered up," and Speed Carlow claimed emphatically that "you
couldn't gargle that brand o' hooch without annexin' a few
queer animals."

In speaking of low dives, the cowboy artist Charles Russell
once described such a place as "a dive that made the other
dives look like a kindergarten or a ladies' finishin' school," and
Calico Starnes told of one down on the Mexican border "where
a skunk would be ashamed to meet his mother."

Joggy Marsh, speaking of a friend who was always "thirsty
as a mud hen on a tin roof," said he lost him in town one day
and went searching the saloons for him. "I fin'lly found 'im,"
said Joggy, "paintin' 'is nose in the Silver Dollar, him bein'
busier'n a prairie dog after a rain with this accomplishment."
Clint Wilson spoke of one drinking as "nosin' his way to the
bottom of a glass," and Tuck McLaren once referred to a heavy

drinker as "wearin' hisself out bendin' 'is elbow to look up the neck of a bottle." Drinking on the trail at night was often spoken of as "takin' a look at the moon through the neck of a bottle."

Snub Davis, in telling of an occasion when he and a friend rode to town to "see the elephant dance," said, "We went in to paint the town red, but after a little session of poker we jes' had 'nough left to buy a couple o' pots o' paint and a mighty small brush." Spike Dodson spoke of a cow hand "eatin' booze till he got to the state where he sees things that ain't there," and Magpie Curry told of another who "got to seein' things that ain't in natural history."

In my wanderings through the cow country I've heard a few descriptions of walking while drunk which are amusing. Tom Foster spoke of a man "so likkered up he couldn't walk, but was jes' feelin' round." Speedy Logan, speaking of a time he was pretty drunk himself, said, "My boots wouldn't track, and I felt like my legs was a burden." Another cow hand, speaking of an old drunken horse trader in town, said, "The way he's spraddlin' down the street you'd think walkin' was a lost art."

The cowman has little use for the prohibitionist. Even if he doesn't drink himself, he feels it to be unjust to legislate away another man's privilege. It is said on the range that a prohibitionist will "take anything that ain't fastened down except a drink." A man might stay "sober as a muley cow" or keep "sober as a watched Puritan" and still not vote for prohibition. Kansas Joe, a puncher of the old Fiddleback, said that in his home state nobody drank liquor without hiding out in the cellar, but that they could drink more in one swallow than the average man could in an hour because they were in the habit of making one drink go as far as it could before they had to hide out again. Clee Taggart, speaking of a drunkard during recent prohibition days, said, "He drank so much hair oil he had to eat moth balls to keep down the fur."

A night "out with the dry cattle" might "take all the tallow" out of a man's bank roll and keep the bartender as "busy as a beaver makin' a new dam"; but the next morning brought remorse, misery, and not a few salty descriptions of his feelings.

Colorado Benson described his feelings by saying, "The next mornin' I had a head so big I couldn't crowd it into a corral." Tucson Williams admitted that "next mornin' I felt like the frazzled end of a misspent life." Center-fire Mahan once said, "Next mornin' I had a taste in my mouth like I'd had supper with a kiyote. If I'd a-had store teeth, I'd taken 'em out and buried 'em." Another "shore had a brindle taste" in his mouth, and Milt Scruggs once said, on a morning after he'd had plenty the night before, "After wakin' up with a head big 'nough to eat hay with the hosses, I reckoned the drought was over." Years later I heard another declare, "I had a dark-brown taste in my disposition and an oversized head." After one of those all-night sessions, Cactus Price claimed, "I'm so shaky I couldn't pour a drink o' whisky into a barrel with the head out." Nevertheless, if he had any money left, he would slip a bottle in the pack so there would be some "hair off the dog" on the trail.

On one occasion, while in a little town in West Texas, I left the hotel at daylight to get my horse from the livery stable for an early start to visit a near-by ranch. In front of the stable I found a puncher I had seen on a bender the night before, now sousing his face and head in the horse trough. I asked him how he felt. He looked at me with bleary eyes, the water dripping from his hair and face, and answered, "Podner, I've shore got one o' them headaches that's built for a hoss."

Once on my way to visit the Swinging L Ranch I met one of its hands in town who offered to ride with me to show the way. But first he stopped at one of the saloons and told the bartender to "prepare a quart of Old Crow for travelin'." This "old bird" hadn't traveled far before its contents began to be lowered considerably. After we had ridden what seemed to me a great distance, I asked him how much farther it was. He pulled the bottle out of the saddle pocket and held it up to the sun. After giving the line of liquid content careful consideration, he made the startling reply, " 'Bout six drinks down the road," adding hastily, with a grin, "plus an eye-opener if I can git by the Old Man with this bottle."

Usually when a cow hand left town, he went "ridin' out o' town with nothin' but a head and some debts," or, as one said, his "head's mighty heavy and pockets plenty light."

Many a cow hand had a secret ambition to become a bartender when he got too stove-up to ride the "snuffy" ones any longer. Not because he wanted to see life from the sober side, or learn the art of "yawnin' on the glasses to give 'em a polish," but because he wanted to remain among his own kind—men who could "talk cow."

In the early days, unless the saloon hired a professional bouncer, the barkeep had to be a fighter, keeping near at hand a bung-starter, a blackjack, or a six-gun. When he reached for the bottle from which you had been pouring your drinks and hammered the cork home with the heel of his hand, he could tell you plainer than words that your credit had run out, or that . in his opinion you had had enough.

CLARK STANLEY

·····>———◆>◦<◆———<·····

Cowboy Songs and Dances*

⟨ CLARK STANLEY ("better known as the Rattle-Snake King") was proprietor of a snake-oil liniment company operating in Rhode Island around the turn of the century. As part of his sales promotion he published in Providence in 1897 a pamphlet entitled *The Life and Adventures of the American Cowboy: Life in the Far West,* nearly half of it consisting of ads for his liniment but including also a collection of cowboy songs (sampled here), the first such collection ever printed. This pamphlet, now a real curiosity, went through a number of editions in the decade after its appearance, each edition containing added bits of cowboy lore and more testimonials from those relieved by the liniment.

THE WESTERN COWBOY was not of special interest to the general public until the year of the Columbian Exposition, when Buffalo Bill introduced his celebrated Wild West Show. The term, cowboy, called up the picture of a handsome, dashing fellow, with wide sombrero, jingling spurs, and the all-powerful six-shooter, who spent his time in daring rescues, in lassoing a fractious wild steer, riding a pitching pony, or bringing the wary coyote or the savage bear to the ground

---

* From *The Life and Adventures of the American Cowboy: Life in the Far West* (Published by the author, 1897).

with unerring shot. One who thus becomes familiar with only the picturesque side of cowboy life fails to realize that the wild steer may turn on his would-be captor, leaving a lasting reminder of his long horns; that the bucking broncho sometimes throws the rider; and that contests with wild beasts do not always result in the hunter's favor. The excitement of the moment gives him a keen pleasure in these contests, but there is nothing attractive in the daily hardships every cowboy must endure.

The same coolness in time of danger, the brave daring, the endurance in fatigue, which made the feats of the Rough Riders possible, is such a necessary part of a cowboy's everyday life and is taken for granted with so much nonchalance that it can but win your sincere respect. At best, his is a rough life and a hard one, yet, lacking not only comforts, but what we have come to regard as necessaries, he is always brave and uncomplaining. He has his faults—so have we all, only his seem graver because they take a more unaccustomed form— yet under a somewhat rough exterior you will always find him a true, courteous gentleman at heart. I speak not of the Western desperado, but of the average cowpuncher, found on the ranches, who to-day is sometimes a college-bred man in search of health. As the Indian and the buffalo are fast disappearing before the advance of civilization, so ere long the cowboy will be a thing of the past, but his part in the development of the country, his heroism, his songs and legends deserve a place in its history. . . .

At night, gathered around the camp fire after herding and roping cattle all day, they sing their own songs, which have true folklore flavor.

"Come, kid, give us Sam Bass." When all is quiet he begins:

I.

Sam Bass was born in Indiana, it was his native home,
And at the age of seventeen young Sam began to roam.
He started out to Texas, a cowboy for to be,
And a kinder hearted fellow you scarcely ever'd see.

II.

Sam used to deal in race stock, known as the Denton mare,
He matched her in scrub races and took her to the fair;
He always coined the money and spent it very free;
He always drank good whiskey wherever he might be.

III.

He started for the Colins ranch in the merry month of May
With a herd of Texas cattle, the black hills for to see.
He sold out at Custer City and there got on a spree,
And a tougher lot of cowboys you never'd hope to see.

And so the song goes on through the numerous exploits of
this hero as he "robbed the U.P. train," and performed various
other daring deeds. As with most epics, the tune is secondary
in importance to the words, and is often a kind of monotonous
chant. The air of this "Sam Bass" is somewhat like that of
"Ninety-nine Blue Bottles Hanging on the Wall," and its verses
almost as endless.

A somewhat mournful song entitled "The Dying Cowboy"
is very popular, perhaps because of the minor strain which
predominates.

"Oh, bury me out on the lone prairie,"
The words came low and mournfully,
From the cold, pale lips of a youth who lay
On his dying couch at the close of day.
He had wasted and pined 'till over his brow
Death shadows were gathering quickly now;
And he thought of his home and his loved ones nigh
As the cowboys came round to see him die.
"Oh, bury me out on the lone prairie
In a narrow grave just six by three,
Where the wild coyotes will howl o'er me;
Oh, bury me out on the lone prairie."

These songs are rarely written, but usually learned around
the mess wagon, where many are doubtless composed or receive various additions according to the fancy of the singer.

For this reason not many of the boys know a complete song, but like most folklore, one finds snatches of it here and there. One particularly bright cowboy often composed very popular ballads, celebrating some event and containing local hints much appreciated by his audience.

The lives of the cowboys are not all work and hardship. They have their amusements, and probably enjoy them more than do those who are surfeited with them. The principal recreations are competitive sports and the dances. The former consist of races on foot or on horseback, of seeing who can best ride the most fractious broncho, exhibitions of skill in roping and tying a wild steer, and wonderful shooting contests.

The dances have an originality all their own. There's a dance over to Stanley's Tuesday, is the common form of invitation to these events, and the word is passed along. Every one is welcome, and unless unavoidably detained, young and old within a radius of fifty miles attend. No social line is drawn in this part of the West; the "help" and the ranchman's wife are "opposite ladies." Cowboy dances last from sunset to sunrise. The music is furnished by a Mexican fiddler, or occasionally by one of the cowboys on a Jewsharp, with which most of them are quite proficient. They confine themselves to square dances, with a very occasional waltz. When all is ready, choose your partners is the command from the director. The fiddler strikes up a rollicking tune, the spurs clink merrily and the dance is in full swing. "Honer yer pardners. Rights the same. Balance you all. Eight hands up and circle to the left. Brake and run away eight."

> First couple balance and swing;
> Promenade the inside ring,
> Promenade the outside ring,
> Balance and swing and cast off six,
> Ladies to the right and gents to the left.
> Swing the one you swung before,
> Down the center and cast off four.
> Swing the one that comes to meet you;
> Down the center and cast off two.

All dance pretty as you can,
Turn your toes and left allemane,
First gent out to the right
Swings the girl that curls her hair,
Then the one that looks so fair,
Then the one that puts on airs,
And now the belle of the ball.

Gents chase and put on style,
Rehash and a little more style.
Little more style, gents, a little more style.
First lady out to the right;
Swing the man that stole the sheep
Now the one that hauled it home,
Now the one that eat the meat,
And now the one that gnawed the bone.

First gent, swing yer opposite pardner,
Then yer turtle dove,
Again your opposite pardner,
And now your own true love.

Birdie hop out and crow hop in.
Three hands round and go it again.
Allemane left; back to pardner
And grand right and left.
Come to yer pardner once and a half,
Yellow hammer right and jay bird left.
Meet yer pardner and all chaw hay,
You know where and I don't care.
Seat your partner in the old arm chair.

It is the etiquette of the cowboy dance, round or square, to
have the music continue as long as any one is dancing on the
floor. Very substantial refreshments are served during the
whole evening at these dances. The refreshments are spread
out on a table, the coffee pot stands on the stove and every
one helps himself whenever and to whatever he wishes. When
a man works as hard as a cowboy at these dances he needs a
square meal, consequently huge meat sandwiches, stewed fruit

and coffee, whose strength would rival Samson's, are provided.
Another favorite dance call is:

> Salute pardners. Lady on the left.
> Eight hands up and circle to the left;
> Circle right back and don't you stop,
> But break in the center and spin the top.
> First lady out to right;
> Swing Daddy Lannigan,
> Then Mother Flannigan,
> Now the old man ag'in.
> Swing pardner round. Left hand lady round.
> Right hand to pardner, round and round.
> Come to the pretty girl,
> Watch her close.
> Come to the pretty girl,
> Double the dose.
> Treat 'em all alike;
> Second lady out to right.
> Swing Mrs. Jinks,
> Then Captain Jinks,
> And now the dude of the army.
> Three hands round and the gent cut a caper.
> Chase the possum, now the coon,
> Then the pretty girl round the moon.
> When you get straight
> Run away eight.

Some of the cowboys are very bright and original in their
dance calls, extemporizing the rhymes and jingles as the dance
progresses. It is, perhaps, the infectious spirit of genuine,
hearty enjoyment which gives these dances their indisputable
charm.

. . . .

As darkness falls and the stars shine out, the cowboy's little
campfire makes a point of light in the vast spaces of desert.
A lonely meal, a half hour's smoke, and soon the dying glow
of the fire falls on a blanket wrapped, soundly sleeping form,

with a pony silently grazing near by, while from the distance comes the wail of the coyote.

> All day on the prairie in the saddle I ride,
> With not even a dog, boys, to trot by my side.
> My fire I kindle with chips gathered round
> And boil my coffee without being ground.
> I wash in a pool, and wipe on a sack,
> I carry my wardrobe all on my back.
> For want of an oven I cook bread in a pot
> And sleep on the ground for want of a cot.
> My ceiling's the skies and my carpet's the grass,
> My music's the lowing of herds as they pass. . . .

AGNES MORLEY CLEAVELAND

Cows Were Our Universe*

⟨ AGNES MORLEY CLEAVELAND and her brother grew up on a New Mexico ranch and had the dream life on the range that some enthusiasts would wish for every child. Any reader whose childhood reaches back to the days of horse instead of motor transportation will read her hilarious, sparkling *No Life for a Lady* with sharp but delicious pangs of homesickness.

THE CATTLE BUSINESS in those days was conducted on horseback. Any rider who knew what to do was on a parity with any other rider who knew what to do, so, as soon as we children had mastered the art of sitting on a horse with some assurance, our value to the business became out of all proportion to our age. The art of horse-sitting is acquired rapidly if one keeps at it from daylight till dark day after day, so we quickly learned to ride by the simple process of riding.

Mounted on a horse, we were useful in direct proportion to our powers of observation and our ability to interpret what we saw, faculties, of course, which are sharpened by interest. Our interest was boundless. Cattle became the circumference of our universe and their behavior absorbed our entire waking hours.

* From *No Life for a Lady* (Boston: Houghton Mifflin Co., 1941).

First it was necessary to know where our cattle were, an extremely difficult thing in a country without fences. The most that we could hope to do was to make an intelligent guess. In general, they tended to range within a few hours' walking distance of one of the various springs, and to stay for considerable periods of time in that district.

Of course, range feed near the watering places is quickly eaten out and trampled off, so that the distance between food and water steadily increases. This is especially true if there is overstocking, and ten miles was not a prohibitive distance for a cow to walk to and from water. It was this long walk which kept them lean in dry years.

While cattle will drink every day if convenient or possible, and be the better for it, they can, nevertheless, thrive reasonably well on every other day's quenching of thirst. And I don't like to think how many days I've known them to go waterless in drought seasons.

"There's lots of cattle watering at the Davenport Spring" was a valuable bit of information, and one a bright-eyed child could relay as well as an adult. If the report were to the effect that it was the same bunch that had previously been watering somewhere else, the report was doubly valuable, and mounted in proportion to the detailed information about each and every animal.

Were there unbranded calves in the bunch old enough to live, however precariously, if forcibly weaned, hence potential "sleepers"? Then no time must be lost in branding them.

You, dear reader, don't know what a sleeper is? I can scarcely believe that such ignorance exists, but I will patiently explain.

A sleeper was a calf which had been earmarked but not branded. Every owner had his individual earmark as well as brand. If an animal was earmarked, the presumption was that it was also branded, both operations being normally performed at the same time. The reason for earmarking is that an earmark can be seen at a greater distance than a brand. The oval of a calf's ears can be cut into an almost endless set of designs, underslopes, crops, swallow forks, ginglebobs, half crops, upper and under slits, and so forth. With two ears to enlarge the possible combinations, it is not difficult to work out one's exclusive earmark. Our own was underslope both ears so that our cattle's ears looked like little supplementary horns.

A sleeper, so it is hoped by the one who has "sleepered" it, will be seen from afar and be presumed to be also branded and its rightful owner will ride on without closer inspection. But the ears will have been only slightly reshaped—just enough to be deceptive. Then, when the opportunity arises, the calf will be taken from its mother and kept in hiding until Nature has completed the weaning process. Its ears are then worked over into its new owner's earmark and it bears the new owner's brand and—so what can the owner do about it?

Spotting sleepers was one of the valuable contributions we children were able to make to our business, for sleepers were common in those days.

To locate a maverick, a calf that had been entirely overlooked and had weaned itself before being either earmarked or branded, was like finding a gold nugget, and we raced home with the news with no less excitement. Sometimes one of us would try to keep the bunch in which the maverick had been discovered within sight while the other carried the news home, or if we thought we could, we'd try to drive the bunch into the nearest available corral. This was not always possible because any bunch with a maverick in it was apt to be pretty wild, having encountered no human beings for a long time.

Another invaluable report would be that of finding a cow "bogged down." Rain puddles sometimes became death traps of sticky mire unless the victims were rescued in time. So "pulling bog" was a routine of the rainy season, and it was of course a tremendous time-saver for the adult wrecking crew to have the bogged-down cow located beforehand. The time came, considerably later—after I abandoned side-saddle, however—when Ray and I pulled them out ourselves, an achievement made possible by the fact that here again the horse did the actual work.

I reconstruct a typical "bog-pulling" scene. Ray wades into the bog and loops his saddle rope around the cow's horns and claws her feet as free as possible from the mud, sometimes an extremely difficult operation if she is lying with her legs tucked under her. If he finds himself in danger of bogging down himself, he lies across the cow while loosening her hooves from the mire. Then I wrap the other end of the saddle rope around the horn of my saddle and give the signal to my horse. He digs his toes into the ground and strains forward while I lean far to one side to avoid being cut in two with the rope. We pull the cow's head a little back over her shoulders to avoid the strain of a direct pull on her neck. Ray meantime has her tail wrapped around his hands and is heaving mightily at the rear. Sometimes she comes and sometimes she doesn't—in the latter case, we shoot her. If she comes, things happen rapidly. Once on her feet with solid ground under them, the cow almost invariably decides that her rescuers are the cause of her woes and proceeds to square accounts by charging at whomsoever is closest at hand.

Fortunately for the rescuer, the cow is apt to be a little dazed and wobbly, and dodging her is only a matter of agility. As Ray grew older, he didn't dodge. In the tone one uses to a naughty child he'd say, "Now, now, sister, none of that!" and seize the angry cow by the horns. A quick twist of the head and down she'd go, unless she decided to behave without this discipline.

The time we rescued a cow from Paddle Cross Lake was probably the most famous instance of this kind of lively work. Paddle Cross Lake was queer, to begin with. For nine months of the year it was no lake but merely a depression—a reddish clay saucer—in the line of natural drainage. After the rainy season began, if it did, Paddle Cross Lake filled with a viscous terra-cotta liquid which cattle appeared to think was water and drank freely with no ill effects. I've drunk it myself as a last resort.

On the day in question we arrived at Paddle Cross with a small bunch of range cattle, a long dry drive. The herd rushed into the lake, some of them belly-deep. At first, no one noticed that one cow had gone in beyond her depth and was firmly mired in the sticky mud which was the lake's floor. Only her nose protruded, letting her breathe. As soon as she was observed, two of the men rode their horses into the lake to rescue her, but the horses began to sink in the ooze and the men dared not ride close to the distressed cow.

For both humanitarian and financial reasons (cattle were high that year) every effort must be made to save the animal. So shedding as much impedimenta as a mixed audience permitted, specifically chaps, boots, spurs, jumper, and hat, Gene dived from his horse and swam to the cow with a rope which he looped over her horns.

Bill, similarly stripped for action, except that he refused to remove his outsize black hat, still sat his horse at a safe distance from the bogging-down point. He took a couple loops of the lariat around his saddle-horn and held the cow's head above water, while Gene strove to claw the cow's feet loose from the mud.

Cowboys are not experts in water, and anyway, the enterprise demanded more of ingenuity than of good diving form. Gene would disappear and emerge by crawling out on the cow. Finally he sent an SOS and Bill swam to assist him, leaving the well-trained pony to keep the rope tight. The comedy of the next few minutes sent the audience into literal hysterics. Bill wouldn't dive because he wouldn't take his hat off, but he would lend a hand to Gene, when the latter came up sputtering after having clawed another hoof loose.

Both were steadying themselves by holding to the cow, who suddenly set up a pathetic mooing, signal that she had given up. Thereafter she refused to help herself at all, even when she was freed from the mud and began to float. Had she been a wind-filled bag she couldn't have been less purposeful or effective in contributing to her own rescue. She flopped on her side and rolled her eyes. Gene got hold of her tail and tried to twist it, with not much success, due to his own unstable position. Bill was valiantly holding her nose out of the water and yelling for Gene to push. Gene pushed and the cow spun around. Bill, his big black hat still on his head, spun with her. The cow was now tail end to shore, and pulling seemed a better technic. This was resorted to, with equally indifferent success, until the horse took a hand. He decided to go to shore himself and went, towing the cow after him, Gene and Bill in splashing pursuit, for by now the cavalcade had got into sufficiently shallow water to offer dubious footing to all concerned, including the cow, had she chosen to avail herself of it, which she didn't. She still floated, wholly oblivious to the language being directed at her.

Only when her sides scraped bottom did she appear to decide that she was still on earth and show signs of returning life—with a vengeance. Scrambling to her feet, she lowered her head, calculated the distance to a nicety, and chased Bill and Gene back into the lake, as far as the rope, still tied to the saddle-horn, would permit.

Help now came from the audience, in the form of shouted instructions, principally, "Take off your hat," "It's your hat she doesn't like." Maybe it was, for she kept a baleful eye upon it while Gene cautiously deployed around and reached the horse —and it was all over. A man, even one dripping Paddle Cross mire from head to heels, on a well-trained horse is master of such a situation. The cow was unceremoniously yanked about face, the rope jiggled off her horns, and she was escorted back to the herd at a clip which would seem to belie her determination to end it all only a few moments before.

Bill waded out, triumphantly wearing his hat.

As youngsters we learned to recognize the individuals among the cattle as though they had been people, and we watched for their coming with the same interest we would have had in the arrival of personal friends. We apportioned the herds among ourselves, each claiming as his own anywhere from a hundred head upward, as the numbers who came in to water varied. And we knew our own dry cows or long yearlings or three-year-old steers or maturing heifers as city children know their schoolmates.

How well I remember them coming in to the home watering troughs, in the later afternoon, coming with a rush the last few hundred yards, bellowing and flipping their tails, drinking until their sides bulged to barrel-like contours, then standing about in stupid relaxation or licking the salt blocks which all good cowmen supply in abundance.

Twice a year roundups were held (we called them "works"), in the spring to brand the new calf crop, and in the fall to segregate the cattle which were to be sent either to Kansas or Nebraska to be corn-fattened for market later, or directly to the slaughterhouses in Chicago.

It was always occasion for deep heartache when we children saw our friends set forth on their last journey, but it was part of life and we had to face it. The one phase of life, however, which I refused to face directly was the branding itself. However much of an accessory to the crime I may have been in the matter of rounding up or even roping the calf, when it came to the actual applying of a hot iron to sentient flesh, I couldn't do it.

However, I hasten to add that, cruel as it sounds, the calves certainly did not suffer to the same extent, emotionally or physically, that a human being would have done. They usually scrambled to their feet, whisked their tails, and galloped off with no evidences of shock or even acute discomfort. A skillful man with the branding iron knew exactly when the hair had been burned away and the flesh merely seared enough to prevent the hair from growing again. I like to think the bawling was more from fright than from suffering.

Another useful function which we children were able to perform and which added to our sense of our own importance was "riding fence line" along the few fences with which we began and the many which came later. To hop off one's horse, with a boot-top bag full of fence staples—which everybody

called "steeples"—and nail a sagging wire back in place satisfied something real in the matter of feeling useful.

When Ray was not yet fourteen, he was the equal of the
average cowpuncher. The ascending scale in open-range cattle
business is from horse wrangler at the lowest rung to range
boss at the highest. Between them lie cook, riders, fence-line
riders (after there were fences), run-of-the-mill waddies. Ray
ran the whole gamut before he was through.

O. HENRY

Art and the Bronco*

([O. HENRY (William Sydney Porter) came to Texas from North Carolina in 1882, at age twenty, to regain his health on a ranch near San Antonio. He rode the range with dictionary in hand, always planning to become a writer. Bank teller and journalist, he left Texas under a cloud, later served time for embezzlement of bank funds, but mastered the art of storytelling during his brief prison stint. Best known for his weekly short stories contributed to the New York *World*, he laid many of his stories in the Southwest. This one is not from *Heart of the West* but from *Roads of Destiny*.

OUT OF THE WILDERNESS had come a painter. Genius, whose coronations alone are democratic, had woven a chaplet of chaparral for the brow of Lonny Briscoe. Art, whose divine expression flows impartially from the fingertips of a cowboy or a dilettante emperor, had chosen for a medium the Boy Artist of the San Saba. The outcome, seven feet by twelve of besmeared canvas, stood, gilt-framed, in the lobby of the Capitol.

The legislature was in session; the capital city of that great Western state was enjoying the season of activity and profit

* From *Roads of Destiny* (New York: Doubleday and Co., 1903).

that the congregation of the solons bestowed. The boarding-houses were corralling the easy dollars of the gamesome law-makers. The greatest state in the West, an empire in area and resources, had arisen and repudiated the old libel of barbarism, lawbreaking, and bloodshed. Order reigned within her borders. Life and property were as safe there, sir, as anywhere among the corrupt cities of the effete East. Pillow-shams, churches, strawberry feasts, and *habeas corpus* flourished. With impunity might the tenderfoot ventilate his "stovepipe" or his theories of culture. The arts and sciences received nurture and subsidy. And, therefore, it behooved the legislature of this great state to make appropriation for the purchase of Lonny Briscoe's immortal painting.

Rarely has the San Saba country contributed to the spread of the fine arts. Its sons have excelled in the solider graces, in the throw of the lariat, the manipulation of the esteemed .45, the intrepidity of the one-card draw, and the nocturnal stimulation of towns from undue lethargy; but, hitherto, it had not been famed as a stronghold of aesthetics. Lonny Briscoe's brush had removed that disability. Here, among the limestone rocks, the succulent cactus, and the drought-parched grass of that arid valley, had been born the Boy Artist. Why he came to woo art is beyond postulation. Beyond doubt, some spore of the afflatus must have sprung up within him in spite of the desert soil of San Saba. The tricksy spirit of creation must have incited him to attempted expression and then have sat hilarious among the white-hot sands of the valley, watching its mischievous work. For Lonny's picture, viewed as a thing of art, was something to have driven away dull care from the bosoms of the critics.

The painting—one might almost say panorama—was designed to portray a typical Western scene, interest culminating in a central animal figure, that of a stampeding steer, life-size, wild-eyed, fiery, breaking away in a mad rush from the herd that, close-ridden by a typical cowpuncher, occupied a position somewhat in the right background of the picture. The landscape presented fitting and faithful accessories. Chaparral, mesquite, and pear were distributed in just proportions. A Spanish dagger-plant, with its waxen blossoms in a creamy aggregation as large as a water-bucket, contributed floral beauty and variety. The distance was undulating prairie, bisected by stretches of the intermittent streams peculiar to the region lined with the rich green of live-oak and water-elm. A richly mottled rattlesnake lay coiled beneath a pale green clump of prickly pear in the foreground. A third of the canvas was ultramarine and lake white—the typical Western sky and the flying clouds, rainless and feathery.

Between two plastered pillars in the commodious hallway near the door of the chamber of representatives stood the painting. Citizens and lawmakers passed there by twos and groups and sometimes crowds to gaze upon it. Many—perhaps a majority of them—had lived the prairie life and recalled easily the familiar scene. Old cattlemen stood, reminiscent and candidly pleased, chatting with brothers of former camps and trails of the days it brought back to mind. Art critics were few in the town, and there was heard none of that jargon of color, perspective, and feeling such as the East loves to use as a curb and a rod to the pretensions of the artist. 'Twas a great picture, most of them agreed, admiring the gilt frame—larger than any they had ever seen.

Senator Kinney was the picture's champion and sponsor. It was he who so often stepped forward and asserted, with the voice of a bronco-buster, that it would be a lasting blot, sir, upon the name of this great state if it should decline to recognize in a proper manner the genius that had so brilliantly transferred to imperishable canvas a scene so typical of the great sources of our state's wealth and prosperity, land—and—er—live-stock.

Senator Kinney represented a section of the state in the extreme West—400 miles from the San Saba country—but the true lover of art is not limited by metes and bounds. Nor was Senator Mullens, representing the San Saba country, lukewarm in his belief that the state should purchase the painting of his constituent. He was advised that the San Saba country was unanimous in its admiration of the great painting by one of

its own denizens. Hundreds of connoisseurs had ~
broncos and ridden miles to view it before its
capital. Senator Mullens desired re-election,
importance of the San Saba vote. He also knew
help of Senator Kinney—who was a power in the ~
the thing could be put through. Now, Senator Kinney
irrigation bill that he wanted passed for the benefit of his ~
section, and he knew Senator Mullens could render him valua
ble aid and information, the San Saba country already enjoy
ing the benefits of similar legislation. With these interests happily dovetailed, wonder at the sudden interest in art at the
state capital must, necessarily, be small. Few artists have un-
covered their first picture to the world under happier auspices
than did Lonny Briscoe.

Senators Kinney and Mullens came to an understanding in
the matter of irrigation and art while partaking of long drinks
in the café of the Empire Hotel.

"H'm!" said Senator Kinney, "I don't know. I'm no art critic,
but it seems to me the thing won't work. It looks like the worst
kind of a chromo to me. I don't want to cast any reflections
upon the artistic talent of your constituent, Senator, but I,
myself, wouldn't give six bits for the picture—without the
frame. How are you going to cram a thing like that down the
throat of a legislature that kicks about a little item in the expense bill of six hundred and eighty-one dollars for rubber
erasers for only one term? It's wasting time. I'd like to help
you, Mullens, but they'd laugh us out of the Senate chamber
if we were to try it."

"But you don't get the point," said Senator Mullens, in his
deliberate tones, tapping Kinney's glass with his long fore-
finger. "I have my own doubts as to what the picture is intended to represent, a bullfight or a Japanese allegory, but I
want this legislature to make an appropriation to purchase.
Of course, the subject of the picture should have been in the
state historical line, but it's too late to have the paint scraped
off and changed. The state won't miss the money and the picture can be stowed away in a lumber-room where it won't

.... Now, here's the point to work on, leaving art
to look after itself the chap that painted the picture is the
grandson of Lucien Briscoe."

"Say it again," said Kinney, leaning his head thoughtfully.
"Of the old, original Lucien Briscoe?"

"Of him. 'The man who,' you know. The man who carved
the state out of the wilderness. The man who settled the Indians. The man who cleaned out the horse thieves. The man
who refused the crown. The state's favorite son. Do you see the
point now?"

"Wrap up the picture," said Kinney. "It's as good as sold.
Why didn't you say that at first, instead of philandering along
about art? I'll resign my seat in the Senate and go back to
chain-carrying for the county surveyor the day I can't make
this state buy a picture calcimined by a grandson of Lucien
Briscoe. Did you ever hear of a special appropriation for the
purchase of a home for the daughter of One-Eyed Smothers?
Well, that went through like a motion to adjourn, and old
One-Eyed never killed half as many Indians as Briscoe did.
About what figure had you and the calciminer agreed upon to
sandbag the treasury for?"

"I thought," said Mullens, "that maybe five hundred—"

"Five hundred!" interrupted Kinney, as he hammered on his
glass with a lead pencil and looked around for a waiter. "Only
five hundred for a red steer on the hoof delivered by a grandson of Lucien Briscoe! Where's your state pride, man? Two
thousand is what it'll be. You'll introduce the bill and I'll get
up on the floor of the Senate and wave the scalp of every
Indian old Lucien ever murdered. Let's see, there was something else proud and foolish he did, wasn't there? Oh, yes; he
declined all emoluments and benefits he was entitled to. Refused his head-right and veteran donation certificates. Could
have been governor, but wouldn't. Declined a pension. Now's
the state's chance to pay up. It'll have to take the picture, but
then it deserves some punishment for keeping the Briscoe
family waiting so long. We'll bring this thing up about the
middle of the month, after the tax bill is settled. Now, Mullens,

you send over, as soon as you can, and get me the figures on the cost of those irrigation ditches and the statistics about the increased production per acre. I'm going to need you when that bill of mine comes up. I reckon we'll be able to pull along pretty well together this session and maybe others to come, eh, Senator?"

Thus did fortune elect to smile upon the Boy Artist of the San Saba. Fate had already done her share when she arranged his atoms in the cosmogony of creation as the grandson of Lucien Briscoe.

The original Briscoe had been a pioneer both as to territorial occupation and in certain acts prompted by a great and simple heart. He had been one of the first settlers and crusaders against the wild forces of nature, the savage and the shallow politician. His name and memory were revered equally with any upon the list comprising Houston, Boone, Crockett, Clark, and Green. He had lived simply, independently, and unvexed by ambition. Even a less shrewd man than Senator Kinney could have prophesied that his state would hasten to honor and reward his grandson, come out of the chaparral at even so late a day.

And so, before the great picture by the door of the chamber of representatives at frequent times for many days could be found the breezy, robust form of Senator Kinney and be heard his clarion voice reciting the past deeds of Lucien Briscoe in connection with the handiwork of his grandson. Senator Mullen's work was more subdued in sight and sound, but directed along identical lines.

Then, as the day for the introduction of the bill for appropriation draws nigh, up from the San Saba country rides Lonny Briscoe and a loyal lobby of cowpunchers, bronco-back, to boost the cause of art and glorify the name of friendship, for Lonny is one of them, a knight of stirrup and chaparreras, as handy with the lariat and .45 as he is with brush and palette.

On a March afternoon the lobby dashed, with a whoop, into town. The cowpunchers had adjusted their garb suitably from that prescribed for the range to the more conventional requirements of town. They had conceded their leather chaparreras and transferred their six-shooters and belts from their persons to the horns of their saddles. Among them rode Lonny, a youth of twenty-three, brown, solemn-faced, ingenuous, bowlegged, reticent, bestriding Hot Tamales, the most sagacious cow pony west of the Mississippi. Senator Mullens had informed him of the bright prospects of the situation; had even mentioned—so great was his confidence in the capable Kinney—the price that the state would, in all likelihood, pay. It seemed to Lonny that fame and fortune were in his hands. Certainly, a spark of the divine fire was in the little brown centaur's breast, for he was counting the two thousand dollars as but a means to future development of his talent. Some day he would paint a picture even greater than this—one, say, twelve feet by twenty, full of scope and atmosphere and action.

During the three days that yet intervened before the coming of the date fixed for the introduction of the bill, the centaur lobby did valiant service. Coatless, spurred, weather-tanned, full of enthusiasm expressed in bizarre terms, they loafed in front of the painting with tireless zeal. Reasoning not unshrewdly, they estimated that their comments upon its fidelity to nature would be received as expert evidence. Loudly they praised the skill of the painter whenever there were ears near to which such evidence might be profitably addressed. Lem Perry, the leader of the claque, had a somewhat set speech, being uninventive in the construction of new phrases.

"Look at that two-year-old, now," he would say, waving a cinnamon-brown hand toward the salient point of the picture. "Why, dang my hide, the critter's alive. I can jest hear him, 'lumpety-lump,' a-cuttin' away from the herd, pretendin' he's skeered. He's a mean scamp, that there steer. Look at his eyes a-wallin' and his tail a-wavin'. He's true and nat'ral to life. He's jest hankerin' fur a cow pony to round him up and send him scootin' back to the bunch. Dang my hide! jest look at that tail of his'n a-wavin'. Never knowed a steer to wave his tail any other way, dang my hide ef I did."

Jud Shelby, while admitting the excellence of the steer, resolutely confined himself to open admiration of the landscape, to the end that the entire picture receive its meed of praise.

"That piece of range," he declared, "is a dead ringer for Dead Hoss Valley. Same grass, same lay of the land, same old Whipperwill Creek skallyhootin' in and out of them motts of timber. Them buzzards on the left is circlin' 'round over Sam Kildrake's old paint hoss that killed hisself over-drinkin' on a hot day. You can't see the hoss for that mott of ellums on the creek, but he's thar. Anybody that was goin' to look for Dead Hoss Valley and come across this picture, why, he'd jest light off'n his bronco and hunt a place to camp."

Skinny Rogers, wedded to comedy, conceived a complimentary little piece of acting that never failed to make an impression. Edging quite near to the picture, he would suddenly at favorable moments emit a piercing and awful "Yi-yi!" leap high and away, coming down with a great stamp of heels and whirring of rowels upon the stone-flagged floor.

"Jeeming Christopher!"—so ran his lines—"thought that rattler was a gin-u-ine one. Ding baste my skin if I didn't. Seemed to me I heard him rattle. Look at the blamed, unconverted insect a-layin' under that pear. Little more, and somebody would a-been snake-bit."

With these artful dodges, contributed by Lonny's faithful coterie, with the sonorous Kinney perpetually sounding the picture's merits, and with the solvent prestige of the pioneer Briscoe covering it like a precious varnish, it seemed that the San Saba country could not fail to add a reputation as an art centre to its well-known superiority in steer-roping contests and achievements with the precarious busted flush. Thus was created for the picture an atmosphere, due rather to externals than to the artist's brush, but through it the people seemed to gaze with more of admiration. There was a magic in the name of Briscoe that counted high against faulty technique and crude coloring. The old Indian fighter and wolf slayer would have smiled grimly in his happy hunting grounds had he known that his dilettante ghost was thus figuring as an art patron two generations after his uninspired existence.

Came the day when the Senate was expected to pass the bill of Senator Mullens appropriating two thousand dollars for the purchase of the picture. The gallery of the Senate chamber was early pre-empted by Lonny and the San Saba lobby. In the front row of chairs they sat, wild-haired, self-conscious, jingling, creaking, and rattling, subdued by the majesty of the council hall.

The bill was introduced, went to the second reading, and then Senator Mullens spoke for it dryly, tediously, and at length. Senator Kinney then arose, and the welkin seized the bellrope preparatory to ringing. Oratory was at that time a living thing; the world had not quite come to measure its questions by geometry and the multiplication table. It was the day of the silver tongue, the sweeping gesture, the decorative apostrophe, the moving peroration.

The Senator spoke. The San Saba contingent sat, breathing hard, in the gallery, its disordered hair hanging down to its eyes, its sixteen-ounce hats shifted restlessly from knee to knee. Below, the distinguished Senators either lounged at their desks with the abandon of proven statesmanship or maintained correct attitudes indicative of a first term.

Senator Kinney spoke for an hour. History was his theme— history mitigated by patriotism and sentiment. He referred casually to the picture in the outer hall—it was unnecessary, he said, to dilate upon its merits—the Senators had seen for themselves. The painter of the picture was the grandson of Lucien Briscoe. Then came the word-pictures of Briscoe's life set forth in thrilling colors. His rude and venturesome life, his simple-minded love for the commonwealth he helped to upbuild, his contempt for rewards and praise, his extreme and sturdy independence, and the great services he had rendered the state. The subject of the oration was Lucien Briscoe; the painting stood in the background serving simply as a means, now happily brought forward, through which the state might bestow a tardy recompense upon the descendant of its favorite son. Frequent enthusiastic applause from the Senators testified to the well reception of the sentiment.

The bill passed without an opposing vote. To-morrow it would be taken up by the House. Already was it fixed to glide through that body on rubber tires. Blandford, Grayson, and Plummer, all wheel-horses and orators, and provided with plentiful memoranda concerning the deeds of pioneer Briscoe, had agreed to furnish the motive power.

The San Saba lobby and its *protégé* stumbled awkwardly down the stairs and out into the Capitol yard. Then they herded closely and gave one yell of triumph. But one of them —Buck-Kneed Summers it was—hit the key with the thoughtful remark:

"She cut the mustard," he said, "all right. I reckon they're goin' to buy Lon's steer. I ain't right much on the parlyment'ry, but I gather that's what the signs added up. But she seems to me, Lonny, the argyment ran principal to grandfather, instead of paint. It's reasonable calculatin' that you want to be glad you got the Briscoe brand on you, my son."

That remark clinched in Lonny's mind an unpleasant, vague suspicion to the same effect. His reticence increased, and he gathered grass from the ground, chewing it pensively. The picture as a picture had been humiliatingly absent from the Senator's arguments. The painter had been held up as a grandson, pure and simple. While this was gratifying on certain lines, it made art look little and slab-sided. The Boy Artist was thinking.

The hotel Lonny stopped at was near the Capitol. It was near to the one o'clock dinner hour when the appropriation had been passed by the Senate. The hotel clerk told Lonny that a famous artist from New York had arrived in town that day and was in the hotel. He was on his way westward to New Mexico to study the effect of sunlight upon the ancient walls of the Zuñis. Modern stone reflects light. Those ancient building materials absorb it. The artist wanted this effect in a picture he was painting and was traveling two thousand miles to get it.

Lonny sought this man out after dinner and told his story. The artist was an unhealthy man, kept alive by genius and indifference to life. He went with Lonny to the Capitol and stood there before the picture. The artist pulled his beard and looked unhappy.

"Should like to have your sentiments," said Lonny, "just as they run out of the pen."

"It's the way they'll come," said the painter man. "I took three different kinds of medicine before dinner—by the table-spoonful. The taste still lingers. I am primed for telling the truth. You want to know if the picture is, or if it isn't?"

"Right," said Lonny. "Is it wool or cotton? Should I paint some more or cut it out and ride herd a-plenty?"

"I heard a rumor during pie," said the artist, "that the state is about to pay you two thousand dollars for this picture."

"It's passed the Senate," said Lonny, "and the House rounds it up tomorrow."

"That's lucky," said the pale man. "Do you carry a rabbit's foot?"

"No," said Lonny, "but it seems I had a grandfather. He's considerable mixed up in the color scheme. It took me a year to paint that picture. Is she entirely awful or not? Some says, now, that that steer's tail ain't badly drawed. They think it's proportioned nice. Tell me."

The artist glanced at Lonny's wiry figure and nut-brown skin. Something stirred him to a passing irritation.

"For Art's sake, son," he said, fractiously, "don't spend any more money for paint. It isn't a picture at all. It's a gun. You hold up the state with it, if you like, and get your two thousand, but don't get in front of any more canvas. Live under it. Buy a couple of hundred ponies with the money—I'm told they're that cheap—and ride, ride, ride. Fill your lungs and eat and sleep and be happy. No more pictures. You look healthy. That's genius. Cultivate it." He looked at his watch. "Twenty minutes to three. Four capsules and one tablet at three. That's all you wanted to know, isn't it?"

At three o'clock the cowpunchers rode up for Lonny, bring-ing Hot Tamales, saddled. Traditions must be observed. To celebrate the passage of the bill by the Senate the gang must ride wildly through the town, creating uproar and excitement. Liquor must be partaken of, the suburbs shot up, and the glory of the San Saba country vociferously proclaimed. A part of the programme had been carried out in the saloons on the way up. Lonny mounted Hot Tamales, the accomplished little beast prancing with fire and intelligence. He was glad to feel Lonny's bowlegged grip against his ribs again. Lonny was his friend, and he was willing to do things for him.

"Come on, boys," said Lonny, urging Hot Tamales into a gallop with his knees. With a whoop, the inspired lobby tore after him through the dust. Lonny led his cohorts straight for the Capitol. With a wild yell, the gang indorsed his now evident intention of riding into it. Hooray for San Saba!

Up the six broad, limestone steps clattered the broncos of the cowpunchers. Into the resounding hallway they pattered, scattering in dismay those passing on foot. Lonny, in the lead, shoved Hot Tamales direct for the great picture. At that hour a downpouring, soft light from the second-story windows bathed the big canvas. Against the darker background of the hall the painting stood out with valuable effect. In spite of the defects of the art you could almost fancy that you gazed out upon a landscape. You might well flinch a step from the convincing figure of the life-sized steer stampeding across the grass. Perhaps it thus seemed to Hot Tamales. The scene was in his line. Perhaps he only obeyed the will of his rider. His ears pricked up; he snorted. Lonny leaned forward in the saddle and elevated his elbows, wing-like. Thus signals the cowpuncher to his steed to launch himself full speed ahead. Did Hot Tamales fancy he saw a steer, red and cavorting, that should be headed off and driven back to herd? There was a fierce clatter of hoofs, a rush, a gathering of steely flank muscles, a leap to the jerk of the bridle rein, and Hot Tamales, with Lonny bending low in the saddle to dodge the top of the frame, ripped through the great canvas like a shell from a mortar, leaving the cloth hanging in ragged shreds about a monstrous hole.

Quickly Lonny pulled up his pony, and rounded the pillars.

Spectators came running, too astounded to add speech to the commotion. The sergeant-at-arms of the House came forth, frowned, looked ominous, and then grinned. Many of the legislators crowded out to observe the tumult. Lonny's cowpunchers were stricken to silent horror by his mad deed.

Senator Kinney happened to be among the earliest to emerge. Before he could speak Lonny leaned in his saddle as Hot Tamales pranced, pointed his quirt at the Senator, and said, calmly:

"That was a fine speech you made to-day, mister, but you might as well let up on that 'propriation business. I ain't askin' the state to give me nothin'. I thought I had a picture to sell to it, but it wasn't one. You said a heap of things about Grandfather Briscoe that makes me kind of proud I'm his grandson. Well, the Briscoes ain't takin' presents from the state yet. Anybody can have the frame that wants it. Hit her up, boys."

Away scuttled the San Saba delegation out of the hall, down the steps, along the dusty street.

Halfway to the San Saba country they camped that night. At bedtime Lonny stole away from the campfire and sought Hot Tamales, placidly eating grass at the end of his stake rope. Lonny hung upon his neck, and his art aspirations went forth forever in one long, regretful sigh. But as he thus made renunciation his breath formed a word or two.

"You was the only one, Tamales, what seen anything in it. It *did* look like a steer, didn't it, old hoss?"

ALFRED HENRY LEWIS

···⇀──⚬⟩⚬⟨⚬──⟨···

Jaybird Bob's Joke*

❪ ALFRED HENRY LEWIS was a sensation in the late nineties when his *Wolfville* (1897) and other Wolfville stories were published by Stokes. Lewis ties together his cowboy and western life stories through his dialect-strong character-narrator called "The Old Cattleman." The stories are tricky anecdotes, usually, but the people in them have the juices of real life and ring true, no matter how inventive or how tall the tale.

WHATEVER MAKES this yere Jaybird Bob believe he's a humorist," said the Old Cattleman one afternoon as we slowly returned from a walk, "whatever it is misleads him to so deem himse'f, is shorely too many for me. Doc Peets tells him himse'f one day he's plumb wrong.

"'You-all's nacherally a somber, morose party,' says Doc Peets this time, 'an' nothin' jocose or jocund about you. Your disp'sition, Jaybird, don't no more run to jokes than a prairie-dog's.'

"'Which I would admire to know why not?' says Jaybird Bob.

"'Well,' goes on Doc Peets, 'you thinks too slow—too much like a cow in a swamp. Your mind moves sluggish that a-way, an' sorter sinks to the hocks each step. If you was born to be funny your intellects would be limber an' frivolous.'

---

* From *Wolfville* (New York: F. A. Stokes Co., 1897).

" 'Bein' all this is personal to me,' says Jaybird Bob, 'I takes leave to regard you as wrong. My jokes is good, high-grade jokes; an' when you-all talks of me bein' morose, it's a mere case of bluff.' An' so Jaybird goes on a-holdin' of himse'f funny ontil we-alls has him to bury.

"No; Jaybird ain't his shore-'nough name; it's jest a handle to his 'dentity, so we-alls picks it up handy and easy. Jaybird's real name is Graingerford—Poindexter Graingerford. But the same is cumbersom an' onwieldy a whole lot; so when he first trails into Wolfville we-alls considers among ourse'fs an' settles it's a short cut to call him 'Jaybird Bob,' that a-way. An' we does.

"It's on the spring round-up this yere Jaybird first develops that he regards himse'f witty. It's in the mornin' as we-alls has saddled up an' lines out to comb the range roundabout for cattle. Thar's a tenderfoot along whose name is Todd, an', as he's canterin' off, Jaybird comes a-curvin' up on his bronco an' reaches over an' tails this shorthorn's pony.

"What's tailin' a pony? It's ridin' up from the r'ar an' takin' a half-hitch on your saddle-horn with the tail of another gent's pony, an' then spurrin' by an' swappin' ends with the whole outfit—gent, hoss, an' all.

"It's really too toomultuous for a joke, an' mebby breaks the pony's neck, mebby the rider's. But whether he saves his neck or no, the party whose pony is thus tailed allers emerges thar-from deshevelled an' wrought-up, an' hotter than a wolf. So no one plays this yere joke much; not till he's ready to get shot at.

"As I says, this Jaybird watches Todd as he rides off. Bein' new on the range that a-way, Todd don't ride easy. A cow saddle ain't built like these yere Eastern hulls, nohow. The stirrup is set two inches further back for one thing, an' it's compiled a heap different other ways. Bein' onused to cow saddles, an' for that matter cow ponies, this Todd lops over for'ard an' beats with his elbows like he's a curlew or some-thin' flyin', an' I reckons it's sech proceedin's makes Jaybird allow he's goin' to be funny an' tail Todd's pony.

"As I explains, he capers along after Todd an' reaches over an' gets a handful of the pony's tail; an' then, wroppin' it 'round his saddle-horn, he goes by on the jump an' spreads Todd an' his bronco permiscus about the scene. This yere Todd goes along the grass on all fours like a jack-rabbit.

"Which Todd, I reckons, is the hostilest gent in south-east Arizona. Before ever he offers to get up, he lugs out his six-shooter an' makes some mighty sincere gestures that a-way to shoot up Jaybird. But he's slow with his weepon, bein' spraddled out on the grass, an' it gives Dave Tutt an' Enright a chance to jump in between an' stop the deal.

"We-alls picks Todd up, an' rounds up his pony—which scrambles to its feet an' is now cavortin' about like its mind is overturned—an' explains to him this yere is a joke. But he's surly an' relentless about it; an' it don't take no hawk to see he don't forgive Jaybird a little bit.

"'Tailin' a gent's pony,' says Todd, 'is no doubt thrillin' amoosement for folks lookin' on, but thar's nothin' of a redeemin' nature in it from the standp'int of the party whose pony's upheaved that a-way. Not to be misonderstood at this yere crisis,' goes on this Todd, 'I wants to announce that from now for'ard life will have but one purpose with me, which'll be to down the next gent whoever tails a pony of mine. The present incident goes as a witticism; but you can gamble the next won't be so regarded.'

"That sorter ends the talk, an' all of us but the cook an' the hoss-hustlers bein' in the saddle by now, we disperses ourse'fs through the scenery to work the cattle an' proceed with the round-up we-alls is on. We notes, though, that tailin' Todd's pony don't go ag'in with safety.

"It's when we-alls rides away that Doc Peets—who's out with the round-up, though he ain't got no cattle-brand himse'f— tells Jaybird he's not a humorist, like I already repeats.

"But, as I su'gests, this Jaybird Bob can't believe it none. He's mighty shore about his jokes bein' excellent good jokes; an' while it's plain Todd ain't got no confidence in him an' distrusts him complete since he tips over his bronco that mornin', it looks like Jaybird can't let him alone. An' them mis-deeds of Jaybird's keeps goin' on, ontil by the merest mistake —for it's shore an accident if ever one happens in the cow country—this yere tenderfoot shoots up Jaybird an' kills him for good.

"It looks to us like it's a speshul Providence to warn folks not to go projectin' about, engaged in what you might call physical jests none. Still, this yere removal of Jaybird don't take place till mighty near the close of the round-up; an' intervenin', he's pirootin' 'round, stockin' the kyards an' settin' up hands on the pore shorthorn continuous.

"One of Jaybird's jokes—'one of his best,' Jaybird calls it— results in stampedin' the herd of cattle we-alls is bringin' along at the time—bein' all cows an' their calves—to a brandin'-pen. Which thar's two thousand, big an' little, in the bunch; an' Jaybird's humor puts 'em to flight like so many blackbirds; an' it takes two days hard ridin' for the whole outfit to bring 'em together ag'in.

"Among other weaknesses this Todd imports from the States is, he's afraid of snakes. Rattlesnakes is his abhorrence, an' if each is a disembodied sperit he can't want 'em further off. He's allers alarmed that mebby, somehow, a rattlesnake will come pokin' in onder his blankets nights, an' camp with him while he's asleep. An' this yere wretched Jaybird fosters them delusions.

"'About them serpents,' I overhears Jaybird say to him one evenin' while we-alls is settin' 'round—all but Moore an' Tutt, who's ridin' herd; ''bout them serpents; a gent can't be too partic'lar. It looks like they has but one hope, which it's to crawl into a gent's blankets an' sleep some with him. Which, if he moves or turns over, they simply emits a buzz an' grabs him: I knows of forty folks who's bit that a-way by snakes, an' nary a one lives to explain the game.

"'Be rattlesnakes thick in Arizona?' I hears Todd say to this Jaybird.

"'Be they thick?' answers Jaybird. 'Well, I shore wishes I had whiskey for all the rattlesnakes thar is yereabouts. I don't

want to go overstatin' the census to a gent who is out playin'
for information, an' who's learnin' fast, but I s'pose now thar
ain't none less than a billion snakes in southeast Arizona alone.
If I could saw off the little passel of cattle I has on this range,
you can gamble I'd pull my freight to-morrow. It's all right
for sech old Cimmarons as Enright, an' sech parties as that
sawbones Peets, to go bluffin' about thar' bein' no rattlesnakes
to speak of, an' that they couldn't p'ison you to death no how;
but you bet I ain't seen forty of my nearest friends cash in
of snake-bites, an' not learn nothin'. An' almost every time it's
a rattlesnake as comes slidin' into bed with 'em while they's
locked in dreams, an' who gets hot an' goes to chewin' of
'em, because they wants to turn out before the snake does.
Rattlesnakes that a-way wants to sleep till it's fourth-drink time
an' the sun's 'way up yonder. An' when a gent goes to rollin'
out of his blankets say at sun-up, it makes 'em monstrous
angry to be disturbed; an' the first he knows of where they be
an' how they looks on early risin', their teeth's in him up to the
gyard, an' before night thar's one less gent to cook for, an' an
extra saddle rides along in the grub-wagon with the blankets
when they next moves camp.'

"Of course all this is a heap impressive to Todd; an' while
Enright an' Peets both tells him Jaybird's havin' fun with him,
you can see he's mortal afraid every night when he spreads
his blankets, an' he makes a circle about where he sleeps at
with a horse-ha'r lariat he's got from a Mexican, an' who tells
him it'll tickle the snakes' necks when they goes to crawl
across it, an' make 'em keep away.

"The way this yere Jaybird manages to stampede the bunch
that time is this a-way. Jaybird comes ridin' in from the cattle
about three hours before sun-up, to turn out Tutt, who is due
to take his place on herd. Jaybird's got a rawhide rope that
he's drugged about in the grass, which makes it damp an'
cold. As Jaybird rides up to camp he sees this Todd rolled in
his blankets, snorin' to beat four of a kind.

"Nacherally Jaybird's out to be joyous in a second. He rides
up close to this he'pless shorthorn as he lays asleep, an' tosses

a loop of his wet rawhide across his countenance where it's
turned up in the moonlight. As it settles down cold an' startlin'
on Todd's skin, Jaybird yells:

"'Snake, Todd! Thar's a rattlesnake on you bigger'n a dog.'

"Jaybird says later as how this Todd behaves tremendous.
He b'iles up into the atmosphere with a howl like a wolf; an',
grabbin' a blanket in each hand, he starts out over the plains
in a state of frenzy. Which the worst is he charges headlong
toward the herd; an' what with them shrieks he volunteers, an'
the blankets flappin' an' wavin', thar ain't a cow in the bunch
who stays in her right mind a moment. Which she springs to
her feet, an', takin' her offspring along, goes surgin' off into
the hills for good. You couldn't head or stop 'em then. It's the
completest case of stampede I ever turns out to behold.

"No; this yere Todd never gathers the rights of the eepisode.
He's that peevish an' voylent by nacher no one tells him it's
Jaybird; an' onless, in the light of knowin' more, he has since
figgered out the trooth, he allows to this day a rattlesnake as
big as a roll of blankets tries to recline on his face that time.

"To keep peace in camp an' not let him go to pawin' 'round
for real trouble with the festive Jaybird, Enright stands in to
cap the game himse'f; an' puts it up in confab with this Todd
the next day as how he sees the rattlesnake, an' that it's mighty
near bein' a whopper.

"'It's shore,' says Enright, when he an' Todd is conversin'
tharon, 'the most giant serpent I ever sees without the aid
of licker. An' when he goes streakin' off into the gloom, bein'
amazed an' rattled by your cries, he leaves, so far as I'm
concerned, a trail of relief behind. You-all can gamble, I wasn't
interruptin' of no sech snake, nor makin' of no pretexts for
his detainment.'

"'What for was his rattles like?' says Todd; an' he gets pale
at the mere sound of Enright's talk.

"'As to them rattles,' says Enright, like he's mighty thoughtful tryin' to recall 'em to mind, 'as to this reptile's rattles, it's
that dark that while I sees 'em I couldn't but jest. So far as I

notes anythin' they looks like a belt full of cartridges, sorter corrugated an' noomerous.'

"Now this yere which I relates, while no doubt burnin' experiences to Todd, is after all harmless enough. An' to people not careful about the basis of their glee it might do some to laugh at. But it all closes up on a play with nothin' gay nor merry in it; leastwise not for Jaybird Bob.

"This yere finish joke of Jaybird's transpires one evenin' as the cook's startin' in to rustle some chuck. The grub-wagon's been stopped in the mouth of Peeled Pine Canyon. Every gent's in camp but this yere tenderfoot Todd. Enright, who's actin' as round-up boss for the outfit—for everybody's cattle's bein' worked together that a-way, like we allers does—has sent Todd peerin' 'round for cattle, 'way off up the valley into which the Peeled Pine Canyon opens. This yere shorthorn's due to be back any time now, 'cause it's only a question of how far up the valley does he go. He don't run no show to be lost, for nothin' less aerial than goats could climb out of the canyon he's in, an' tharfore he's bound to find camp.

"Of course, knowin' every gent's station in the day's ridin', we-alls is plenty aware that this tenderfoot Todd is some'ers above us in the valley. None of the rest of us is turnin' our minds to him probably, except Jaybird Bob. It all of a bump like a buckin' pony strikes Jaybird that he's missin' a onusual chance to be buoyant.

"'What for a play would it be,' says Jaybird, rousin' up from where he lays watchin' of the cook slice salt hoss for the fryin'-pan, 'what for a game would it be, I says, for a passel of us to lay out up the draw, an' bush-whack this yere ontaught person Todd as he comes ridin' down to camp? We-alls could hop out at him, a-whoopin' an' shoutin', an' bein' wropped up in blankets, he allows it's shore Injuns an' goes plumb locoed.'

"'You-all will keep harrowin' away at this Todd party, Jaybird,' says Enright, 'ontil you arises from the game loser. Now I don't reckon none I'd play Apache if I'm you. Thar's too much effort in bein' an Apache that a-way. I'd lay yere an' think up some joke which don't demand so much industry, an' ain't calc'lated to scare an innocent gent to death.'

"But Jaybird won't listen. He falls into admiration of his scheme; an' at last Tutt an' Jack Moore allows they'll go along an' play they's aborigines with Jaybird an' note how the tenderfoot stands the racket.

"'As long as this yere Jaybird's bound to make the play,' says Jack Moore to Enright, talkin' one side, 'it's a heap better to have the conserv'tive element represented in the deal. So I puts it up, it's a good sage move for me an' Tutt to stand in. We-alls will come handy to pull Jaybird an' this shorthorn apart if they gets their horns locked in the course of them gaities.'

"Enright takes the same view; so Jaybird an' Moore an' Tutt wanders off up the canyon a mile, an' lays in wait surreptitious to head off Todd. Jack tells me the story when him an' Tutt comes ridin' back with the corpse.

"'This is how we does,' says Jack. 'Me an' Tutt an' deceased —which last is Jaybird all right enough—is ensconced behind a p'int of rocks. Jaybird's got his blanket wropped 'round him so he looks like a savage. It ain't long when we-alls hears the tenderfoot comin' down the canyon; it's likely he's half-mile away. He's runnin' onto us at a road-gait; an' when he's about two hundred yards off Jaybird turns out a yell to make you shiver, shakes a load or two outen his gun, goes surgin' out from 'round the p'int of rocks, an' charges straight at this on-thinkin' tenderfoot. It is due to trooth to say, me an' Tutt follows this Jaybird's suit, only not so voylent as to whoops.

"'Does it scare up the tenderfoot? Well, it shorely alarms him a heap. He takes Jaybird for an Injun an' makes no ques-tion; which the same is nowise strange; I'd took him for a savage myse'f, only, bein' in the deal that a-way, I knows it's Jaybird. So, as I remarks, it horrifies the tenderfoot no end, an' at the first sight of Jaybird he whirls his pony an' lights out up that valley like antelope.

"'Nacherally we-alls follows; Jaybird leadin', a-whoopin', an' a-shootin', an' throwin' no end of sperit into it. It's a success.

this piece of wit is, up to this juncture, an' Jaybird puts a heap of zest into it.

" 'The weak spot in all this yere humor grows out of the idees this tenderfoot's been gainin', an' the improvements he's been makin', while stragglin' about in our s'ciety. I onhesitatin'ly states that if this yere joke is pulled off by Jaybird when Todd first enters our midst, it might have been the vict'ry of his life. But Jaybird defers it too long. This tenderfoot has acquired a few Western ways; enough to spoil the fun an' send pore Jaybird a-curvin' to his home on high.

" 'This is what that shorthorn does which teaches me he's learnin'. While he's humpin' off up the canyon, an' me an' Jaybird an' Tutt is stampedin' along in pursoot, the fugitive throws loose his six-shooter, an' without even turnin' his head or lookin' back at us, he onhooks the entire bundle of lead our way.

" 'Which the worst feature of it is, this back-handed, blind shootin' is a winner. The very first shot smites Jaybird plumb through the hat, an' he goes off his pony without even mentionin' about it to either Tutt or me.

" 'That's all thar is to the report. Dave an' me pulls up our broncos, abandons the joke, lays Jaybird across his saddle like a sack of corn, an' returns to state the case.'

" 'Whatever did you-alls do with this frightened stranger?' asks Enright.

" 'Which we never does nothin',' says Jack. 'The last I beholds, he's flyin' up the valley, hittin' nothin' but the high places. An' assoomin' his project is to get away, he's succeedin' admirable. As he vanishes, I should jedge from his motions he's reloadin' his gun; an' from the luck he has with Jaybird, Tutt an' me is led to believe thar's no real object in followin' him no further. I don't press my s'ciety on no gent—shorely not on some locoed tenderfoot that a-way who's pulled his gun an' is done blazin' away erratic, without purpose or aim.'

" 'Don't you an' Tutt know where he is at?' demands Enright.

" 'Which we shorely don't,' says Jack. 'If his hoss holds, an' he don't swerve none from the direction he's p'inting out in when he fades from view, he's goin' to be over in the San Simon country by to-morrow mornin' when we eats our grub; an' that's half way to the Borax desert. If you yearns for my impressions,' concloods Jack, 'drawn from a-seein' of him depart, I'm free to say I don't reckon you-alls is goin' to meet this yere tenderfoot none soon.'

"An' that's about the size of it. Jack calls the turn. Jaybird's last joke alarms this tenderfoot Todd plumb outen Arizona, an' thar ain't none of us ever sees ha'r, horn, nor hoof-mark of him no more. An' he takes with him, this Todd does, the boss pony in our bunch."

STEWART EDWARD WHITE

The Drive*

❲ STEWART EDWARD WHITE was a professional writer
(with an output of better than a book a year) whose subjects ranged from children's stories to psychical research;
but his fiction has the ring of truth, especially when he is
recalling his early youth spent camping and ranching in
California and Arizona, as in the story collection from
which "The Drive" is taken, *Arizona Nights*. White was
well educated (a University of Michigan graduate) but
savvied the lives and lingo of men whose only schooling
was on horseback. If the reader thinks the drama of "The
Drive" looks like material for Hollywood, he is dead right;
no fewer than five films have been made from *Arizona
Nights*.

A CRY AWAKENED ME. It was still deep night. The moon
sailed overhead, the stars shone unwavering like candles,
and a chill breeze wandered in from the open spaces of the desert. I raised myself on my elbow, throwing aside the blankets and
the canvas tarpaulin. Forty other indistinct, formless bundles
on the ground all about me were sluggishly astir. Four figures
passed and repassed between me and a red fire. I knew them
for the two cooks and the horse wranglers. One of the latter
was grumbling.

249

"Didn't git in till moon-up last night," he growled. "Might as well trade my bed for a lantern and be done with it."

Even as I stretched my arms and shivered a little, the two wranglers threw down their tin plates with a clatter, mounted horses and rode away in the direction of the thousand acres or so known as the pasture.

I pulled on my clothes hastily, buckled in my buckskin shirt, and dove for the fire. A dozen others were before me. It was bitterly cold. In the east the sky had paled the least bit in the world, but the moon and stars shone on bravely and undiminished. A band of coyotes was shrieking desperate blasphemies against the new day, and the stray herd, awakening, was beginning to bawl and bellow.

Two crater-like dutch ovens, filled with pieces of fried beef, stood near the fire; two galvanised water buckets, brimming with soda biscuits, flanked them; two tremendous coffee pots stood guard at either end. We picked us each a tin cup and a tin plate from the box at the rear of the chuck wagon; helped ourselves from a dutch oven, a pail, and a coffee pot, and squatted on our heels as close to the fire as possible. Men who came too late borrowed the shovel, scooped up some coals, and so started little fires of their own about which new groups formed.

While we ate, the eastern sky lightened. The mountains under the dawn looked like silhouettes cut from slate-coloured paper; those in the west showed faintly luminous. Objects about us became dimly visible. We could make out the windmill, and the adobe of the ranch houses, and the corrals. The cowboys arose one by one, dropped their plates into the dishpan, and began to hunt out their ropes. Everything was obscure and mysterious in the faint grey light. I watched Windy Bill near his tarpaulin. He stooped to throw over the canvas. When he bent, it was before daylight; when he straightened his back, daylight had come. It was just like that, as though someone had reached out his hand to turn on the illumination of the world.

The eastern mountains were fragile, the plain was ethereal,

like a sea of liquid gases. From the pasture we heard the shout-
ings of the wranglers, and made out a cloud of dust. In a moment the first of the remuda came into view, trotting forward
with the free grace of the unburdened horse. Others followed
in procession: those near sharp and well defined, those in the
background more or less obscured by the dust, now appearing
plainly, now fading like ghosts. The leader turned unhesitat-
ingly into the corral. After him poured the stream of the
remuda—two hundred and fifty saddle horses—with an unceas-
ing thunder of hoofs.

Immediately the cook-camp was deserted. The cowboys
entered the corral. The horses began to circle around the edge
of the enclosure as around the circumference of a circus ring.
The men, grouped at the centre, watched keenly, looking for
the mounts they had already decided on. In no time each
had recognised his choice, and, his loop trailing, was walking
toward that part of the revolving circumference where his
pony dodged. Some few whirled the loop, but most cast it with
a quick flip. It was really marvellous to observe the accuracy
with which the noose would fly, past a dozen tossing heads,
and over a dozen backs, to settle firmly about the neck of
an animal perhaps in the very centre of the group. But again,
if the first throw failed, it was interesting to see how the selected pony would dodge, double back, twist, turn, and hide
to escape a second cast. And it was equally interesting to observe how his companions would help him. They seemed to
realise that they were not wanted, and would push themselves
between the cowboy and his intended mount with the utmost
boldness. In the thick dust that instantly arose, and with the
bewildering thunder of galloping, the flashing change of group-
ing, the rush of the charging animals, recognition alone would
seem almost impossible, yet in an incredibly short time each
had his mount, and the others, under convoy of the wranglers,
were meekly wending their way out over the plain. There, until
time for a change of horses, they would graze in a loose and
scattered band, requiring scarcely any supervision. Escape?
Bless you, no, that thought was the last in their minds.

In the meantime the saddles and bridles were adjusted. Always in a cowboy's "string" of from six to ten animals the boss assigns him two or three broncos to break in to the cow business. Therefore, each morning we could observe a half dozen or so men gingerly leading wicked looking little animals out to the sand "to take the pitch out of them." One small black, belonging to a cowboy called the Judge, used more than to fulfil expectations of a good time.

"Go to him, Judge!" someone would always remark.

"If he ain't goin' to pitch, I ain't goin' to make him," the Judge would grin, as he swung aboard.

The black would trot off quite calmly and in a most matter of fact way, as though to shame all slanderers of his lamb-like character. Then, as the bystanders would turn away, he would utter a squeal, throw down his head, and go at it. He was a very hard bucker, and made some really spectacular jumps, but the trick on which he based his claims to originality consisted in standing on his hind legs at so perilous an approach to the perpendicular that his rider would conclude he was about to fall backwards, and then suddenly springing forward in a series of stiff-legged bucks. The first manoeuvre induced the rider to loosen his seat in order to be ready to jump from under, and the second threw him before he could regain his grip.

"And they say a horse don't think!" exclaimed an admirer.

But as these were broken horses—save the mark!—the show was all over after each had had his little fling. We mounted and rode away, just as the mountain peaks to the west caught the rays of a sun we should not enjoy for a good half hour yet.

I had five horses in my string, and this morning rode "that C S horse, Brown Jug." Brown Jug was a powerful and well-built animal, about fourteen two in height, and possessed of a vast enthusiasm for cow-work. As the morning was frosty, he felt good.

At the gate of the water corral we separated into two groups. The smaller, under the direction of Jed Parker, was to drive the mesquite in the wide flats; the rest of us, under the command of Homer, the round-up captain, were to sweep the country even as far as the base of the foothills near Mount Graham. Accordingly we put our horses to the full gallop.

Mile after mile we thundered along at a brisk rate of speed. Sometimes we dodged in and out among the mesquite bushes, alternately separating and coming together again; sometimes we swept over grassy plains apparently of illimitable extent; sometimes we skipped and hopped and buck-jumped through and over little gullies, barrancas, and other sorts of malpais— but always without drawing rein. The men rode easily, with no thought to the way nor care for the footing. The air came back sharp against our faces. The warm blood stirred by the rush flowed more rapidly. We experienced a delightful glow. Of the morning cold only the very tips of our fingers and the ends of our noses retained a remnant. Already the sun was shining low and level across the plains. The shadows of the cañons modelled the hitherto flat surfaces of the mountains.

After a time we came to some low hills helmeted with the outcrop of a rock escarpment. Hitherto they had seemed a termination of Mount Graham, but now, when we rode around them, we discovered them to be separated from the range by a good five miles of sloping plain. Later we looked back and would have sworn them part of the Dos Cabesas system, did we not know them to be at least eight miles distant from that rocky rampart. It is always that way in Arizona. Spaces develop of whose existence you had not the slightest intimation. Hidden in apparently plane surfaces are valleys and prairies. At one sweep of the eye you embrace the entire area of an eastern State; but nevertheless the reality as you explore it foot by foot proves to be infinitely more than the vision has promised.

Beyond the hill we stopped. Here our party divided again, half to the right and half to the left. We had ridden, up to this time, directly away from camp, now we rode a circumference of which headquarters was the centre. The country was pleasantly rolling and covered with grass. Here and there were clumps of soapweed. Far in a remote distance lay a slender dark line across the plain. This we knew to be mesquite; and once entered, we knew it, too, would seem to spread out vastly. And then this grassy slope, on which we now rode, would show merely as an insignificant streak of yellow. It is also like that in Arizona. I have ridden in succession through grass land, brush land, flower land, desert. Each in turn seemed entirely to fill the space of the plains between the mountains.

From time to time Homer halted us and detached a man. The business of the latter was then to ride directly back to camp, driving all cattle before him. Each was in sight of his right- and left-hand neighbour. Thus was constructed a drag-net whose meshes contracted as home was neared.

I was detached, when of our party only the Cattleman and Homer remained. They would take the outside. This was the post of honour, and required the hardest riding, for as soon as the cattle should realise the fact of their pursuit, they would attempt to "break" past the end and up the valley. Brown Jug and I congratulated ourselves on an exciting morning in prospect.

Now, wild cattle know perfectly well what a drive means, and they do not intend to get into a round-up if they can help it. Were it not for the two facts, that they are afraid of a mounted man, and cannot run quite so fast as a horse, I do not know how the cattle business would be conducted. As soon as a band of them caught sight of any one of us, they curled their tails and away they went at a long, easy lope that a domestic cow would stare at in wonder. This was all very well; in fact we yelled and shrieked and otherwise uttered cow-calls to keep them going, to "get the cattle started," as they say. But pretty soon a little band of the many scurrying away before our thin line, began to bear farther and farther to the east. When in their judgment they should have gained an opening, they would turn directly back and make a dash for liberty. Accordingly the nearest cowboy clapped spurs to his horse and pursued them.

It was a pretty race. The cattle ran easily enough, with long, springy jumps that carried them over the ground faster than appearances would lead one to believe. The cow-pony, his nose stretched out, his ears slanted, his eyes snapping with joy of the chase, flew fairly "belly to earth." The rider sat slightly forward, with the cowboy's loose seat. A whirl of dust, strangely insignificant against the immensity of a desert morning, rose from the flying group. Now they disappeared in a ravine, only to scramble out again the next instant, pace undiminished. The rider merely rose slightly and threw up his elbows to relieve the jar of the rough gully. At first the cattle seemed to hold their own, but soon the horse began to gain. In a short time he had come abreast of the leading animal. The latter stopped short with a snort, dodged back, and set out at right angles to his former course. From a dead run the pony came to a stand in two fierce plunges, doubled like a shot, and was off on the other tack. An unaccustomed rider would here have lost his seat. The second dash was short. With a final shake of the head, the steers turned to the proper course in the direction of the ranch. The pony dropped unconcernedly to the shuffling jog of habitual progression.

Far away stretched the arc of our cordon. The most distant rider was a speck, and the cattle ahead of him were like maggots endowed with a smooth, swift onward motion. As yet the herd had not taken form; it was still too widely scattered. Its units, in the shape of small bunches, momently grew in numbers. The distant plains were crawling and alive with minute creatures making toward a common tiny centre.

Immediately in our front the cattle at first behaved very well. Then far down the long gentle slope I saw a break for the upper valley. The manikin that represented Homer at once became even smaller as it departed in pursuit. The Cattleman moved down to cover Homer's territory until he should return, and I in turn edged farther to the right. Then another break from another bunch. The Cattleman rode at top speed to head it. Before long he disappeared in the distant mesquite. I found myself in sole charge of a front three miles long.

The nearest cattle were some distance ahead, and trotting along at a good gait. As they had not yet discovered the chance left open by unforeseen circumstance, I descended and took in on my cinch while yet there was time. Even as I mounted, an impatient movement on the part of experienced Brown Jug told me that the cattle had seen their opportunity.

I gathered the reins and spoke to the horse. He needed no further direction, but set off at a wide angle, nicely calculated, to intercept the truants. Brown Jug was a powerful beast. The spring of his leap was as whalebone. The yellow earth began to stream past like water. Always the pace increased with a growing thunder of hoofs. It seemed that nothing could turn us from the straight line, nothing check the headlong momentum of our rush. My eyes filled with tears from the wind of our going. Saddle strings streamed behind. Brown Jug's mane whipped my bridle hand. Dimly I was conscious of soapweed, sacatone, mesquite, as we passed them. They were abreast and gone before I could think of them or how they were to be dodged. Two antelope bounded away to the left; birds rose hastily from the grasses. A sudden *chirk, chirk, chirk,* rose all about me. We were in the very centre of a prairie-dog town, but before I could formulate in my mind the probabilities of holes and broken legs, the *chirk, chirk, chirk*ing had fallen astern. Brown Jug had skipped and dodged successfully.

We were approaching the cattle. They ran stubbornly and well, evidently unwilling to be turned until the latest possible moment. A great rage at their obstinacy took possession of us both. A broad shallow wash crossed our way, but we plunged through its rocks and boulders recklessly, angered at even the slight delay they necessitated. The hard land on the other side we greeted with joy. Brown Jug extended himself with a snort.

Suddenly a jar seemed to shake my very head loose. I found myself staring over the horse's head directly down into a deep and precipitous gully, the edge of which was so cunningly concealed by the grasses as to have remained invisible to my blurred vision. Brown Jug, however, had caught sight of it at the last instant, and had executed one of the wonderful stops possible only to a cow-pony.

But already the cattle had discovered a passage above, and

were scrambling down and across. Brown Jug and I, at more sober pace, slid off the almost perpendicular bank, and out the other side.

A moment later we had headed them. They whirled, and without the necessity of any suggestion on my part Brown Jug turned after them, and so quickly that my stirrup actually brushed the ground. After that we were masters. We chased the cattle far enough to start them well in the proper direction, and then pulled down to a walk in order to get a breath of air.

But now we noticed another band, back on the ground over which we had just come, doubling through in the direction of Mount Graham. A hard run set them to rights. We turned. More had poured out from the hills. Bands were crossing everywhere, ahead and behind. Brown Jug and I set to work.

Being an indivisible unit, we could chase only one bunch at a time; and, while we were after one, a half dozen others would be taking advantage of our preoccupation. We could not hold our own. Each run after an escaping bunch had to be on a longer diagonal. Gradually we were forced back, and back, and back; but still we managed to hold the line unbroken. Never shall I forget the dash and clatter of that morning. Neither Brown Jug nor I thought for a moment of sparing horseflesh, nor of picking a route. We made the shortest line, and paid little attention to anything that stood in the way. A very fever of resistance possessed us. It was like beating against a head wind, or fighting fire, or combating in any other way any of the great forces of nature. We were quite alone. The Cattleman and Homer had vanished. To our left the men were fully occupied in marshalling the compact brown herds that had gradually massed—for these antagonists of mine were merely the outlying remnants.

I suppose Brown Jug must have run nearly twenty miles with only one check. Then we chased a cow some distance and into the dry bed of a stream, where she whirled on us savagely. By luck her horn hit only the leather of my saddle skirts, so we left her; for when a cow has sense enough to "get on the peck," there is no driving her farther. We gained nothing, and had to give ground, but we succeeded in holding a semblance of order, so that the cattle did not break and scatter far and wide. The sun had by now well risen, and was beginning to shine hot. Brown Jug still ran gamely and displayed as much interest as ever, but he was evidently tiring. We were both glad to see Homer's grey showing in the fringe of mesquite.

Together we soon succeeded in throwing the cows into the main herd. And, strangely enough, as soon as they had joined a compact band of their fellows, their wildness left them and, convoyed by outsiders, they set themselves to plodding energetically toward the home ranch.

As my horse was somewhat winded, I joined the "drag" at the rear. Here by course of natural sifting soon accumulated all the lazy, gentle, and sickly cows, and the small calves. The difficulty now was to prevent them from lagging and dropping out. To that end we indulged in a great variety of the picturesque cow-calls peculiar to the cowboy. One found an old tin can which by the aid of a few pebbles he converted into a very effective rattle.

The dust rose in clouds and eddied in the sun. We slouched easily in our saddles. The cowboys compared notes as to the brands they had seen. Our ponies shuffled along, resting, but always ready for a dash in chase of an occasional bull calf or yearling with independent ideas of its own.

Thus we passed over the country, down the long gentle slope to the "sink" of the valley, whence another long gentle slope ran to the base of the other ranges. At greater or lesser distances we caught the dust, and made out dimly the masses of the other herds collected by our companions, and by the party under Jed Parker. They went forward toward the common centre, with a slow ruminative movement, and the dust they raised went with them.

Little by little they grew plainer to us, and the home ranch, hitherto merely a brown shimmer in the distance, began to take on definition as the group of buildings, windmills, and corrals we knew. Miniature horsemen could be seen galloping forward to the open white plain where the herd would be held.

Then the mesquite enveloped us; and we knew little more, save the anxiety lest we overlook laggards in the brush, until we came out on the edge of that same white plain.

Here were more cattle, thousands of them, and billows of dust, and a great bellowing, and dim, mounted figures riding and shouting ahead of the herd. Soon they succeeded in turning the leaders back. These threw into confusion those that followed. In a few moments the cattle had stopped. A cordon of horsemen sat at equal distances holding them in.

"Pretty good haul," said the man next to me; "a good five thousand head."

N. HOWARD (JACK) THORP
and
NEIL M. CLARK

Five-Hundred-Mile Horse Race*

❪ N. HOWARD (JACK) THORP was the first person to attempt a systematic study and collection of cowboy songs and range ballads, his 1908 publication of a score of songs following Clark Stanley's haphazard gathering of 1897 and preceding John A. Lomax's extensive 1910 anthology. Thorp was himself a cowboy, cattleman, and top rider, a man who had, in Frank Dobie's words, "the perspective of both range and civilization. . . . No other range man excepting Ross Santee has put down so much everyday horse lore in such a fresh way." Characterized by Dobie as "a great story," "Five-Hundred-Mile Horse Race" is from Thorp's posthumously published reminiscences, *Pardner of the Wind*, set down in collaboration with Neil McCullough Clark.

Oh, music springs under the galloping hoofs,
    Out on the plains;
Where mile after mile drops behind with a smile,
And tomorrow seems always to tempt and beguile—
    Out on the plains.

I

COWBOYS' ENDURANCE RACES are a thing of the past now, but in their day, sponsored by different people and especially Buffalo Bill, they had a peculiar place in the West

* From *Pardner of the Wind* (Caldwell, Idaho: The Caxton Printers, Ltd., 1945).

and were a picturesque part of the life. I got the detailed story of one such race, which was run in the early eighties, from Jack Best, who was one of the contestants. He rode in this race, he told me, the year he went north with a trail herd from southern New Mexico, which was about the time when my brother and I had a ranch south of Stanton, Nebraska, on Maple Creek. The conditions of the race were as follows: it was to start at Deadwood, South Dakota, and finish at Omaha, Nebraska. No horse entered would be over fifteen hands. He must be a qualified cow horse, and carry a rider and saddle, six-gun and chaps, all to weigh not less than one hundred and ninety pounds. The nearest distance from Deadwood to Omaha was approximately five hundred and thirty miles, but the riders could choose their routes to suit themselves. Each rider was allowed a helper to drive his buckboard or hack, which went along to carry chuck, horse feed, and bedding. Creeks and rivers had to be forded as they were come to. Starting time was a Saturday morning at six o'clock, in Deadwood, and the contestants had to check in at the fair grounds at Omaha not later than midnight the following Saturday in order to qualify. The condition of the horse on arrival was supposed to count 60 per cent, the time of arrival 40 per cent. There were four purses. The first prize was one thousand dollars in cash, and Buffalo Bill in person was to hand the money to the winner.

Following is the account of the ride Jack Best made in that race, in my words but as if he were telling it, as in fact he did tell it to me.

II

A bucking horse reared high, and pitched through the crowd that had gathered to see the first stage of the big race, which was just about to start. Suddenly the bucker fell. Somebody piled on his head to prevent his scrambling to his feet and trampling the rider, who was pinned underneath. When they worked the horse off, it was found that the rider, Hank Singleton, had a broken leg. That was a hard line of luck for Hank, who was one of the ten entrants in the race. What had happened was that he had left the corral riding the young horse which bucked, and leading Once Again, the horse he meant to ride in the race. The noise of the crowd frightened the young horse, and whirling, he got the rope of the led horse under his tail, clamped down on it, became more frightened, started pitching, then lost his footing and fell.

Hank, with a broken leg, was out of the race before it began. But his sister was following on another horse, intending to lead the young saddle horse back to the corral; however, as soon as she saw that her brother was being cared for, she went to the judges and asked for a chance to take his place. They gave her permission to do so. When we started, therefore, there were nine men riders, and one girl.

I don't remember the names of all the horses that lined up at the start, but the four that went the whole way and finished were a black named Coaly, a bay named Ranger, a sorrel named Hornet, and my own little horse, Johnnie Dun. Of all ten horses in the race, Johnnie Dun was the smallest in height, standing just fourteen-two hands. He had a dark line down his back, a black mane and tail, was glass-eyed, wore a naught-size shoe, and was branded Diamond A. He had a fast walk, a good running fox trot, an easy lope, and like all of his color and kind, a lot of bottom. For a month before the race, Dunnie had been getting his exercise daily to make him hard and fit. Starting at ten miles a day, with three feeds of oats and good mountain hay, I had increased the training distance daily, and the week before the start of the event he was going thirty miles every day, and was as hard as rocks.

A good deal of fun was poked at Johnnie Dun when we lined up to start, because he was so small; the other horses were all around fifteen hands. Now my own idea was that some of them were too fat, and others too long coupled, to stand a long, hard grind. However, the gamblers thought otherwise. They were makin' books and layin' all kinds of odds, and at Deadwood, Ranger and Hornet seemed to be the general favorites. Once Again, ridden now by Singleton's sister, was also carrying a lot of money to win. But Johnnie Dun was the joke horse of the race, as far as the gamblers went, and nobody was willing to make a bet on such a long shot except one old cowhand who, a year or so previously, had ridden Dunnie up the trail from New Mexico, and had a feeling of affection for him. More because of that than any real belief that he could win, this feller placed a twenty-five-dollar bet that I would finish in the money, that is, that I'd be one of the first four. The gamblers gave him odds of four to one that number eight, which was Dunnie's number that I wore on a card on my back, wouldn't show.

Amid a lot of shouting and excitement, we received our final instructions, and got away. Three of the ten starters went off in a high lope, cutting a great swath, throwing dust and gravel as they sped down the flat. Five galloped, trotted, or fox-trotted. Dunnie was fishing at the bit and wanted to make as showy a start as anybody. But I figured that a five-hundred-mile race wasn't going to be won in the first mile, and I held him down to a flat-foot walk. The Singleton girl, whose number was nine, did the same thing with her mount, Once Again; in fact, she rode at my side, taking it easy, and we chatted and got acquainted. Her father, she said, was driving her hack; he had a pair of spotted ponies hitched to it. I told her that my brother Bill was driving our outfit, and he had a pair of long-legged mules that could walk around five miles an hour and not worry. Bill, I might as well remark here, carried a keg of water, plenty of food, a few bales of hay, and two sacks of oats; also a bucket and sponge, a bottle of rubbing alcohol, and a blanket for Dunnie in case the nights were cold or rainy. The girl asked what I thought of her horse. I had to tell her the truth, which was that I was afraid he was too soft and fat. "But if you hold him down the first few days," I said, "you might have a chance. Don't expect me to pull you out of any bogs, though!" Helping a girl was one thing, but that thousand-dollar purse at the end of the long grind was another.

"Cowboy," she said, understanding perfectly well what I was thinking, "this is a hoss race!"

At eleven o'clock, five hours after the start, she and I were still riding along together, and my original opinion about her horse was unchanged. My hack had stopped, and when I came up to it, Bill was cooking up a meal. "Good luck!" I said, and pulled off the road. The girl went on to overtake her own outfit.

I unsaddled Dunnie, fed him, had a good dinner myself, and rested. The five-hour ride hadn't been more than a good morning's exercise for either of us, but I once read about a party of men who were left afoot in a desert, with very little food, at a place where they were at least fifty miles from water. If they had lost their heads thinking about it, they might have tried to get to that moisture quick and died of exhaustion. But their leader had a watch, and he made a rule that the party should walk fifteen minutes, then rest ten, walk fifteen and rest ten, and keep it up; and by not ever lettin' any of the party tire themselves out, he got them through to water safely. My idea in this race was something like that for Dunnie. By one o'clock I was saddled and on my way again. We had covered almost twenty-five miles, and had left the town of Calcite some distance behind.

The tracks of the hacks showed that all of the riders, like ourselves, were making a beeline for the town of Interior. However, I didn't catch up with any of them that first afternoon; they seemed to smell the Omaha "moisture," and were making for it as fast and hard as they could go. My brother, with our hack, passed me with his mules at a trot, and handed me a couple of doughnuts he had brought from Deadwood. "I'll camp about six," he said. "That should bring us five miles or so beyond Box Elder Creek, and I'll have supper ready when you come." He whipped up and drove on. I held Dunnie to his slow and steady pace. About an hour after getting out of the hills, I came to Box Elder Creek, and here both Dunnie and I had a good drink. He stood in the water for a few minutes, cooling off his legs and feet. Refreshed by this short rest, we rode on several miles more and reached the camp which Bill had made in a mott of timber.

On the wheel of the buckboard, Bill had rigged up what he called a buggy-o-meter, by means of which he could figure out more or less correctly the miles we traveled. It was based on the number of revolutions of the wheel, times its circumference. After consulting this contraption and doing the necessary multiplying, Bill announced that we had covered something more than forty-eight miles so far. I was well satisfied with that. After watering Dunnie, I threw him some hay, stripped off the saddle, threw a sheet over him, then ate my own supper. I must say that Bill, without being a regular *cocinero,* could toss up some mighty fine grub over a campfire, and it sure tasted good to a feller who half the time was hungrier than a red-headed woodpecker.

After we ate, Bill and I went into a huddle. As I said, I had a general idea of how I meant to run the race, and of how I thought a man and a horse might win it. You probably gathered that my plan did not depend very much on speed in any given short distance, but I knew, from long experience with cow ponies, that a horse that was given specially good care, many times would travel a long distance faster and in better shape than a naturally better horse that was ridden harder and faster for short distances, but wasn't given equal care. My main thought, accordingly, was to keep Dunnie going, not fast or hard, but steadily, for just as much of the time as was possible without wearing him down, letting him rest frequently. That first evening, therefore, knowing that the moon would soon be up, I decided to put a few more miles behind me as soon as Dunnie finished his supper. By nine o'clock I felt good and rested, and Dunnie looked as fit as when we started, so I saddled him and pulled out. Within five miles, Bill caught up and passed me. Soon I saw a rig camped beside the road. Behind the buckboard and the spotted ponies was the Singleton girl's fat horse, Once Again. The girl and her father were apparently fast asleep, so I kept right on, and in another six miles or so, came to the camp Bill had made. He said that some other outfit was camped immediately ahead, but whose it was he didn't know. He also said that according to the buggy-o-meter we had put fifty-nine miles behind us, just about half the distance to our first goal, the town of Interior.

I offered Dunnie water, but he didn't want any. I sponged off his back, legs, and shoulders with alcohol, rubbed him dry, and threw a sheet and blanket over him, then broke out some good hay for him, fed him grain, and finally turned into my own hot-roll for a good night's sleep.

Bill called me at four. I smelled the coffee and bacon he had ready and waiting, and he told me that he had already given Dunnie a good rubbing with a flannel cloth to take out any stiffness that the first day's trip might have caused. Now as part of my equipment I was carrying two double Navajo saddle blankets. One had been used the day before, and was sweaty and liable to cause chafing. I gave that one to Bill and asked him to wash it out at the first creek he came to. The other one, which was clean, I put under the saddle. On a long ride, no horse is better than his back, and I meant to keep Dunnie's back in good shape if it was in my power to do so.

In the course of the first two miles or so that morning, I came to a camp and saw the horse, Ranger, which carried number one in the race. His rider and helper were just eating breakfast as I went by at an easy trot. About a mile further on I passed number ten, and close by, numbers two and six. I was fox-trotting along easily when the sorrel horse named Hornet (number three in the race) came out of the brush, and his rider and I rode along together for a while. This feller was long and skinny, and when he was standing on the ground he looked like a rattlesnake on stilts. Some distance on we passed number seven, then in a little while number four, who was just saddling up. Most of those horses had gone a lot faster while they were going, the day before, than Dunnie. Yet here we were, right along with them. Hornet's rider remarked that the weather was sure cool. Yes, I agreed, it sure was. He remarked that I was traveling pretty slow, wasn't I? Yes, I said, I reckon I was. He said he guessed he would try to make better time. I told him not to let me stop him. So he struck out at a high lope, and

as I watched horse and rider disappear, I thought of a saying
of my old Swiss grandmother:

> A long race,
> A slow pace.

Dunnie and I weren't going to be hurried. We continued to
keep our slow and easy gait, and one after another, all the
horses in the race, except Once Again, with the Singleton girl
aboard, caught up and passed us.

Bill and I camped for grub and rest at eleven o'clock, and it
was close to noon before Once Again finally put in an appearance, following close behind the girl's rig, and carrying his
head low. I knew by the look of him that he wasn't going to
get much farther. Father and daughter pulled up close to us.

"Light an' take a load off your saddle," I said.

Bill invited them to eat dinner with us. The girl seemed dis-
couraged as she looked after her horse, but declared she would
keep going till that night anyhow. Then if Once Again didn't
perk up, she said, she would drop out. I rode off from that
camp at about one o'clock. But before I went, the Singleton
girl had a talk with Bill and me that showed her heart was in
the right place.

"Jack," she said, "from what you've told me, you live a long
ways from here, an' don't know a whole lot about people in
these parts."

I told her I was practically born poppin' longhorns out o'
the tornial along the Rio Grande.

"Well," she said, "all the horses in this race are local horses,
except Coaly and your Johnnie Dun. Coaly is supposed to have
been sent here by a ring of gamblers, to win the race. He's a
clean thoroughbred, and his rider has a reputation for winning,
no matter how. Ranger and Hornet are carryin' most of the
Deadwood gamblers' money, but the big money has been bet
in Lincoln and Omaha on this big black horse, Coaly.

"If you don't think Coaly is fast," she went on, "you don't
know the feel of cactus when you're settin' in the middle of it.
If those other riders ever find that you fellers have any sort

of a look-in to win, they won't stop at much. At least, that's my notion. They'll try to dope or cripple your horse, if they can, or they'll put you out some other way. Keep your eyes peeled. Remember that there's probably a hundred thousand dollars at stake."

Her own horse, she admitted, was in no condition to compete. "I'll probably drop out; but I wish you boys luck. That's why I'm warnin' you to be on the lookout. Take care of yourself, and your horse."

Bill and I felt grateful, and said so.

"That's all right," she replied. "I may hop the train and see you in Omaha. *Adios.*"

I climbed aboard Dunnie and rode off, and never saw her again.

III

The next few days were a steady grind of riding, resting, eating, riding, resting, eating, with a few highlights and incidents along the way. Nearly every night we made our last camp ahead of the others, or got an earlier start next day, and nearly every morning the others passed me, one by one, until Dunnie and I were again at the tail of the procession. On Monday morning, for example, I left camp at five o'clock, and in the next two hours passed seven of the outfits camped along the road. I was just thinking that another horse must be ahead or dropped out, when suddenly I passed Coaly's camp as the rider and his helper were having breakfast.

"Come and have coffee," they called.

I shook my head and thanked them, saying I had eaten, and kept right on. Shortly after crossing Pass Creek, the brown horse, number seven, galloped by under a full head of steam. His rider waved. "I'll order supper for you in Omaha!" he shouted.

I felt like saying, "Brother, you'll never get to Omaha on *that horse!*"—but I didn't. And as a matter of fact, neither did he—get to Omaha, I mean.

They all passed me, horses and rigs both. As Bill went by, he called, "I'm goin' to stop at nine today, Jack, an' we'll have some coffee and rest a while." That was our regular routine—ride, rest, ride. And whenever we were making one of those rests, even a short one, I would sponge Dunnie's head, wash out his nostrils, take off the saddle, give him an alcohol rub, and let him munch some hay. In half an hour we would be going again, refreshed like a prize fighter after the rest between rounds. I gave the horse every attention I could think of that would keep him fit, and anybody with eyes could see that under that kind of treatment he was standing up well; but I was thinking a lot, and very seriously, about that thoroughbred, Coaly, and about what the Singleton girl had said about the money that was down on him, and about those other horses, Ranger and Hornet, both of which were built bigger and stronger than Dunnie. I figured that the load of money on these three would not have been wagered unless it was supposed that one of them was almost sure to win. However, neither Bill nor I ever had any notion of quitting. We were raised with horses, and we felt that if any of the other riders thought they could run any rani-cum-boogerie on us, they were welcome to try. It was real competition that we were up against. Dad, who had been a horseman all his life, used to say, when he matched one of his horses in a race, "I may not win myself, but I'll sure make the other feller think he has been to a hoss race."

We passed Norris on Black Pine Creek in the middle of Monday morning, and got to White River at about eleven o'clock. All the other riders were bunched up there, afraid of the water, but Bill never even stopped; he drove right in, hollering to me to keep on the lower side of the team. Twice we struck swimming water, but it didn't cause us any trouble, in fact, Dunnie seemed to enjoy the swim and the look and feel of the clear water. We went into camp on the far side, and soon all the other riders came across. I laid up here till one-thirty, and when I pulled out, some of the other riders trailed along with me. Soon, however, my speed proved too slow for their liking, and they galloped on ahead. Bill and I camped at six on the other side of Mission, about a hundred and seventy-five miles from Deadwood, laid up till eleven, then rode for another hour, camping at midnight at Rock Creek, where we found seven other outfits camped. This was the only night when so many of us were together. The missing outfits, I discovered, were numbers seven and nine, one being the Singleton girl on Once Again, and the other the rider who had promised when he passed me, to order supper for me in Omaha. There was one other casualty. Number ten, who was camped next to us, said his horse had been sick half the night with colic, and he would have to drop out and turn back. That left only seven of us.

Next day Bill and I had a piece of luck, the only important bit of luck that came our way from first to last in all the five hundred miles of the race. I left at five o'clock, just as most of the others were lighting their campfires; and eight o'clock saw me crossing the Keyapaha River. Bill caught up and passed me there. Nine miles further on he was waiting for me; none of the other riders had caught up yet.

"We're campin' here till they pass," he said.

He had news.

One by one the riders went by us, and when the last one was out of sight, we went too—but by a different road. The news Bill had picked up was that for many miles the straight road ahead was a quagmire. He and I turned to the left, paralleling the muddy stretch on higher ground. Our way was a few miles farther, but the going was fine, and when we hit the Niobrara that evening at the town of Riverview, and got Nebraska instead of Dakota under our feet, we learned that we were ahead of everybody. And by eleven that night when we set out again and put ten more miles behind us, none of the other riders had yet appeared. In fact, it was not till nine o'clock next morning that I saw any of them. At that time Hornet and Ranger caught up with me. The two horses were coated with dried mud up to their knees, and looked drawn and tired, and the riders told me they had pulled through twenty miles of heavy bog mud the day before, and that all the hacks but one got stuck. They said there was another horse right behind, but they didn't know which one it was, and two more of the riders had dropped out.

Tired though Hornet and Ranger were after that hard mud, their riders could not long bear to crawl along at the slow and steady pace which I made Dunnie take. They galloped on ahead. But when I reached Bill's camp at eleven o'clock, there they were, waiting for their own hack (they were both using the same one now), and smelling Bill's coffee with hungry looks. They ate with us, and before we were through, their hack came along.

Following my usual routine, I pulled out again at one-thirty, walking Dunnie for an hour, then fox-trotting him for another hour. We camped again at six. About nine, three riders and two hacks passed—the horses were Ranger, Coaly, and Hornet. They all camped near us, but Bill and I pulled out again at eleven, and as I was passing, Hornet's rider told me that another horse had now dropped out and there were only four of us left in the race. Covering another ten miles in the dark before turning in for the long sleep, we found we were about three hundred and ten miles on our journey, and we had Thursday, Friday, and Saturday yet to go. Those next two hundred miles, we knew, would furnish the real test. Coaly already looked awful; Ranger and Hornet seemed to be dead tired. Dunnie, thanks to the care I constantly gave him, looked fine. But he probably wasn't as much of a horse, I knew, as the others were. The race, I told myself, was still far from over.

The others overtook me the next day at about nine o'clock, as usual, and I let them go ahead.

"Don't hurry," Bill said, grinning like a mountain cat over a fresh-killed deer, "we've got 'em licked."

But no rooster ever ought to crow till his chickens are hatched. It was eleven o'clock when I next caught up with Bill; and I didn't find him at the side of the road with a fire built, and coffee on to boil, and beans in the pan, and biscuits comin' up.

> Bacon in the pan,
> Coffee in the pot;

> Get up an' get it—
> Get it while it's hot.

No, his hack was standing in the middle of the road, tip-tilted like a stovepipe hat on a drunk's head. He had hit a boulder and knocked every spoke out of the right hind wheel.

"So we've got 'em licked, have we!" says I, lighting to inspect the damage. Without Bill and the hack to take care of all the little chores and leave me free to care for Dunnie, I knew I wouldn't stand any chance at all of taking the race. "*Now* what are we goin' to do?"

"*We* aren't goin' to do a thing," said Bill, who was peeled down to his undershirt and sweatin' with an ax. "You fork your horse an' hit the road. I'll have this fixed an' beat you in to O'Neill yet."

I never thought he could do it, but he sure did. He cut a long pole and tied it on top of the front axle and under the rear one, with the end of the pole dragging along behind. The hack sagged a little on the pole corner, but it stayed up, and when Bill waved his whip and spoke kind words to those long-legged mules of his, riding on three wheels and a bob-sled, he split the breeze about as fast as on four wheels. When I got to O'Neill I found him strutting around like a turkey gobbler in a hen pen, admiring the hack, which now had four good wheels and looked the same as ever. Bill had rustled an old wheel from somebody's buggy shop, and though it had taken our last cent of cash money to buy it, once more we had hopes of shaking the hand of Buffalo Bill and sharing the promised purse. O'Neill was called three hundred and forty miles from Deadwood.

I left there at one o'clock, riding along the Elkhorn River. Bill passed me, but none of the other riders or hacks came in sight. At six-thirty I rode into the camp Bill had made, and smelled something that made my stomach get right up and wave its hat. As a special celebration, Bill had borrowed a chicken and fried it for our supper. I took good care of my half of the fowl, as well as Dunnie, giving the little horse an alcohol rub and bandaging his legs with wet cloths. We went on again after eleven for about an hour and a half, the buggy-o-meter tallying three hundred and eighty miles when we stopped for the night. One hundred and fifty miles still to go, and two days to make it in!

Next day none of the riders appeared until Bill and I were nooning. Then all three came by together, trailing behind their two hacks, and when they saw us, they camped a little beyond. Their horses, with heads hanging, looked gaunt and tired. Presently the three riders strolled over to where we were.

"Keep your eyeballs oiled," said Bill, when he saw them coming. But a cowhand foaled in Texas and busted out in New Mexico didn't need that warning.

It was easy to see that the three had some serious business on their minds. I hunkered down near Dunnie, just in case their intentions had any reference to him. But as it turned out, they were mostly interested in mathematics and long division. They started edging into the subject by pointing out what all of us knew by heart, namely, that there were four prizes offered for this race—$1,000, $500, $300, and $200—making a grand total of $2,000.

"Cut the deck deeper, fellers," said Bill, "Jack and I don't *sabe.*"

"Only four of us," Hornet's rider pointed out, "are left, and it's still anybody's race." He then went on to say that $2,000 could be cut four ways, making four even piles of $500 each. "Why not make a pool of it," he said, "we can let the horses take it easier. We'll cut cards to see who comes in first, but whatever the cards say, we'll split the money four ways even. That's the way she lays with us. How about you two?"

A certain kind of smell always means a skunk. This Hornet feller had been friendly enough to me, even if he was so skinny that a man would need an extra batch of luck to hit him with a handful of gravel, but his talk wasn't the kind I liked to trouble my ears with. I'm no professor with a deck of cards, but I have met people who can make them act real educated. It passed through my mind that tens of thousands of dollars had been bet on each of the other three horses left in the race, and only twenty-five dollars on Dunnie; and it seemed as plain as plowed ground that if we did cut cards with those three, there was one rider present who would not cut the high card, and the name of his horse was Johnnie Dun. I shook my head, and Bill, backing me up, said "No!"

"It's still a hoss race, fur's I'm concerned," I said.

"Reckon I know how you feel," said Hornet's rider smoothly. "That prize money is warm in your pocket already, ain't it? But," rising to his feet, "you know there's never any certainty in a hoss race—*is* there?"

That was the end of the parley. "We'll have to watch those *hombres* like hawks," said Bill when we were alone again. "If I ever heard a plain warnin', that's it."

"An' we're only two against five."

"They may not try to pull anything; and again, they may. We won't camp near them again. And nobody hangs around our camp any time, day or night. Whenever you use the water bucket, Jack, put it away in a gunnysack an' tie the end good— don't give 'em any possible chance to dope Dunnie."

Now it was that same afternoon as I was passing through the town of Neleigh, that a crowd cheered me. One fellow came running out and thrust a bottle of whiskey into my hand. "Go it, old Diamond-A!" he yelled, adding that he used to work for that outfit down in Deming, New Mexico. About five miles farther on I caught up with Bill and offered him a jolt of the rye, and I sure didn't have to twist his arm to make him take it. We ate supper, and I hit the hay, Bill keeping one eye wide open. At nine-thirty he called me. We went eight miles farther, passing Warnersville before we made our last night camp. About midnight the hacks of our rivals pulled up and passed, and presently the three riders trailed along too. We saw them apparently make camp at a little distance, but we did not call attention to ourselves in any way. I think Bill slept with one eye open all night, expecting somebody to creep up out of the dark and try something on Dunnie. I turned in and told him to call me at four.

Well, we were expecting a surprise from those other riders, but not the surprise we got.

Dunnie and I at this point had only seventy miles to go to the fair grounds at Omaha, and we had until twelve o'clock midnight to do it—just twenty-four hours. Easy? After the grind we had been through? Don't you think it!

IV

I was up and ready to go at four-thirty next morning. It was still only half light, and I saw no signs of activity in the camp of the other riders. Since it was the last big day, I tied a bright new silk handkerchief around my neck, and pulled out aboard Dunnie all dressed up for the home stretch. The little horse still looked good. Nothing had happened to us so far; maybe nothing would. As Hornet's rider had said, the prize money was already hot in my pocket. And then I passed the camp of the other riders.

It wasn't a camp any more. In fact, it was as quiet as a hoss-thief after a hanging—not because the other riders weren't awake yet, but because they had gone. In the dark of the night they had stolen a march on us. At what time they had left, neither Bill nor I had any idea. But gone they were, and by now they might be ten, twenty, or even twenty-five miles ahead. Bill saw the possibilities at a glance; and with his mules at a keen trot left me behind.

"Keep your eyes open," he hollered. "I might leave a message for you at the station in Nickerson."

I figured my chances as I rode. If those riders had traveled all night, as seemed likely, even if their horses couldn't strike a lope and hold it, I realized that maybe just by walking they could make it to the fair grounds ahead of me. I had a powerful itch to make Dunnie lay out his legs and run. Though he was tired, I knew he still had a lot up his sleeve. But I decided against changing my style of riding, even if I was to lose the race for it. I walked the little horse for an hour, then fox-trotted him for an hour, then walked him, and kept it up, like the party in the desert walking fifteen minutes and resting ten.

Two farmers came out of a cross lane. "Here comes another cowboy from the Black Hills," they yelled, wavin' their hats. "Go it, sonny!"

A little later I met a team and a buggy coming towards me, and I hailed the driver. "Seen anything of three men on horseback," I asked, "an' a couple o' hacks?"

Yes, he said with a grin, he had seen 'em.

"How far ahead?"

"About ten miles."

"How are they makin' it?"

"A slow walk, an' about played out."

"*Bueno!*" I went on feeling a little better.

I caught up with Bill about thirty miles from the last night's camp. It was then ten-thirty in the morning. He had met a fellow who told him that the other riders were now only about four miles ahead and going very slowly. It was hard to sit down for two hours and a half in the face of those facts, and just do nothing but rest, knowing that every minute carried them yards closer to the winning line and the big prize; but that's what we did, for I knew what the rest would do for Dunnie. He had lost some flesh during the long grind, but he still didn't look drawn or gaunt. When I left that camping place, at one o'clock, I had forty-odd miles to go, and eleven hours to make it in.

Bill and I passed through Nickerson together at about four. He then went on ahead, and when I caught up with him at six, he had a good supper cooked. He had passed the other outfits, he said, and they had passed him in turn while he was fixing supper. He said they looked about all in, and were urging their dead-tired horses for all they were worth.

This was our last camp. I fed Dunnie once more, and gave him a final rubdown with the last few drops of alcohol. But we were up and off at seven. Bill hit a six-mile gait and I stayed alongside till we came to the last hack. Right ahead of it we saw the other one. It was then nine-thirty, with thirteen miles to go. At ten we overtook the three riders and a dozen or so of Buffalo Bill's cowboys who had come out to escort us in.

"Let's pull around 'em!" said Bill.

We did so. The cowboys from the show gave a rousing cheer as Dunnie and I tore out on the last stretch. "Tore" isn't just the word. We were making two miles to the others' one, but neither Bill nor I knew how much reserve power those other horses might have. They might not be nearly as tired as they looked. We had been assured that the big black was a thoroughbred, and though he certainly seemed to be dead on his feet, I knew you never could tell just how much last-minute power a really good horse might have. There was no question as to Dunnie's being in the best condition of any of the horses, but if I let this Coaly horse get too close, could he in a last-quarter drive beat me? Blood, I knew, will tell. In consequence, I decided to go at a saddle gait and put just as much distance as possible between us.

Three of the cowboys from the show rode along with Bill and me. At eleven-fifteen they sent word to the fair grounds that we would soon be in, as we had only three more miles to go. Just about then, Bill yelled at me:

"Here they come, Jack. Look out!"

I took a quick look over my shoulder. We were now inside the city limits. Although it was late, the town was lighted up and was almost as bright as day. The sidewalks were lined with people, and the crowds got denser, the yells louder, the nearer we came to the finish line. In my quick look back I saw the thoroughbred, Coaly, come pounding up from behind. He passed me and took the lead.

"Don't race him!" Bill yelled excitedly. "Push him at a good gallop, but keep just behind. He'll come back to you in a mile."

And pretty soon one of the cowboys said, "There's only a mile more to go, buddy."

Away we hammered. People shouted, and waved hats and handkerchiefs. Dunnie, being the smaller horse, got more 'n his share of the cheering—"Come on, you little buckskin!" But Coaly, though he looked to be gutted, was a wonder and got plenty of the yells too—"Come on, you black!" Once when the big horse stumbled, I thought sure he would fall. But with a thoroughbred's great grit, he recovered himself and kept on. Hornet and Ranger were left blocks behind. Bill threw the leather into his galloping mules and kept pace with me.

Inch by inch, Dunnie edged up on the big black. Now we were abreast of him. I could see that he was really dead on his feet. But he was trained to be a race horse, and a race horse he was to the last, even when he was running on nothing but breeding and nerve. A great horse—greater than Johnnie Dun— but not as well taken care of during the long week of that race. I gave Dunnie the spurs in earnest for almost the first time in five hundred miles, and with a spurt of speed that the black simply couldn't match, we shot ahead and through the fair- ground gate, breaking the string that was stretched between the posts, two good lengths in the lead. That was all. Just two lengths in a five-hundred-mile race.

A wild, screaming mob pulled me out of the saddle and carried me to the judges' stand, right up to say "Howdy!" to Buffalo Bill himself—and to this day I don't know what he said to me, but the check he handed me said one thousand dollars!

FRANK S. HASTINGS

···➤──➤◉◄◉──◄···

Old Gran'pa*

¶ FRANK S. HASTINGS, manager of the S.M.S. Ranch at Stamford, Texas, wrote a series of autobiographical sketches which appeared in the *Breeder's Gazette* (Chicago) during 1920 and were issued by that magazine in book form in 1921, with the title *A Ranchman's Recollections*. Hastings added to his extensive familiarity with life on the range a knowledge of the cattle industry on through meat packing and refrigeration. "Old Gran'pa," though, is a classic horse story; Frank Dobie calls it "the most pulling cowhorse story I know."

THE COOL NIGHT AIR was stirring caressingly, and we were both under the spell of it all. The mares had steadied down to normal. We were crossing a prairie near Rice Springs, once a famous roundup ground in the open range days. Mage raised his six-feet-five up in the buggy, looked all around, and, as he sat down, said: "This here's the place; here's where me an' Old Gran'pa won our first ditty."

The moon had risen high enough to flood a great flat until we could see a mile or more. I saw just a beautiful expanse of curly mesquite grass, blending its vivid green with the soft silver moonlight, but Mage saw great crowds lined on either side of a straight half-mile track; two riders; the one on a mid-

* From *A Ranchman's Recollections* (Chicago: *Breeder's Gazette*, 1921).

279

night black and the other on a speed-mad sorrel, in deadly contest for supremacy. The stillness of the night—which to me was the calm benediction of peace and rest—was broken for him by wild cheers as a boy and a sorrel horse crossed the line, victors. His face was tense, his eyes shone with the fire of strain and excitement, and then slowly he came back to the stillness and to the moonlight, and to me.

I waited a minute, and asked, "What was it, Mage?" He did not answer until we had crossed the flat. Then, with a little short laugh, peculiar to him before telling a story, he began: "As fur as thet's consarn it wus this away—"

But here let me tell some true things I knew about Old Gran'pa. He was a famous cow pony, originally known as Sorrel Stud. Mage broke him as a three-year-old, and had ridden him some eighteen years. The last few years of that time Stud had come to be known as Old Gran'pa. He was still alive, but had been turned out under good keep, winter and summer, to end his days in peace. He was very fast, and was considered among the top cutting horses of his time. Mage's worship of this horse is only typical of every cowboy's love for his pet horse. But to his story:

"It wus this away: We hed fenced some, but allus hed lots o' strays on the open range, an' Shorty Owen [who, by the way, stood 6 feet and 6 inches], tole me early in the spring he would send me out to gather strays when the big roundups begin, an' 'lowed I best be gettin' my plunder rounded up. That wus 'fore you cum, but you know he wus the S. M. S. range boss, an' mighty nigh raised me. He tuk to me the day I hit the ranch. 'Kid,' he says, 'you ain't never hed no chanct an' I'm agoin' to giv you one.'

"Shorty taught me to ride—hobbled my feet unter a three-year-ole steer onct, an' turned him a-loose. We hed it roun' an roun' with the hole outfit hollerin', 'Stay with 'im, Kid!' I stayed all right, but when he pitched into a bunch o' mesquites I sure would 'a' left 'im if these here preachers is right 'bout 'free moral agency,' but them hobbles helt me back, and I stayed

fer the benediction. Since thet time I never hev seed a hoss I
wus scart to climb on.

"Shorty cut Sorrel Stud out to me when he wus a bronc, an'
said, 'Break him right, Kid; I think you got a cow hoss if he
ain't spoilt in the breakin'.' An' I done it without ever hittin'
him a lick. As fur as thet's consarn, I never did hit him but
onct, an' thet wus the time him an' me both failed, only Shorty
said we didn't fail; we jes' went to the las' ditch. But thet's
another story.

"I wisht you could a-seed Sorrel Stud in his prime. He wus
a hoss! I thought 'bout it today when you hed yore arms
round his neck an' a-talkin' to him 'bout me, an' I wondered if
any body 'cept me could understan' that Sorrel Stud and Ole
Gran'pa wus the same hoss. But when I got up an' thumbed
him, an' made him pitch me off jest to show you what a twenty-
year-ole hoss could do, did you see the fire come into them
eyes, an' them ears lay back? Hones' to God, Frank, he wus a
hoss!

"I know I wus jest a tough kid when I come, but a-tween
Shorty Owen an' maybe a little doin' right fer right's sake I
tried to live an hones' life. But they's two things me and St.
Peter may hev to chew 'bout a little at the gate. You know
what a fool I am 'bout tomatoes? Well, onct I stole a dozen
cans from the chuck wagon and hid 'em out in the cedar
brakes. But the boys at the wagon hed me so plum scart 'bout
Injuns thet I never did git to them tomatoes. Well, Ole Gran'pa
is jest as plum a fool 'bout oats as I be 'bout tomatoes. I'll
admit I stole this here outfit's oats fer him ten years, till the
High Boss wus out onct from New York and seed Ole Gran'pa
go to a fire. Of course I wus up, an' he sed he guessed he could
pay fer Gran'pa's oats the rest o' his days. Joe wus mighty
perticular 'bout company oats. We hed to haul 'em 60 miles,
but I think he slipped a mess to White Pet onct in a while
hisself. I used to wait 'til the boys hed hit their hot rolls, then
I'd slip out to the barn, get my big John B. full o' oats, steal
to the corner o' the hoss pasture, an' Ole Gran'pa wus allus

waitin' fur me an' he'd never leave a stray oat to give us away.
"They called me 'the S. M. S. Kid.' I wus 'bout sixteen. I
could ride some an' I allus hed a little money back from my
wages. So when Shorty Owen tole me I wus agoin' I used thet
an' all I made up to goin' time fer an outfit. I hed a good
season saddle, a Gallup; but I bought a bridle with plenty o'
do-dads on it. Then you know my Injun likin' fer color: I
bought a yaller swet blanket, an' a top red Navajo blanket fer
Gran'pa. He kinda leaned to color too. I set up all night with
Swartz an' made him finish a pair o' top stitched boots, an' I
hed enuff left fer new duckin' pants, red flannel shirt, an' a
plaid fer change, shop-made bit and spurs, both inlaid, a
yaller silk handkerchief, a new hot roll, an' a twelve-dollar
beaver John B. Then Shorty Owen cut out my mount. In course
I hed Sorrel Stud; he wus six years old, right in his prime, an'
I kep' him shinin'. Then there war nine more, all good ones—
Blutcher, Alma, Polecat, Tatterslip, Bead Eye, Louscage, Possum, Silver Dollar, an' Badger, three of 'em from Shorty's own
mount.

" 'Kid,' says Shorty, 'you got as good as the best o' 'em. I
wants fer you to mind thet on this here work you're representin'
this here outfit. Keep yore head, an' come back with it up.
But I'd bet my life on you, an' this here outfit is trailin' you
to the las' ditch.' "

Mage's voice was getting low here, and he swallowed on
the last words, paused for a moment, then with that laugh
of his continued: "Well, I'm stringin' 'em out a mile here,
when I ought to have 'em bunched. Thet wus a great summer.
I worked in the big outfit with men an' hosses thet knowed
how to turn a cow, an' the captain o' the roundup got to
puttin' me an' Stud into the thick o' it purty reg'ler. It allus
seemed thet when I rode Stud, Split Miller rode a little hoss
called Midnight, an' he sure wus a hoss; black as midnight,
'cept fer a white star in the forehead, short-coupled an' quicker
then forked lightnin'. He would cut with the bridle off, and
fast? He was a cyclone. Every night 'roun' the camp fire Split
kep' pickin' a load in to me 'bout the Stud. Onct it wus, 'Well,

Kid, I seed you hed the little scrub out watchin' Midnight work.' Or, 'Say, Kid, I believe if you hed somethin' to ride you'd be a hand.' I swelled up some, but I 'membered what Shorty Owen sed, 'Keep yore head an' come back with it up.' An' Split wusn't mean. He jest luved to josh. Two or three times the captain said, 'Split, let the Kid alone.' But he'd shoot one at me as he rode by in the work, and wus allus badgerin' me fer a race.

"Then I kinda fell into watchin' Midnight run somethin'; an' I'd start Stud in the same direction to pace him. An' I cum alive; the Stud was full as fast. I jest naturally supposed thet Midnight could beat anything, but I kep' a-tryin' an' my eyes kep' a-openin'. One night Split got mighty raw, an' finally says, 'Kid, I'll jest give you twenty dollars to run a half-mile race, standin' start, saddle agin saddle.' An' then I fergot Shorty's instructions an' los' my head.

" 'Split,' I ses, 'you been pickin' on me ever sinct I cum to this here work. Me an' Stud don't need no twenty dollars to run you. An even break's good enuff fer us, saddle fer saddle, bridle fer bridle, blanket fer blanket, spur fer spur.'

" 'Good enuff, Kid,' ses Split, 'got enything else—eny money?'

" 'No,' I ses, 'I ain't got no money, but I got sum damned good rags an' a new hot roll.'

"Then the captain o' the roundup tuk a hand. But my blood was up, an' they put cash allowance on all my plunder an' I bet it 'gainst money. They give me $12 fer my Swartz boots, $8 fer my John B., $5 fer my cordaroy coat, $4 fer my shirts, an' $2 fer my duckin's. It war Wednesday, an' the race wus to be pulled off Saturday evenin', straight half-mile, standin' start at the pop o' a gun. The captain tuk the thing in charge an' sed he'd lick eny damned puncher thet tried to run a sandy on the Kid. It was all settled, but by the time I hed crawled into my hot roll thet night I 'membered the talk Shorty Owen give me. Stud wus kinda mine, but he war a company hoss, arter all, to work on an' not fer racin', an' I sure wus in a jackpot fer losin' my head. Well, the nex' day I tuk Stud off to practice fer a standin' start. You know how I say

'Now!' when I'm workin' on a hoss and jest as I want him to do somethin'. Well, Stud he'd been trained thet a-way, with jest a little touch o' the spur, an' I figured to say 'Now!' as the gun popped an' touch him thet a-way, an' he got the idee.

"Thet night I tuk him to the track an' put him over it four or five times. An' onct when we wus restin' a-tween heats I says to him, 'Stud, if me an' you loses this here race looks like we'd hev to steal off home in the night an' both o' us mighty nigh naked.' Everybody knocked off work Saturday. You know how even in them days word gits 'bout by the grapevine. Well, by noon they wus ridin' and drivin' in from all directions. The wimin folks brought pies and cakes. The cusey cooked up two sacks o' flour an' we hed to kill two beeves. Everybody et at the chuck wagon an' it wus sum picnic. I tol' the fellers not to bet on me an' Stud, but they wus plenty o' money on both sides. An' a girl with black eyes an' hair an' jest as purty as a bran' new red wagon, ses, 'Kid, if you win I'm agoin' to knit you sum hot roll socks.' An' Ole Pop Sellers ses, 'Better look at them feet an' begin figurin' on yarn, 'cause the Kid's agoin' to win.' But Split hed a girl, too, an' she up an' ses, 'If the Kid's dependin' on them there socks to keep warm he's mighty apt to git frost-bit this winter.' Well, you know the josh thet goes 'round when a big bunch o' cow people git together. An' they wus a plenty, until I wus plumb flustrated. When the time cum, a starter on a good hoss wus to see thet we got off fair an' then ride with us as sort o' pace-maker an' try an' see the finish. But his hoss wusn't in Midnight's an' Stud's class.

"Split hed seemed to figure thet Midnight didn't need no trainin', he hed run so meny races an' never been beat. So all Split did wus saddle Midnight and stan' 'round an' josh. But me an' Stud was addled, an' I warmed him up a bit, talkin' to him all the time. I wus worited 'bout urgin' him in a tight place. I hed played with my spurs on him, but he never hed been spurred in his life 'cept a signal touch to turn or jump. I allus carried a quirt on the horn o' my saddle, but 'cept to tap him in a frenly way or in work he hed never knowed its use. What wus I a-goin' to do in a pinch? I knowed he would use his

limit under my word, but what if he didn't? Did I hev to hit
him? If I owned this here ranch I'd hev give it all to be out
o' the race an' not look like a quitter. Well, the time wus cum.
Stud hed been frettin' an' I wus stewin', but when we toed
the line sumthin' funny happened: We both seemed to settle
down an' wus as cam as this here night. I jest hed time to give
him one pat an' say, 'God A'mighty, Stud, I'm glad I got you,'
when the starter hollered, 'Git ready!' An' the gun popped! I
yelled, 'Now!' at the same time, an' we wus off.

"Midnight wus a mite the quickest, but Stud caught his
neck in the third jump an' I helt him there. I wanted Midnight
to lead, but kep' pushin' him. We didn't change a yard in the
fust quarter an' Split yelled, 'Kid, yer holdin' out well, but
I got to tell you farewell.' An' he hit Midnight a crack with
his quirt. Stud heard it singin' through the air an' jumped like
he wus hit hisself. In thirty yards we wus nose an' nose; ten
more, a nose ahead. Then I knowed we hed to go fer it. I wus
ridin' high over his neck, spurs ready, my quirt helt high, an'
I kep' talkin' to him an' saying, 'Good boy, Stud!' The crowd
wus a-yellin' like demons. We wus in the last eighth, nose an'
nose, an' I let out one o' them Injun yells an', 'Now, Stud! Now!'

"It seemed like he'd been waitin' fer it. I could feel his heart
beatin' faster. There wus a quiver wint through him like a
man nervin' hisself fer some big shock. An' I could see him
gainin'—slow, but gainin'. The crowd hed stoppt yellin'. It
cum sudden. They wus so still you could hear 'em breathe.
I guess we must a-bin three feet ahead, with a hundred yards
to go. Split was a-cussin' an' spurrin', an' whippin'. I didn't hev
no mind to yell in all thet stillness, I wus ready to spur, ready
to whip, an' my heart wus a-bleedin'. I don't think now thet
I could a-done it to win, an' I jest whispered, 'Now, Stud!
Now! Now!'

"I thought he wus a-runnin' a-fore, but he shot out like a
cry o' joy when a los' child is foun'; an' we crossed the line a
length an' a half ahead. I seed the black-eyed girl with her
arms 'round Pop Sellers' neck an' a-jumpin' up an' down. Pop
wus jumpin' too, like a yearlin', an' the crowd wus doin' an

Injun dance generally. Stud didn't seem to sense the race wus over, an' wus still hittin' the breeze. I checked him in slow, pattin' him on the neck, an' talkin' to him like a crazy man, 'til he stood still, all a-quiver, his nostrils red as fire an' eyes still blazin'. Then I clum down an' throwed my arms 'roun' his neck and ses, 'God A'mighty, Stud, I didn't hev to hit you.' Stud's eyes seemed to softin' an' he laid his head down over my shoulder. I wus cryin' like a baby, huggin' him hard. The boys wus ridin' to us an' Stud raised his head an' whinnied. I guess it wus jest the other hosses comin', but I thought he sed, 'Didn't we raise hell with 'em?' An' I ses, 'You bet we did, Stud, but it wus you done it.'

"News travels fast, an' long 'fore I got in with my strays they knowed all 'bout it at headquarters. I kep' thinkin' 'bout what Shorty sed, 'Come back with yore head up,' but I hed mine down when he met me at the corral. I knowed we hadn't no hosses to race fer money. He looked kinda hard at my extra saddled hoss an' roll o' plunder and ses, 'Kid, this ain't no racin' stable. There here is a cow outfit, an' our best hosses is fer cuttin', not racin'.' I didn't say a word, jest unsaddled an' started fer the dog-house, when I herd him cumin'. He caught up with me, grabbed me by both shoulders an' turned me 'roun'. I saw a great big tear stealin' down his cheek, an' he ses, 'God A'mighty, Kid, I wisht you wus my boy.' Then he turned away quick an' wus gone, while I set down on the groun' an' blubbered in my ole fool way thet I hev never got over. When pay day cum Shorty handed me my wage check, which had growed sum, an' sed, 'Kid, when a boy does a man's work he gits a man's pay. You begin doin' a man's work when you went to gather them strays, an' you cum back the same way.'

"Then he started to go on, but turned and sed, 'Say, Kid, if I owned this here S. M. S. Ranch, hosses an' cattle, I'd a-give the whole damned outfit to a-seed you an' Stud cum over thet line.'"

ROSS SANTEE

···→··—➡➤●◄➡—·◆··

The Rough String*

❡ ROSS SANTEE is an artist as well as a writer and his
books are valued from the double points of view of both
picture and text, a distinction he holds in common with
three other contributors to this Reader: Charlie Russell,
Frederic Remington and Tom Lea. Dobie pays him this
tribute: "Passages in 'Cowboy' combine reality and ele-
mental melody in a way that almost no other range writer
excepting Charles M. Russell has achieved."

I LIKE 'EM," said the Pecos Kid, "for an outlaw horse is usually
gamer than a gentle one. I've rode the rough string an'
been a-snappin' broncs since I was old enough to make a hand.
An' a outlaw has always interested me a heap more than a
gentle horse. For when you find an outlaw horse that's really
game he's just about the gamest thing I know."

Every cow outfit of any size has its rough string. And to me
the horses that make up the rough string and the peeler who
rides them are one of the most interesting things about a cow
outfit. For the rough string is made up of broncs and old outlaw
horses that the average cow-puncher can't ride. The peeler
who rides them usually draws a few dollars a month more than
a regular puncher. Often for the trifling sum of ten dollars

* From *Men and Horses* by Ross Santee. Copyright, 1926, Ross Santee. Reprinted by permission of the publishers Appleton-Century-Crofts, Inc.

extra he rides these wild devils and does the work of a regular
hand. It is more of a matter of pride than anything else with
a peeler. The Pecos Kid rode the rough string at the Bar F Bar
for years without any extra pay. For the wilder they came the
more they interested Pecos. The best riders always draw the
worst horses. And I never saw the Pecos Kid on a gentle horse
in my life.

"Mebbe I've given the horse the worst of it," said Pecos.
"But horses is a heap like humans anyway. For every one of
them is different. But whenever you see an outlaw horse, nine
cases out of ten you can trace it back to the ignorance or
cruelty of some cow-puncher.

.   .   .   .

"About the gamest horse I ever rode was one they gave me
at the Diamond D's. An' he was about the sorriest one for
looks I ever saw. I was just a button at the time, an' when I
rode in there one night an' hit 'em for a job a-peelin' broncs
the boss just laughed at me. It made me sore as hell. An' I
told him if he didn't think that I could ride, to trot one of his
rough ones out. An' if I couldn't ride him I'd go on down the
road that night. That sort of interested him, an' he told me to
come on inside an' eat, an' if I thought I could handle the
rough string he'd stake me to a job.

"Next morning they led old Sontag out. I had some trouble
a-gettin' my wood on him. For he was the outfightin'est horse
I've ever seen. He tried to use his teeth an' strike with those
front feet of his. But I finally got his foot tied up an' got
my tree laced on.

"When they turned him loose he broke into an' went sky-
high with me. I think he was the hardest buckin' horse I ever
rode. He had me pullin' leather on the second jump. But by
pullin' everything in sight I managed to keep my seat. And,
say! when that horse finally quit I was about the worst done-up
kid you ever saw, for I was limber as a rag. But I'd won myself
a job. But if that horse had taken one more jump I know they'd
have had to pick me up.

"The rest of the rough string was made up of broncs. The

feed was short that spring, an' so old Sontag come in for most of the hard ridin'. An' what a horse he was! For he could do the work of any other six I had. But he never did quit pitching. It made no difference if I rode him two days straight. He always broke into with me when I topped him off next morning. An' like as not he'd kick at me when I got off that night. But the more I seen of him the more I liked the horse, an' I finally got so I could ride him when he bucked without a-pullin' leather.

Bronco

Drawing by Charles M. Russell, from *Bucking the Sagebrush*, by Charles J. Steedman (Putnam, 1904)

"I worked there till the outfit shipped their second bunch of steers. That was along in June. An' then I quit. For I was quite a rambler in them days, an' I never stayed long in one place.

"The night before I left I made a trade, an' the boys all hurrahed me. But next mornin' when I pulled my freight I had old Sontag under me. An' a lucky thing I did. For that horse I traded for Sontag, for all his looks, was an awful yellow pup.

"I'd always worked in the mountains, an' desert country was all new to me, but it interested me a heap. I wasn't goin' no place in particular, just driftin', but the third night out I camped on the edge of the desert with an old prospector. He knowed the desert like a book, an' he told me about this water-hole I'd strike about half-way across. He said it was a good place to camp, an' I wouldn't have no trouble a-makin' the rest of the way across the second day.

"I started next mornin' before daylight. I was packin' a canteen of water in the saddle-horn. But while old Sontag pitched with me that mornin' the canteen fell to the ground. The old desert rat handed it up to me after the horse had quit his buckin'. An' as he did, old Sontag just missed the old man, takin' a shot at him with one of them hind feet of his. An' as I rode out of hearing that old man was still a-cussin' me.

"It was cool when I started. But even then there was a feel about the place I didn't like. It was somethin' you can't explain. An' I wondered then about the horse. I'd used him pretty hard the last few weeks. An' I knowed if anything went wrong with him the game was up with me. I tried to think about somethin' else, but my mind was always comin' back to this. An' once I come near turnin' him around an' headin' back. But, hell! thinks I, it's just because the desert's new to me.

"I was plenty thirsty when the sun came up. But I figured on nursin' that old canteen along. An' I rode for several hours before I went to take a drink. I knowed it the minute that I touched the string. An' it made me sick all over. For the canteen was empty. I couldn't account for it at first, but finally I found a little hole. It was where the canteen had struck a rock when it fell to the ground that mornin'.

"Oh, well, I thought, it won't be long till I strike that water-hole; then everything will be all right. But the place was like a furnace now. An' the wind that seemed to come from every-where felt like a red-hot blast.

"I tried to talk to old Sontag to keep my nerve from quittin' me. But my tongue was so swelled an' thick I couldn't make it work.

"It's funny what a man will think of when he gets in a place like that. You'd suppose he'd think of all the water-holes he'd ever known in all his life. But, instead, the only thing I could think of was a little spring I used to drink at when I was just a kid. I could even see the water-cress. An' them little bugs that skipped around on top. . . .

"I wouldn't admit it at first. But finally I knowed I'd missed the water-hole. The nearest water I knowed of was at the Colorada, and I knowed it was all of sixty miles. Could old Sontag make it? I shut my eyes and tried to keep from thinkin'. Old Sontag was still a-goin' strong. But I knowed no other horse I ever rode could make it there, an' I had my doubts of him.

"I guess I went batty as a loon, for I took to seein' things. The movin' shadow that we made looked like a brook to me, an' I could see green grass and shady trees.

"When I woke up I couldn't imagine where I was. The moon was shinin' in my face, an' some woman was holdin' my head in her lap. I knew she was talkin' to me, but I couldn't understand a word she said. Then all at once it come over me that the woman was a Mexican. She wouldn't give me anything to drink at first, but instead she made me suck a wet rag that she kept dipping in an olla at her side.

"It wasn't but a little while before I could set up an' look around. An' the first thing I seen when I set up was old Sontag. But he looked more like a ghost than any other thing I know. He was caked with sweat an' so thin an' drawn that both cinches hung loose on him. But I don't guess I've ever seen a horse, before or since, that looked so good to me.

"While I was watchin' him a Mexican went over to unsaddle him. But the minute he come near, old Sontag raised that hammer head of his an' let drive with one hind foot. Man! what a horse he was!

"You know when a man fools with bad horses all his life most people thinks there's somethin' wrong with him. Mebbe there is. For a peeler seldom quits until he's hurt or too broke up to ride no more. A man that fools with bad ones is bound to be gettin' throwed. An' any time you hear somebody say he's never been bucked off, you can bet your life that he ain't done much ridin'. Mebbe I've just been lucky, for I've been throwed as much as any one who rides, but the only time I was ever hurt was once when I was ridin' an old gentle horse.

"The horse was just trottin' down the road when he stubbed his toe with me. But when the dust cleared up an' I got to my feet I found I'd sprained both wrists an' broke my collar-bone."

WALTER PRESCOTT WEBB

The Cattle Kingdom*

⟨[WALTER PRESCOTT WEBB'S *The Great Plains* has probably been the most controversial single volume on American history published in this century. Henry Steele Commager has called it in the *New York Times* the most influential single volume on American history of the past fifty years. Webb, glory of the University of Texas faculty, minces no words about the supreme importance of the American West in shaping our national character.

THE CATTLE KINGDOM was a world within itself, with a culture all its own, which, though of brief duration, was complete and self-satisfying. The cattle kingdom worked out its own means and methods of utilization; it formulated its own law, called the code of the West, and did it largely upon extra-legal grounds. The existence of the cattle kingdom for a generation is the best single bit of evidence that here in the West were the basis and the promise of a new civilization unlike anything previously known to the Anglo-European-American experience. The Easterner, with his background of forest and farm, could not always understand the man of the cattle kingdom. One went on foot, the other went on horseback; one carried his law in books, the other carried it strapped round his waist. One

* From *The Great Plains* (Boston: Ginn and Co., 1931).

represented tradition, the other represented innovation; one responded to convention, the other responded to necessity and evolved his own conventions. Yet the man of the timber and the town made the law for the man of the plain; the plainsman, finding this law unsuited to his needs, broke it, and was called lawless. The cattle kingdom was not sovereign, but subject. Eventually it ceased to be a kingdom and became a province. The Industrial Revolution furnished the means by which the beginnings of this original and distinctive civilization have been destroyed or reduced to vestigial remains. Since the destruction of the Plains Indians and the buffalo civilization, the cattle kingdom is the most logical thing that has happened in the Great Plains, where, in spite of science and invention, the spirit of the Great American Desert still is manifest.

The cattle kingdom had its origin in Texas before the Civil War. After the war it expanded, and by 1876 it had spread over the entire Plains area. The physical basis of the cattle kingdom was grass, and it extended itself over all the grassland not occupied by farms. Within a period of ten years it had spread over western Texas, Oklahoma, Kansas, Nebraska, North and South Dakota, Montana, Wyoming, Nevada, Utah, Colorado, and New Mexico; that is, over all or a part of twelve states. For rapidity of expansion there is perhaps not a parallel to this movement in American history.

. . . .

From the time of the Texas revolution until the Civil War, cattle grew wild in Texas and multiplied at a rapid and constant rate. Sporadic attempts were made to market these cattle in New Orleans, in California after the gold rush, and even in the North; but nothing about the industry was standardized until after the Civil War. The cattle had little more value than the wild animals of the Plains. The history of cattle in southern Texas from the Texas revolution to the Civil War is summed up very briefly as follows:

In 1837 and 1838 the "cowboys" gathered herds of from three hundred to a thousand head of the wild unbranded cattle of the

Nueces and Rio Grande country, and drove them for sale to cities of the interior. In 1842 the driving of cattle to New Orleans began. The first shipment from Texas was by a Morgan steamer in 1848, but up to 1849 there were very few outlets for the stock, which had increased enormously since 1830. There is a report of a drive of 1500 to Missouri in 1842, but the earliest perfectly authenticated record of a business venture of that kind found was for 1846, when Edward Piper . . . drove 1000 head of Texas cattle to Ohio, where he fed and sold them. From 1846 to 1861 the drives increased. In 1850 drives began to California. The first drive to Chicago was in 1856. From the beginning of the northern drives in 1846 until the war of the rebellion there was always some movement of cattle out of Texas, but it was irregular. A large proportion of the cattle driven was sold on the plains. Some cattle went into California, Arizona, and New Mexico. Besides such drives there were only the shipments from the seaboard cities to New Orleans and Cuba.[1]

But these early drives and sales, by land and by sea, were not only irregular but inconsequential. The stock in the Nueces valley continued to increase; the valley became, in fact, a veritable hive from which the cattle swarmed to the north and west. The estimate of 1830 gave Texas 100,000 head, the census of 1850 gave it 330,000 head, and that of 1860 gave it 3,535,768 head. On this basis the increase from 1830 to 1850 was only about 330 per cent, but in the next ten years it was 1070 per cent. One investigator judged in 1880 that the number for 1860 should have been 4,785,400 head. If this number is correct, then the increase for the decade 1850 to 1860 would amount to 1450 per cent. Whether such figures violate the biological law governing cattle or prove the estimates and enumeration wrong does not greatly concern us. There is no disputing the fact that cattle were multiplying in southern Texas (and most of them were still in southern Texas) at a rate that would make some disposition of them in the near future imperative if they were not to become a pest. Even as early as 1849 a ranchman of Live Oak County found the country overrun with wild, unbranded cattle, and wrote that

[1] Tenth Census, *Statistics of Agriculture*, p. 965.

"upon the prairies he had often come upon old branding-irons, unrecognized by the people living there." Each year, up to the time of the Civil War, cattle were becoming more numerous and less valuable.

Then came the Civil War, which temporarily arrested the development of the cattle business. A few cattle were delivered to the Confederate forces; but after the Mississippi River fell into the hands of the Union army this outlet for Texas cattle was closed, and the movement of Texas cattle to the Confederate army was stopped. But the breeding went on without abatement, and one writer maintains that the foundations of several fortunes in cattle were laid by the men who remained in Texas while their neighbors were in the armies. Cattle accumulated; the calves remained unbranded, mingling with the old stock hardened and toughened by age and the experiences of precarious survival. Just how tough these Texas cattle became cannot be known in this day of short-horned beef and milk stock. The longhorns yielded little beef and less milk, but they had remarkable ability to survive. Writing about 1876 Colonel [Richard Irving] Dodge declared that "the domestic cattle of Texas, miscalled tame, are fifty times more dangerous to footmen than the fiercest buffalo." The following extracts from Colonel Dodge's chapter on the wild cattle of Texas will give some idea of the bovine influence that was to permeate the cattle kingdom.

I should be doing injustice to a cousin-german of the buffalo, did I fail to mention as game the wild cattle of Texas. It is the domestic animal run wild, changed in some of his habits and characteristics by many generations of freedom and self-care. I have already spoken of the ferocious disposition of some of the so-called tame cattle of Texas. A footman is never safe when a herd is in his vicinity; and every sportsman who has hunted quail in Texas will have experienced the uneasiness natural to any man around whom a crowd of long-horned beasts are pawing the earth and tossing their heads in anger at his appearance.

I admit some very decided frights, and on more than one occasion have felt exceedingly relieved when an aggressive young bull has gone off bellowing and shaking his head, his face and eyes full of No. 8 shot, and taking the herd with him. I speak, I am sorry to say, of an experience now more than twenty years old.[2] Texas was a new country then, and certainly an aggressive country. Every bush had its thorn; every animal, reptile, or insect had its horn, tooth, or sting; every male human his revolver; and each was ready to use his weapon of defense on any unfortunate sojourner, on the smallest, or even without the smallest, provocation. . . .

The tame cow is nearly as dangerous as the bull; while in its wild state, the cow, except in defense of her calf, is as timid as a deer. The wild bull is "on his muscle" at all times; and though he will generally get out of the way if unmolested, the slightest provocation will convert him into a most aggressive and dangerous enemy.

The wild cattle are not found in herds. A few cows and their calves may associate together for mutual protection, but the bulls are almost always found alone. Should two meet, a most desperate combat determines the mastery then and there, very frequently with the life of one of the combatants.

He who would enjoy the favours of a cow must win his way to them by a series of victories. The result of this is that the number of bulls is greatly disproportioned to the number of cows; and this disproportion is increased by the fact that it seems impossible for the bull to keep his mouth shut, and when not actually eating he is bellowing, or moaning, or making some hideous noise which indicates his whereabouts to the hunter.[3]

Colonel Dodge then relates an army story which illustrates the prowess of one of these ferocious longhorns:

There is an old army story to the effect that, when General Taylor's little army was on the march from Corpus Christi to Matamoras, a soldier on the flank of the column came upon and fired at a bull. The bull immediately charged, and the soldier, taking to his heels, ran into the column. The bull, undaunted by the numbers of enemies, charged headlong, scattering several regiments like chaff, and finally escaped unhurt, having demoralised and put to

[2] Colonel Dodge was referring to conditions soon after the Mexican War, probably in the early fifties. He refers here to southwest Texas, and records in the lines quoted that he had come into a new environment, the southern Plains.

[3] Dodge, *The Hunting Grounds of the Great West* (London, 1877), pp. 148-149.

flight an army which a few days after covered itself with glory by victoriously encountering five times its numbers of human enemies.[4]

Considerable space has been devoted to the diamond-shaped territory below San Antonio, the Nueces valley, where cattle throve and multiplied without care. This area has been called the cradle of the Plains cattle industry, and such it was. But it becomes clear from what Colonel Dodge tells and from what we know from other sources that he who would tend the rough occupants of that cradle would best do it on horseback with a rope and a six-shooter. If the Plains Indian created the mounted Texas Ranger and compelled the Texan to recognize the six-shooter as his own weapon, then the Texas longhorn kept him on horseback and rendered the six-shooter desirable after the Indian had departed.

The value of the six-shooter to the man who handled these cattle is brought out in the following incident, which occurred about 1860:

On this occasion it became necessary or desirable to rope a large and powerful steer, with horns long and well set for hooking and sharp as a lance. He showed fight and would not drive to the pen, and a young man galloped forth from the crowd on a fleet horse and roped him. But before the steer could be thrown, the lasso being put to the horn of the saddle, he jerked the horse down, and in the fall one leg of the rider was caught beneath him. The young man spurred with the loose foot, but the horse, being stunned by the fall, was unable to get up and held his rider pinned to the ground. The steer having been "brought up" at the end of the rope by the fall of the horse, and seeing both horse and rider prostrate on the prairie, turned and with neck bowed, charged upon them. It was an awful moment. There appeared no escape, as the party was some distance away, and the whole thing was the work of a moment. Some persons in such a situation would have been paralyzed—would have lost all presence of mind. But not so with the young man: His hand was instantly on his revolver, and drawing it he shot the furious animal through the brain, when the delay of a moment would have been fatal.[5]

[4] *Ibid.*, p. 152.
[5] D. E. McArthur, *The Cattle Industry of Texas, 1685–1918* (manuscript), pp. 84–85.

Thus we see the elements of the cattle industry of the West coming together in the Nueces country, the southern point of the Great Plains. There Mexican cattle came into the presence of the mounted Texan armed with rope and six-shooter—the cowboy. But as yet the area was limited and regular markets were nonexistent. Indians and buffaloes still roamed over the empire of grass on the Plains. In the meantime industrial giants were arising in the North—giant cities hungry for meat. The agricultural South was much nearer, but now prostrate before the industrial North. Then the cattle swarmed, passed out of the valley along the timber line, on the natural highway of the prairie, by San Antonio, Austin, Fort Worth, on and on, taking meat to the giants of the North—the first tie to rebind the North and the South after the Civil War.

. . . .

The price situation in 1865 was as follows: cattle in Texas could be bought for $3 and $4 per head, on the average; but even so, there were no buyers. The same cattle in the Northern markets would have brought $30 or $40, "and mature Texas beeves which cost in Texas $5 each by the herd were worth $50 each in other sections of the United States." [6] It was easy for a Texan with a pencil and a piece of paper to "figure up" a fortune. If he could buy five million cattle at $4 and sell them in the North at $40 each, his gross profit would amount to the sum of $180,000,000 on an investment of $20,000,000 plus the cost of transportation! This exercise in high finance is, of course, fanciful, but it does show what men did on a small scale. Five million cattle? No. Three thousand? Yes. Profit, $108,000. How the Texans needed the money in those hard days! They took vigorous measures to connect the four-dollar cow with a forty-dollar market. As a matter of fact they did within fifteen years actually deliver to the North the five million head of cattle, and more, though the actual profits fell short of the paper figures. At the same time the number of cattle remaining on the breeding ground in Texas was greater than before by more than eight hundred thousand head.

[6] Tenth Census, *Statistics of Agriculture*, p. 966.

When the Texans started their rangy longhorns northward—
and they were fortunate in having such tough customers for
such a perilous journey—they had no intention of setting up a
new economic kingdom: they were merely carrying their herds
to market. The fact that the market happened to be twelve or
fifteen hundred miles away was no fault of theirs. And if we
follow the history of their drives for five years, we see that
they were groping, experimenting, trying this and that, until
by the familiar system of trial and error, which has characterized all progress in the Plains country, they came at length,
and after great sacrifice, upon success. They beat out the trail,
learned to avoid the timber and the farmer, to whip the Indian,
to cross the quicksanded rivers; they reached the railroad,
found buyers and a steady market, and heard once more the
music made by real money rattling in the pocket. And the
North had meat, sometimes tough and unsavory, but the worst
of it good enough for factory workers and the pick-and-shovel
men of the railroads and too good for the Indians of the reserva-
tion under the corrupt régime of Grant Republicans.

As has been stated, the purpose of the Texans in making
the first drives to the north was to find a market for their cattle.
Their immediate objective was a railhead from which the cattle
could be shipped East. An examination of the railroad maps of
1866 will show that several railroads had nosed their way
across the Mississippi and followed population to the edge of
the Great Plains. Among these roads was the Missouri Pacific,
which had reached Sedalia, Missouri.

It is estimated that two hundred and sixty thousand head of
Texas cattle crossed Red River for the northern markets in
1866. The objective of most of these herds was Sedalia, Missouri, which offered rail facilities to St. Louis and other cities.
But disaster awaited the Texans and their herds in southeastern
Kansas, southern Missouri, and northern Arkansas, where
armed mobs met the herds with all possible violence.[7] The

[7] J. G. McCoy's *Historic Sketches of the Cattle Trade of the West and
Southwest* (Kansas City, 1874) is the pioneer work on the Texas cattle drive,
and has been used by all later writers in the field. *Prose and Poetry of the Live*

pretext for this opposition was that the cattle would bring the Texas fever among Northern cattle, but in some cases, at least, robbery and theft were the real motives.

The southwestern Missouri roads leading to Sedalia were the scenes of the worst of the work of these outlaws. . . . When outright murder was not resorted to as the readiest means of getting possession of a herd of cattle, drovers were flogged until they had promised to abandon their stock, mount their horses, and get out of the country as quick as they could. A favorite scheme of the milder-mannered of these scoundrels to plunder the cattlemen was that of stampeding a herd at night. This was easily done, and having been done the rogues next morning would collect as many of the scattered cattle as they could, secrete them in an out-of-the-way place—much of the country being hilly and timbered—and then hunt up the owner and offer to help him, for an acceptable money consideration per head, in recovering his lost property. If the drover agreed to pay a price high enough to satisfy the pirates, they next day would return with many, if not all, of the missing cattle; but if not, the hold-ups would keep them, and later take them to the market and pocket the entire proceeds.[8]

The Texas drovers soon learned to avoid this region. Some turned to the east and others to the west, away from the bandit-infested country around Baxter Springs. Those who turned east did so in the northeastern part of the Indian Territory, driving along the Missouri-Arkansas boundary and laying their course toward St. Louis or some rail point east of Sedalia. This route had few attractions. The country was timbered and broken, and the cattle reached the market in poor condition. Other drovers turned west along the southern boundary of Kansas for one hundred and fifty miles, until they were beyond the settlements and well out on the grassy plains. When far enough north they turned eastward, most of them reaching the railroad

Stock Industry of the United States (Denver, 1905), prepared by authority of the National Live Stock Association, is perhaps the most thorough and comprehensive work on the subject.

[8] Prose and Poetry of the Live Stock Industry of the United States, p. 433; McCoy, op. cit., Chap. II.

at St. Joseph, Missouri, and shipping direct to Chicago. Other cattle found their way to feeding pens in Iowa and Illinois. To the west some cattle went as far north as Wyoming.

On the whole the season of 1866 was disastrous to the Texans. It was a year of groping experiment, trial, and error. But one clear fact emerges from the welter of uncertainty of that year, and that is that the cattle trail of the future would lie to the west. Ferocious Plains Indians were there on horseback, but they were to be preferred to the Missourians. Why the Texans who had raised their cattle on the prairies, or, at least, gathered them there, did not immediately realize that it would be best to drive on the prairie may seem strange; yet what they had done was perfectly natural, namely, to seek the most direct route to market. In spite of the losses which most of them experienced, the drovers saw that they had an unlimited market for their cattle if they could only find a way of getting them safely through. They met buyers as well as thieves. Their future problem was to establish permanent relations with the buyers and avoid—or, better, kill, as they sometimes did—the thieves.

The man who first saw the desirability of establishing a permanent and fairly safe point of contact between the Eastern buyer and the Texan drover was J. G. McCoy, who, with his two brothers, was engaged in a large live-stock shipping business in Illinois. McCoy, a dreamer with a practical bent, conceived the notion that there must be a strategic point where the cattle trail from Texas would cut the railroads then pushing west. At this point of intersection Texas cattle drovers would be met by Northern and Eastern buyers, and all would prosper together. "The plan," says McCoy, "was to establish at some accessible point a depot or market to which a Texan drover could bring his stock unmolested, and there, failing to find a buyer, he could go upon the public highways to any market in the country he wished. In short, it was to establish a market whereat the Southern drover and Northern buyer would meet upon an equal footing, and both be undisturbed by mobs or swindling thieves." [9] In other words, McCoy proposed to establish, and did establish, the first cow town of the West—Abilene, Kansas. This act constituted the third step in the founding of the cattle kingdom.

At first McCoy was uncertain where this town should be, and he spent much time studying maps, trying to decide whether it should be on the Western prairies or on some Southern river. At this stage of his meditation a business trip took him to Kansas City, where he met some men who were interested in a herd of cattle reported to be coming up from Texas, destination unknown. McCoy became more interested. He went to Junction City and proposed to purchase land there for a stockyard, but found the price too high. He next made the rounds of the railroad offices. The president of the Kansas Pacific promised aid, but showed only mild enthusiasm for the plan, which he thought impractical. The president of the Missouri Pacific ordered McCoy out of his office, declaring that McCoy had no cattle, had never had any, and probably never would have any. A few hours later McCoy had signed a contract with the general freight agent of the Hannibal and St. Joe Railroad granting favorable rates from the Missouri River to Chicago. McCoy thought that this incident—the action of the official of the Missouri Pacific—turned the cattle business permanently from St. Louis to Chicago.

McCoy now had rail connection on the Kansas Pacific to the Missouri River, and thence on the Hannibal and St. Joe to Chicago and other markets farther east. He now hurried back to Kansas to select the site of his town on the Kansas Pacific. Neither Salina nor Solomon City was hospitable to the idea of being a cow town, and McCoy finally selected Abilene, the county seat of Dickinson County. In McCoy's words,

Abilene in 1867 was a very small, dead place, consisting of about one dozen log huts, low, small, rude affairs, four fifths of which were covered with dirt for roofing; indeed, but one shingle roof could be

[9] J. G. McCoy, *op. cit.*, p. 40.

seen in the whole city. The business of the burg was conducted in two small rooms, mere log huts, and of course the inevitable saloon, also in a log hut, was to be found.[10]

Just how poor the town must have been is indicated by the fact that the saloon-keeper supplemented his income and provided himself amusement by tending a colony of prairie dogs and selling them to Eastern tourists as curiosities. The time was near when the saloon-keepers of Abilene would have too much business to stoop to prairie-dog culture. However, the presence of the prairie-dog town tells us significantly that Abilene was across the line, a town of the West. Says McCoy [11]:

Abilene was selected because the country was entirely unsettled, well watered, excellent grass, and nearly the entire area of country was adapted to holding cattle.[12] And it was the [farthest] point east at which a good depot for cattle business could have been made.

McCoy labored with energy, zeal, and intelligence. Pine lumber was brought from Hannibal, Missouri, and hard wood from Lenape, Kansas. The work of building stockyards, pens, and loading chutes went forward rapidly, and within sixty days Abilene had facilities to accommodate three thousand head of cattle; but as yet it was a cow town without any cows.

McCoy had not overlooked the cows, however. As soon as he chose Abilene he sent to Kansas and the Indian Territory a man well versed in the geography of the country and "accustomed to life on the prairie," "with instructions to hunt up every straggling drove possible—and every drove was straggling, for they had nowhere to go—and tell the drovers of Abilene, and what was being done there toward making a market and outlet for Texan cattle." This man rode almost two hundred miles into the Indian Territory, cut the fresh trail of cattle going north, followed it, overtook the herd, and

[10] *Ibid.*, p. 44. Abilene was far enough out on the Plains to use lumber sparingly.

[11] *Ibid.*, p. 50.

[12] McCoy means that the country was open and level and had plenty of grass for forage.

informed the owner that a good, safe place with adequate shipping facilities awaited him at Abilene.

This was joyous news to the drover, for the fear of trouble and violence hung like an incubus over his waking thoughts alike with his sleeping moments. It was almost too good to be believed; could it be possible that someone was about to afford a Texan drover any other reception than outrage and robbery? They were very suspicious that some trap was set, to be sprung on them; they were not ready to credit the proposition that the day of fair dealing had dawned for Texan drovers, and the era of mobs, brutal murder, and arbitrary proscription ended forever.

Yet they turned their herds toward the point designated, and slowly and cautiously moved on northward, their minds constantly agitated with hope and fear alternately.[13]

The first herd to reach Abilene was driven from Texas by a man named Thompson, but was sold to some Northern men in the Indian Territory and by them driven to Abilene. Another herd owned by Wilson, Wheeler, and Hicks, and en route for the Pacific states, stopped to graze near Abilene and was finally sold there. On the fifth of September the first cattle were shipped from Abilene to Chicago. A great celebration was held that night, attended by many stock-raisers and buyers brought by excursion from Springfield, Illinois, and other points. Southern men from Texas and Northern men from Lincoln's home town sat down to "feast, wine, and song," heralding the initiation of the cattle kingdom, which was to rise immediately after the fall of the cotton kingdom. Who can say that Abilene was less significant than Appomattox?

. . . .

Abilene! Abilene may be defined. It was the point where the north-and-south cattle trail intersected the east-and-west railroad. Abilene was more than a point. It is a symbol. It stands for all that happened when two civilizations met for conflict, for disorder, for the clashing of great currents which carry on

[13] McCoy, *op. cit.*, p. 51.

their crest the turbulent and disorderly elements of both civilizations—in this case the rough characters of the plain and of
the forest. On the surface Abilene was corruption personified.
Life was hectic, raw, lurid, awful. But the dance hall, the
saloon, and the red light, the dissonance of immoral revelry
punctuated by pistol shots, were but the superficialities which
hid from view the deeper forces that were working themselves
out round the new town. If Abilene excelled all later cow towns
in wickedness, it also excelled them in service—the service of
bartering the beef of the South for the money of the North.

Through Abilene passed a good part of the meat supply of a
nation. That part of the story belongs to the East, and we are
not concerned with it here. But Abilene's service was no less
to the West. From Abilene and other like towns Texas cattle,
blended with American cattle, swarmed out to the West and
covered the Great Plains—the empire of grass—from the California mountains to the Illinois prairies. Not all the cattle that
reached Abilene were fit for market, and at times there was no
market. In such cases the surplus cattle were "held on the
prairie" or established on permanent ranches to be fattened.

In this way the cattle kingdom spread from Texas and
utilized the Plains area, which would otherwise have lain idle
and useless. Abilene offered the market; the market offered
inducement to Northern money; Texas furnished the base
stock, the original supply, and a method of handling cattle on
horseback; the Plains offered free grass. From these conditions
and from these elements emerged the range and ranch cattle
industry, perhaps the most unique and distinctive institution
that America has produced. This spread of the range cattle
industry over the Great Plains is the final step in the creation
of the cattle kingdom.

The first step was made when the Spaniards and Mexicans
established their ranches in the Nueces country of southern
Texas, where natural conditions produced a hardy breed of
cattle that could grow wild; the second step occurred when
the Texans took over these herds and learned to handle them
in the only way they could have been handled—on horseback;

the third step was taken when the cattle were driven north-ward to market; the fourth came when a permanent depot was set up at Abilene which enabled trail-driving to become stand-ardized; the fifth took place when the overflow from the trail went west to the free grass of the Great Plains.